Charles Kingsley

Westminster Sermons

With a Preface

Charles Kingsley

Westminster Sermons
With a Preface

ISBN/EAN: 9783744704700

Printed in Europe, USA, Canada, Australia, Japan

Cover: Foto ©Suzi / pixelio.de

More available books at **www.hansebooks.com**

WESTMINSTER SERMONS

WITH A PREFACE

BY

CHARLES KINGSLEY

London:
MACMILLAN AND CO.
AND NEW YORK.
1890

CONTENTS.

PAGE

SERMON XII.

PREFACE.

I VENTURE to preface these Sermons—which were preached either at Westminster Abbey, or at one of the Chapels Royal—by a Paper read at Sion College, in 1871; and for this reason. Even when they deal with what is usually, and rightly, called "vital" and "experimental" religion, they are comments on, and developments of, the idea which pervades that paper; namely—That facts, whether of physical nature, or of the human heart and reason, do not contradict, but coincide with, the doctrines and formulas of the Church of England, as by law established.

*   *   *   *   *

Natural Theology, I said, is a subject which seems to me more and more important; and one which is just now somewhat forgotten. I therefore desire to say a few words on it. I do not pretend to teach : but only to suggest; to point out certain problems of natural Theology, the further solution of which ought, I think, to be soon attempted.

I wish to speak, be it remembered, not on natural religion, but on natural Theology. By the first, I understand what can be learned from the physical universe of man's duty to God and to his neighbour; by the latter, I understand what can be learned concerning God Himself. Of natural religion I shall say nothing. I do not even affirm that a natural religion is possible: but I do very earnestly believe that a natural Theology is possible; and I earnestly believe also that it is most important that natural Theology should, in every age, keep pace with doctrinal or ecclesiastical Theology.

Bishop Butler certainly held this belief. His *Analogy of Religion, Natural and Revealed, to the Constitution and Course of Nature*—a book for which I entertain the most profound respect—is based on a belief that the God of nature and the God of grace are one; and that therefore, the God who satisfies our conscience ought more or less to satisfy our reason also. To teach that was Butler's mission; and he fulfilled it well. But it is a mission which has to be re-fulfilled again and again, as human thought changes, and human science develops; for if, in any age or country, the God who seems to be revealed by nature seems also different from the God who is revealed by the then popular religion: then that God, and the religion which tells of that God, will gradually cease to be believed in.

For the demands of Reason—as none knew better than good Bishop Butler—must be and ought to be satisfied. And therefore; when a popular war arises between the reason of any generation and its Theology: then it behoves the ministers of religion to inquire, with all humility and godly fear, on which side lies the fault;

whether the Theology which they expound is all that it should be, or whether the reason of those who impugn it is all that it should be.

For me, as—I trust—an orthodox priest of the Church of England, I believe the Theology of the National Church of England, as by law established, to be eminently rational as well as scriptural. It is not, therefore, surprising to me that the clergy of the Church of England, since the foundation of the Royal Society in the seventeenth century, have done more for sound physical science than the clergy of any other denomination; or that the three greatest natural theologians with which I, at least, am acquainted—Berkeley, Butler, and Paley—should have belonged to our Church. I am not unaware of what the Germans of the eighteenth century have done. I consider Goethe's claims to have advanced natural Theology very much over-rated : but I do recommend to young clergymen Herder's *Outlines of the Philosophy of the History of Man* as a book—in spite of certain defects—full of sound and precious wisdom. Meanwhile it seems to me that English natural Theology in the eighteenth century stood more secure than that of any other nation, on the foundation which Berkeley, Butler, and Paley had laid; and that if our orthodox thinkers for the last hundred years had followed steadily in their steps, we should not be deploring now a wide, and as some think increasing, divorce between Science and Christianity.

But it was not so to be. The impulse given by Wesley and Whitfield turned—and not before it was needed—the earnest minds of England almost exclusively to questions of personal religion; and that impulse, under many unexpected forms, has continued ever since. I only state the fact: I do not deplore it; God forbid. Wisdom is justified of all her children; and as, according to the wise American, "it takes all sorts to make a world," so it takes all sorts to make a living Church. But that the religious temper of England for the last two or three generations has been unfavourable to a sound and scientific development of natural Theology, there can be no doubt.

We have only, if we need proof, to look at the hymns—many of them very pure, pious, and beautiful—which are used at this day in churches and chapels by persons of every shade of opinion. How often is the tone in which they speak of the natural world one of dissatisfaction, distrust, almost contempt. " Change and decay in all around I see," is their key-note, rather than "O all ye works of the Lord, bless Him, praise Him, and magnify Him for ever." There lingers about them a savour of the old monastic theory, that this earth is the devil's planet, fallen, accursed, goblin-haunted, needing to be exorcised at every turn before it is useful or even safe for man. An age which has adopted as its most popular hymn a paraphrase of the mediæval monk's "Hic breve vivitur," and in which stalwart public-school boys are bidden in their chapel-worship to tell the Almighty God of Truth that they lie awake weeping at night for joy at the thought that they will die and see " Jerusalem the Golden," is doubtless a pious and devout age : but not—at least as yet—an age in which natural Theology is likely to attain a high, a healthy, or a scriptural development.

Not a scriptural development. Let me press on you, my clerical brethren, most earnestly this one point. It is time that we should make up our minds what tone Scripture does take toward nature, natural science, natural Theology. Most of you, I doubt not, have made up your minds already; and in consequence have no fear of natural science, no fear for natural Theology. But I cannot deny that I find still lingering here and there certain of the old views of nature of which I used to hear but too much some five-and-thirty years ago—and that from better men than I shall ever hope to be—who used to consider natural Theology as useless, fallacious, impossible; on the ground that this Earth did not reveal the will and character of God, because it was cursed and fallen ; and that its facts, in consequence, were not to be respected or relied on. This, I was told, was the doctrine of Scripture, and was therefore true. But when, longing to reconcile my conscience and my reason on a question so awful to a young student of natural science, I went to my Bible, what did I find ? No word of all this. Much—thank God, I may say one continuous undercurrent—of the very opposite of all this. I pray you bear with me, even though I may seem impertinent. But what do we find in the Bible, with the exception of that first curse? That, remember, cannot mean any alteration in the laws of nature by which man's labour should only produce for him henceforth thorns and thistles. For, in the first place, any such curse is formally abrogated in the eighth chapter and 21st verse of the very same document—"I will not again curse the earth any more for man's sake. While the earth remaineth, seed-time and harvest, cold and heat, summer and winter, day and night, shall not cease." And next : the fact is not so ; for if you root up the thorns and thistles, and keep your land clean, then assuredly you will grow fruit-trees and not thorns, wheat and not thistles, according to those laws of nature which are the voice of God expressed in facts.

And yet the words are true. There is a curse upon the earth : though not one which, by altering the laws of nature, has made natural facts untrustworthy. There is a curse on the earth; such a curse as is expressed, I believe, in the old Hebrew text, where the word "*admah*" —correctly translated in our version "the ground"— signifies, as I am told, not this planet, but simply the soil from whence we get our food ; such a curse as certainly is expressed by the Septuagint and the Vulgate versions : "Cursed is the earth"—ἐν τοῖς ἔργοις σου; "in opere tuo," "in thy works." Man's work is too often the curse of the very planet which he misuses. None should know that better than the botanist, who sees whole regions desolate, and given up to sterility and literal thorns and thistles, on account of man's sin and folly, ignorance and greedy waste. Well said that veteran botanist, the venerable Elias Fries, of Lund:—

"A broad band of waste land follows gradually in the steps of cultivation. If it expands, its centre and its cradle dies, and on the outer borders only do we find green shoots. But it is not impossible, only difficult, for man, without renouncing the advantage of culture itself, one day to make reparation for the injury which he has inflicted: he is appointed lord of creation. True it is that thorns and thistles, ill-favoured and poisonous plants, well named by botanists rubbish plants, mark the track which man has proudly traversed through the earth. Before him lay original nature in her wild but sublime beauty. Behind him he leaves a desert, a deformed and ruined land; for childish desire of destruction, or thoughtless squandering of vegetable treasures, has destroyed the character of nature ; and, terrified, man himself flies from the arena of his actions, leaving the impoverished earth to barbarous races or to animals, so long as yet another spot in virgin beauty smiles before him. Here again, in selfish pursuit of profit, and consciously or unconsciously following the abominable principle of the great moral vileness which one man has expressed—' Après nous le Déluge,'—he begins anew the work of destruction. Thus did cultivation, driven out, leave the East, and perhaps the deserts long ago robbed of their coverings; like the wild hordes of old over beautiful Greece, thus rolls this conquest with fearful rapidity from East to West through America; and the planter now often leaves the already exhausted land, and the eastern climate, become infertile through the demolition of the forests, to introduce a similar revolution into the Far West."

As we proceed, we find nothing in the general tone of Scripture which can hinder our natural Theology being at once scriptural and scientific.

If it is to be scientific, it must begin by approaching Nature at once with a cheerful and reverent spirit, as a noble, healthy, and trustworthy thing; and what is that, save the spirit of those who wrote the 104th, 147th, and 148th Psalms; the spirit, too, of him who wrote that Song of the Three Children, which is, as it were, the flower and crown of the Old Testament, the summing up of all that is most true and eternal in the old Jewish faith; and which, as long as it is sung in our churches, is the charter and title-deed of all Christian students of those works of the Lord, which it calls on to bless Him, praise Him, and magnify Him for ever?

What next will be demanded of us by physical science? Belief, certainly, just now, in the permanence of natural laws. That is taken for granted, I hold, throughout the Bible. I cannot see how our Lord's parables, drawn from the birds and the flowers, the seasons and the weather, have any logical weight, or can be considered as aught but capricious and fanciful "illustrations"—which God forbid—unless we look at them as instances of laws of the natural world, which find their analogues in the laws of the spiritual world, the kingdom of God. I cannot conceive a man's writing that 104th Psalm who had not the most deep, the most earnest sense of the permanence of natural law. But more: the fact is expressly asserted again and again. "They continue this day according to Thine ordinance, for all things serve Thee." "Thou hast made them fast for ever and ever. Thou hast given them a law which shall not be broken——"

Let us pass on. There is no more to be said about this matter.

But next: it will be demanded of us that natural Theology shall set forth a God whose character is consistent with all the facts of nature, and not only with those which are pleasant and beautiful. That challenge was accepted, and I think victoriously, by Bishop Butler, as far as the Christian religion is concerned. As far as the Scripture is concerned, we may answer thus—

It is said to us—I know that it is said—You tell us of a God of love, a God of flowers and sunshine, of singing birds and little children. But there are more facts in nature than these. There is premature death, pestilence, famine. And if you answer—Man has control over these; they are caused by man's ignorance and sin, and by his breaking of natural laws :—What will you make of those destructive powers over which he has no control; of the hurricane and the earthquake; of poisons, vegetable and mineral; of those parasitic Entozoa whose awful abundance, and awful destructiveness, in man and beast, science is just revealing—a new page of danger and loathsomeness? How does that suit your conception of a God of love?

We can answer—Whether or not it suits our conception of a God of love, it suits Scripture's conception of Him. For nothing is more clear—nay, is it not urged again and again, as a blot on Scripture?—that it reveals a God not merely of love, but of sternness; a God in whose eyes physical pain is not the worst of evils, nor animal life—too often miscalled human life—the most precious of objects; a God who destroys, when it seems fit to Him, and that wholesale, and seemingly without either pity or discrimination, man, woman, and child, visiting the sins of the fathers on the children, making the land empty and bare, and destroying from off it man and beast? This is the God of the Old Testament. And if any say—as is too often rashly said—This is not the God of the New: I answer, But have you read your New Testament? Have you read the latter chapters of St Matthew? Have you read the opening of the Epistle to the Romans? Have you read the Book of Revelation? If so, will you say that the God of the New Testament is, compared with the God of the Old, less awful, less destructive, and therefore less like the Being—granting always that there is such a Being—who presides over nature and her destructive powers? It is an awful problem. But the writers of the Bible have faced it valiantly. Physical science is facing it valiantly now. Therefore natural Theology may face it likewise. Remember Carlyle's great words about poor Francesca in the Inferno: "Infinite pity: yet also infinite rigour of law. It is so Nature is made. It is so Dante discerned that she was made."

There are two other points on which I must beg leave to say a few words. Physical science will demand of our natural theologians that they should be aware of their importance, and let—as Mr Matthew Arnold would say—their thoughts play freely round them. I mean questions of Embryology, and questions of Race.

On the first there may be much to be said, which is, for the present, best left unsaid, even here. I only ask you to recollect how often in Scripture those two plain old words—beget and bring forth—occur; and in what important passages. And I ask you to remember that marvellous essay on Natural Theology—if I may so call it in all reverence—namely, the 139th Psalm; and judge for yourself whether he who wrote that did not consider the study of Embryology as important, as significant, as worthy of his deepest attention, as an Owen, a Huxley, or a Darwin. Nay, I will go further still, and say, that in those great words—"Thine eyes did see my substance, yet being imperfect; and in Thy book all my members were written, which in continuance were fashioned, when as yet there was none of them,"—in those words, I say, the Psalmist has anticipated that realistic view of embryological questions to which our most modern philosophers are, it seems to me, slowly, half unconsciously, but still inevitably, returning.

Next, as to Race. Some persons now have a nervous fear of that word, and of allowing any importance to difference of races. Some dislike it, because they think that it endangers the modern notions of democratic equality. Others because they fear that it may be proved that the Negro is not a man and a brother. I think the fears of both parties groundless. As for the Negro, I not only believe him to be of the same race as myself, but that—if Mr Darwin's theories are true—science has proved that he must be such. I should have thought, as a humble student of such questions, that the one fact of the unique distribution of the hair in all races of human beings, was full moral proof that they had all had one common ancestor. But this is not matter of natural Theology. What is matter thereof, is this.

Physical science is proving more and more the immense importance of Race; the importance of heredi-tary powers, hereditary organs, hereditary habits, in all organized beings, from the lowest plant to the highest animal. She is proving more and more the omnipresent action of the differences between races: how the more " favoured " race—she cannot avoid using the epithet—

exterminates the less favoured; or at least expels it, and forces it, under penalty of death, to adapt itself to new circumstances; and, in a word, that competition between every race and every individual of that race, and reward according to deserts, is, as far as we can see, an universal law of living things. And she says—for the facts of History prove it—that as it is among the races of plants and animals, so it has been unto this day among the races of men.

The natural Theology of the future must take count of these tremendous and even painful facts. She may take count of them. For Scripture has taken count of them already. It talks continually—it has been blamed for talking so much—of races; of families; of their wars, their struggles, their exterminations; of races favoured, of races rejected; of remnants being saved, to continue the race; of hereditary tendencies, hereditary excellencies, hereditary guilt. Its sense of the reality and importance of descent is so intense, that it speaks of a whole tribe or a whole family by the name of its common ancestor; and the whole nation of the Jews is Israel, to the end. And if I be told this is true of the Old Testament, but not of the New: I must answer,— What? Does not St Paul hold the identity of the whole Jewish race with Israel their forefather, as strongly as any prophet of the Old Testament? And what is the central historic fact, save One, of the New Testament, but the conquest of Jerusalem; the dispersion, all but

K. S. 2

destruction of a race, not by miracle, but by invasion, because found wanting when weighed in the stern balances of natural and social law?

Think over this. I only suggest the thought: but I do not suggest it in haste. Think over it, by the light which our Lord's parables, His analogies between the physical and social constitution of the world, afford; and consider whether those awful words—fulfilled then, and fulfilled so often since—"The kingdom of God shall be taken from you, and given to a nation bringing forth the fruits thereof," may not be the supreme instance, the most complex development, of a law which runs through all created things, down to the moss which struggles for existence on the rock.

Do I say that this is all? That man is merely a part of nature, the puppet of circumstances and hereditary tendencies? That brute competition is the one law of his life? That he is doomed for ever to be the slave of his own needs, enforced by an internecine struggle for existence? God forbid. I believe not only in nature, but in Grace. I believe that this is man's fate only as long as he sows to the flesh, and of the flesh reaps corruption. I believe that if he will

> Strive upward, working out the beast,
> And let the ape and tiger die;

if he will be even as wise as the social animals; as the ant and the bee, who have risen, if not to the virtue of all-embracing charity, at least to the virtues of self-sacrifice and patriotism: then he will rise towards a higher sphere; towards that kingdom of God of which it is written—"He that dwelleth in love, dwelleth in God, and God in him."

Whether that be matter of natural Theology, I cannot tell as yet. But as for all the former questions; and all that St Paul means when he talks of the law, and how the works of the flesh bring men under the law, stern and terrible and destructive, though holy and just and good,—they are matter of natural Theology; and I believe that here, as elsewhere, Scripture and Science will be ultimately found to coincide.

But here we have to face an objection which you will often hear now from scientific men, and still oftener from non-scientific men; who will say—It matters not to us whether Scripture contradicts or does not contradict a scientific natural Theology; for we hold such a science to be impossible and naught. The old Jews put a God into nature; and therefore of course they could see, as you see, what they had already put there. But we see no God in nature. We do not deny the existence of a God. We merely say that scientific research does not reveal Him to us. We see no marks of design in physical phenomena. What used to be considered as marks of design can be better explained by considering them as the results of evolution according to necessary laws; and you and Scripture make a mere assumption when you ascribe them to the operation of a mind like the human mind.

2—2

Now on this point I believe we may answer fearlessly—If you cannot see it, we cannot help you. If the heavens do not declare to you the glory of God, nor the firmament show you His handy-work, then our poor arguments will not show them. "The eye can only see that which it brings with it the power of seeing." We can only reassert that we see design everywhere; and that the vast majority of the human race in every age and clime has seen it. Analogy from experience, sound induction—as we hold—from the works not only of men but of animals, has made it an all but self-evident truth to us, that wherever there is arrangement, there must be an arranger; wherever there is adaptation of means to an end, there must be an adapter; wherever an organization, there must be an organizer. The existence of a designing God is no more demonstrable from nature than the existence of other human beings independent of ourselves; or, indeed, than the existence of our own bodies. But, like the belief in them, the belief in Him has become an article of our common sense. And that this designing mind is, in some respects, similar to the human mind, is proved to us—as Sir John Herschel well puts it—by the mere fact that we can discover and comprehend the processes of nature.

But here again, if we be contradicted, we can only reassert. If the old words, "He that made the eye, shall he not see? he that planted the ear, shall he not hear?" do not at once commend themselves to the intellect of any person, we shall never convince that person by any arguments drawn from the absurdity of conceiving the invention of optics by a blind man, or of music by a deaf one.

So we will assert our own old-fashioned notion boldly: and more; we will say, in spite of ridicule—That if such a God exists, final causes must exist also. That the whole universe must be one chain of final causes. That if there be a Supreme Reason, he must have reason, and that a good reason, for every physical phenomenon.

We will tell the modern scientific man—You are nervously afraid of the mention of final causes. You quote against them Bacon's saying, that they are barren virgins; that no physical fact was ever discovered or explained by them. You are right: as far as regards yourselves. You have no business with final causes; because final causes are moral causes: and you are physical students only. We, the natural Theologians, have business with them. Your duty is to find out the How of things: ours, to find out the Why. If you rejoin that we shall never find out the Why, unless we first learn something of the How, we shall not deny that. It may be most useful, I had almost said necessary, that the clergy should have some scientific training. It may be most useful—I sometimes dream of a day when it will be considered necessary—that every candidate for Ordination should be required to have passed creditably in at least one branch of physical science, if it be only to teach him the method of sound scientific thought. But our having learnt the How, will not make it needless, much less impossible, for us to study the Why. It will merely make more clear to us the things of which we have to study the Why; and enable us to keep the How and the Why more religiously apart from each other.

But if it be said—After all, there is no Why. The doctrine of evolution, by doing away with the theory of creation, does away with that of final causes,—Let us answer boldly,—Not in the least. We might accept all that Mr Darwin, all that Professor Huxley, all that other most able men, have so learnedly and so acutely written on physical science, and yet preserve our natural Theology on exactly the same basis as that on which Butler and Paley left it. That we should have to develop it, I do not deny. That we should have to relinquish it, I do.

Let me press this thought earnestly on you. I know that many wiser and better men than I have fears on this point. I cannot share in them.

All, it seems to me, that the new doctrines of evolution demand is this:—We all agree—for the fact is patent—that our own bodies, and indeed the body of every living creature, are evolved from a seemingly simple germ by natural laws, without visible action of any designing will or mind, into the full organization of a human or other creature. Yet we do not say on that account—God did not create me: I only grew. We hold in this case to our old idea, and say—If there be evolution, there must be an evolver. Now the new physical theories only ask us, it seems to me, to extend this conception to the whole universe; to believe that not individuals merely, but whole varieties and races; the total organized life on this planet; and, it may be, the total organization of the universe, have been evolved just as our bodies are, by natural laws acting through circumstance. This may be true, or may be false. But all its truth can do to the natural Theologian will be to make him believe that the Creator bears the same relation to the whole universe, as that Creator undeniably bears to every individual human body.

I entreat you to weigh these words, which have not been written in haste; and I entreat you also, if you wish to see how little the new theory, that species may have been gradually created by variation, natural selection, and so forth, interferes with the old theory of design, contrivance, and adaptation, nay, with the fullest admission of benevolent final causes—I entreat you, I say, to study Darwin's "Fertilization of Orchids"—a book which, whether his main theory be true or not, will still remain a most valuable addition to natural Theology.

For suppose that all the species of Orchids, and not only they, but their congeners—the Gingers, the Arrowroots, the Bananas—are all the descendants of one original form, which was most probably nearly allied to the Snowdrop and the Iris. What then? Would that be one whit more wonderful, more unworthy of the wisdom and power of God, than if they were, as most believe, created each and all at once, with their minute and often imaginary shades of difference? What would the natural Theologian have to say, were the first theory true, save that God's works are even more wonderful that he always believed them to be? As for the theory being impossible: we must leave the discussion of that to physical students. It is not for us clergymen to limit the power of God. "Is anything too hard for the Lord?" asked the prophet of old; and we have a right to ask it as long as time shall last. If it be said that natural selection is too simple a cause to produce such fantastic variety: that, again, is a question to be settled exclusively by physical students. All we have to say on the matter is—That we always knew that God works by very simple, or seemingly simple, means; that the whole universe, as far as we could discern it, was one concatenation of the most simple means; that it was wonderful, yea, miraculous, in our eyes, that a child should resemble its parents, that the raindrops should make the grass grow, that the grass should become flesh, and the flesh sustenance for the thinking brain of man. Ought God to seem less or more august in our eyes, when we are told that His means are even more simple than we supposed? We held him to be Almighty and All-wise. Are we to reverence Him less or more, if we hear that His might is greater, His wisdom deeper, than we ever dreamed? We believed that His care was over all His works; that His Providence watched perpetually over the whole universe. We were taught—some of us at least—by Holy Scripture, to believe that the whole history of the universe was made up of special Providences. If, then, that should be true which Mr Darwin eloquently writes—"It may be metaphorically said that natural selection is daily and hourly scrutinizing, throughout the world, every variation, even the slightest; rejecting that which is bad, preserving and adding up that which is good, silently and incessantly working whenever and wherever opportunity offers at the improvement of every organic being,"—if that, I say, were proven to be true: ought God's care and God's providence to seem less or more magnificent in our eyes? Of old it was said by Him without whom nothing is made, "My Father worketh hitherto, and I work." Shall we quarrel with Science, if she should show how those words are true? What, in one word, should we have to say but this?—We knew of old that God was so wise that He could make all things: but, behold, He is so much wiser than even that, that He can make all things make themselves.

But it may be said—These notions are contrary to Scripture. I must beg very humbly, but very firmly, to demur to that opinion. Scripture says that God created. But it nowhere defines that term. The means, the How, of Creation is nowhere specified. Scripture, again, says that organized beings were produced, each according to their kind. But it nowhere defines that term. What a kind includes; whether it includes or not the capacity of varying—which is just the question in point—is nowhere specified. And I think it a most important rule in Scriptural exegesis, to be most cautious as to limiting the meaning of any term which Scripture itself has not limited, lest we find ourselves putting into the teaching of Scripture our own human theories or prejudices. And consider—Is not man a kind? And has not mankind varied, physically, intellectually, spiritually? Is not the Bible, from beginning to end, a history of the variations of mankind, for worse or for better, from their original type?

Let us rather look with calmness, and even with hope and goodwill, on these new theories; for, correct or incorrect, they surely mark a tendency towards a more, not a less, Scriptural view of Nature. Are they not attempts, whether successful or unsuccessful, to escape from that shallow mechanical notion of the universe and its Creator which was too much in vogue in the eighteenth century among divines as well as philosophers; the theory which Goethe, to do him justice—and after him Mr Thomas Carlyle—have treated with such noble scorn; the theory, I mean, that God has wound up the universe like a clock, and left it to tick by itself till it runs down, never troubling Himself with it; save possibly—for even that was only half believed—

by rare miraculous interferences with the laws which He Himself had made? Out of that chilling dream of a dead universe ungoverned by an absent God, the human mind, in Germany especially, tried during the early part of this century to escape by strange roads; roads by which there was no escape, because they were not laid down on the firm ground of scientific facts. Then, in despair, men turned to the facts which they had neglected; and said—We are weary of philosophy: we will study you, and you alone. As for God, who can find Him? And they have worked at the facts like gallant and honest men; and their work, like all good work, has produced, in the last fifty years, results more enormous than they even dreamed. But what are they finding, more and more, below their facts, below all phenomena which the scalpel and the microscope can show? A something nameless, invisible, imponderable, yet seemingly omnipresent and omni-potent, retreating before them deeper and deeper, the deeper they delve: namely, the life which shapes and makes; that which the old schoolmen called "forma formativa," which they call vital force and what not—metaphors all, or rather counters to mark an unknown quantity, as if they should call it x or y. One says—It is all vibrations: but his reason, unsatisfied, asks—And what makes the vibrations vibrate? Another—It is all physiological units: but his reason asks—What is the "physis," the nature and innate tendency of the units? A third—It may be all caused by infinitely numerous "gemmules:" but his reason asks him—What puts infinite order into these gemmules, instead of infinite anarchy? I mention these theories not to laugh at them. I have all due respect for those who have put them forth. Nor would it interfere with my theological creed, if any or all of them were proven to be true to-morrow. I mention them only to show that beneath all these theories, true or false, still lies that unknown x. Scientific men are becoming more and more aware of it; I had almost said, ready to worship it. More and more the noblest-minded of them are engrossed by the mystery of that unknown and truly miraculous element in Nature, which is always escaping them, though they cannot escape it. How should they escape it? Was it not written of old—"Whither shall I go from Thy presence, or whither shall I flee from Thy Spirit?"

Ah that we clergymen would summon up courage to tell them that! Courage to tell them, what need not hamper for a moment the freedom of their investigations, what will add to them a sanction—I may say a sanctity —that the unknown x which lies below all phenomena, which is for ever at work on all phenomena, on the whole and on every part of the whole, down to the colouring of every leaf and the curdling of every cell of protoplasm, is none other than that which the old Hebrews called—by a metaphor, no doubt: for how can man speak of the unseen, save in metaphors drawn from the seen?—but by the only metaphor adequate to express the perpetual and omnipresent miracle; The Breath of God; The Spirit who is The Lord, and The Giver of Life.

In the rest, let us too think, and let us too observe. For if we are ignorant, not merely of the results of experimental science, but of the methods thereof: then we and the men of science shall have no common ground whereon to stretch out kindly hands to each other.

But let us have patience and faith; and not suppose in haste, that when those hands are stretched out it will be needful for us to leave our standing-ground, or to cast ourselves down from the pinnacle of the temple to earn popularity; above all, from earnest students who are too high-minded to care for popularity themselves.

True, if we have an intelligent belief in those Creeds and those Scriptures which are committed to our keeping, then our philosophy cannot be that which is just now in vogue. But all we have to do, I believe, is to wait. Nominalism, and that "Sensationalism" which has sprung from Nominalism, are running fast to seed; Comtism seems to me its supreme effort: after which the whirligig of Time may bring round its revenges: and Realism, and we who hold the Realist creeds, may have our turn. Only wait. When a grave, able, and authoritative philosopher explains a mother's love of her newborn babe, as Professor Bain has done, in a really eloquent passage of his book on the *Emotions and the Will*[1], then the end of that philosophy is very near; and an older, simpler, more human,

---

[1] Second edition, pp. 78, 79.

and, as I hold, more philosophic explanation of that natural phenomenon, and of all others, may get a hearing.

Only wait: and fret not yourselves; else shall you be moved to do evil. Remember the saying of the wise man—"Go not after the world. She turns on her axis; and if thou stand still long enough, she will turn round to thee."

SERMON I.

THE MYSTERY OF THE CROSS. A GOOD FRIDAY SERMON.

PHILIPPIANS II. 5—8.

Let this mind be in you, which was also in Christ Jesus: who, being in the form of God, thought it not robbery to be equal with God: but made Himself of no reputation, and took upon Him the form of a slave, and was made in the likeness of men: and being found in fashion as a man, He humbled Himself, and became obedient unto death, even the death of the Cross.

THE second Lesson for this morning's service, and the chapter which follows it, describe the Passion of our Lord Jesus Christ, both God and Man. They give us the facts, in language most awful from its perfect calmness, most pathetic from its perfect simplicity. But the passage of St Paul which I have chosen for my text gives us an explanation of those facts which is utterly amazing. That He who stooped to die upon the Cross is Very God of Very God, the Creator and Sustainer of the Universe, is a thought so overwhelming, whenever we try to comprehend even a part of it in our small imaginations, that it is no wonder if, in all ages, many a pious soul, as it contemplated the Cross of

Christ, has been rapt itself into a passion of gratitude, an ecstasy of wonder and of love, which is beautiful, honourable, just, and in the deepest sense most rational, whenever it is spontaneous and natural.

But there have been thousands, as there may be many here to-day, of colder temperament; who would distrust in themselves, even while they respected in others, any violence of religious emotion : yet they too have found, and you too may find, in contemplating the Passion of Christ, a satisfaction deeper than that of any emotion; a satisfaction not to the heart, still less to the brain, but to that far deeper and diviner faculty within us all—our moral sense; that God-given instinct which makes us discern and sympathise with all that is beautiful and true and good.

And so it has befallen, for eighteen hundred years, that thousands who have thought earnestly and carefully on God and on the character of God, on man and on the universe, and on their relation to Him who made them both, have found in the Incarnation and the Passion of the Son of God the perfect satisfaction of their moral wants; the surest key to the facts of the spiritual world; the complete assurance that, in spite of all seeming difficulties and contradictions, the Maker of the world was a Righteous Being, who had founded the world in righteousness; that the Father of Spirits was a perfect Father, who in His only-begotten Son had shewn forth His perfectness, in such a shape and by such acts that men might not only adore it, but sympathise with it; not only thank Him for it, but copy it; and become, though at an infinite distance, perfect as their Father in heaven is perfect, and full of grace and truth, like that Son who is the brightness of His Father's glory, and the express image of His person. Such a satisfaction have they found in looking upon the triumphal entry into Jerusalem of Him who knew that it would be followed by the revolt of the fickle mob, and the desertion of His disciples, and the Cross of Calvary, and all the hideous circumstances of a Roman malefactor's death.

But there have been those, and there are still, who have found no such satisfaction in the story which the Gospel tells, and still less in the explanation which the Epistle gives; who have, as St Paul says, stumbled at the stumblingblock of the Cross.

It would be easy to ignore such persons, were they scoffers or profligates: but when they number among their ranks men of virtuous lives, of earnest and most benevolent purposes, of careful and learned thought, and of a real reverence for God, or for those theories of the universe which some of them are inclined to substitute for God, they must at least be listened to patiently, and answered charitably, as men who, however faulty their opinions may be, prove, by their virtue and their desire to do good, that if they have lost sight of Christ, Christ has not lost sight of them.

To such men the idea of the Incarnation, and still more, that of the Passion, is derogatory to the very notion of a God. That a God should suffer, and that a God should die, is shocking—and, to do them justice, I believe they speak sincerely—to their notions of the may be wrapped up, is real and true, and will be so as long as evil exists within this universe. Were it not true, there would be something wanting to the perfect justice and the perfect benevolence of God.

But is this all? If this be all, what have we Christians learnt from the New Testament which is not already taught us in the Old? Where is that new, deeper, higher revelation of the goodness of God, which Jesus of Nazareth preached, and which John and Paul and all the apostles believed that they had found in Jesus Himself? They believed, and all those who accepted their gospel believed, that they had found for that word "grace," a deeper meaning than had ever been revealed to the prophets of old time; that grace and goodness, if they were perfect, involved self-sacrifice.

And does not our own highest reason tell us that they were right? Does not our own highest reason, which is our moral sense, tell us that perfect goodness requires, not merely that we should pity our fellow-creatures, not merely that we should help them, not merely that we should right them magisterially and royally, without danger or injury to ourselves: but that we should toil for them, suffer for them, and if need be, as the highest act of goodness, die for them at last? Is not this the very element of goodness which we all confess to be most noble, beautiful, pure, heroical, divine? Divine even in sinful and fallen man, who must forgive because he needs to be forgiven; who must help others because he needs help himself; who, if he suffers for others, deserves to suffer, and probably will suffer, in himself. But how

much more heroical, and how much more divine in a
Being who needs neither forgiveness nor help, and who is
as far from deserving as He is from needing to suffer!
And shall this noblest form of goodness be possible to
sinful man, and yet impossible to a perfectly good God?
Shall we say that the martyr at the stake, the patriot
dying for his country, the missionary spending his life for
the good of heathens; ay more, shall we say that those
women, martyrs by the pang without the palm, who in
secret chambers, in lowly cottages, have sacrificed and do
still sacrifice self and all the joys of life for the sake of
simple duties, little charities, kindness unnoticed and unknown by all, save God—shall we say that all who have
from the beginning of the world shewn forth the beauty
of self-sacrifice have had no divine prototype in heaven?
—That they have been exercising a higher grace, a nobler
form of holiness, than He who made them, and who, as
they believe, and we ought to believe, inspired them with
that spirit of unselfishness, which if it be not the Spirit of
God, whose spirit can it be? Shall we say this, and so
suppose them holier than their own Maker? Shall we say
this, and suppose that they, when they attributed self-
sacrifice to God, made indeed a God in their own image,
but a God of greater love, greater pity, greater graciousness because of greater unselfishness, than Him who
really exists?

Shall we say this, the very words whereof confute
themselves and shock alike our reason and our conscience? Or shall we say with St John and with St
Paul, that if men can be so good, God must be in-

finitely better; that if man can love so much, God must love more; if man, by shaking off the selfishness which is his bane, can do such deeds, then God, in whom is no selfishness at all, may at least have done a deed as far above theirs as the heavens are above the earth? Shall we not confess that man's self-sacrifice is but a poor and dim reflection of the self sacrifice of God, and say with St John, "Herein is love, not that we loved God, but that He loved us, and sent His Son to be the propitiation for our sins;" and with St Paul, "Scarcely for a righteous man would one die, but God commendeth His love to us in this, that while we were yet sinners, Christ died for us"? Shall we not say this: and find, as thousands have found ere now, in the Cross of Calvary the perfect satisfaction of our highest moral instincts, the realization in act and fact of the highest idea which we can form of perfect condescension, namely, self-sacrifice exercised by a Being of whom perfect condescension, love and self-sacrifice were not required by aught in heaven or earth, save by the necessity of His own perfect and inconceivable goodness?

We reverence, and rightly, the majesty of God. How can that infinite majesty be proved more perfectly than by condescension equally infinite? We adore, and justly, the serenity of God, who has neither parts nor passions. How can that serenity be proved more perfectly, than by passing, still serene, through all the storm and crowd of circumstance which disturb the weak serenity of man; by passing through poverty, helplessness, temptation, desertion, shame, torture, death; and passing through them all

victorious and magnificent; with a moral calm as undisturbed, a moral purity as unspotted, as it had been from
all eternity, as it will be to all eternity, in that abysmal
source of being, which we call the Bosom of the Father?
It is the moral majesty of God, as shewn on Calvary,
which I uphold. Shew that Calvary was not inconsistent
with that; shew that Calvary was not inconsistent with
the goodness of God, but rather the perfection of that
goodness shewn forth in time and space: then all other
arguments connected with God's majesty may go for
nought, provided that God's moral majesty be safe.
Provided God be proved to be morally infinite—that
is, in plain English, infinitely good; provided God be
proved to be morally absolute—that is, absolutely unable to have His goodness affected by any circumstance
outside Him, even by the death upon the Cross: then let
.the rest go. All words about absoluteness and infinity
and majesty, beyond that, are physical—metaphors drawn
from matter, which have nothing to do with God who is
a Spirit.

But God's infinite power too often means, in the
minds of men, only some abstract notion of boundless
bodily strength. God's omniscience too often means,
only some physical fancy of innumerable telescopic or
microscopic eyes. God's infinite wisdom too often means,
only some abstract notion of boundless acuteness of brain.
And lastly—I am sorry to have to say it, but it must be
said,—God's infinite majesty too often means, in the
minds of some superstitious people, mere pride, and
obstinacy, and cruelty, as of the blind will of some

enormous animal which does what it chooses, whether right or wrong.

If the mystery of the Cross contradict any of these carnal or material notions, so much the more glory *to* the mystery of the Cross. One spiritual infinite, one spiritual absolute, it does not contradict: and that is the infinite and absolute goodness of God.

Let all the rest remain a mystery, so long as the mystery of the Cross gives us faith for all the rest.

Faith, I say. The mystery of evil, of sorrow, of death, the Gospel does not pretend to solve: but it tells us that the mystery is proved to be soluble. For God Himself has taken on Himself the task of solving it; and has proved by His own act, that if there be evil in the world, it is none of His; for He hates it, and fights against it, and has fought against it to the death.

It simply says—Have faith in God. Ask no more of. Him—Why hast Thou made me thus? Ask no more—Why do the wicked prosper on the earth? Ask no more—Whence pain and death, war and famine, earth-quake and tempest, and all the ills to which flesh is heir?

All fruitless questionings, all peevish repinings, are precluded henceforth by the passion and death of Christ.

Dost thou suffer? Thou canst not suffer more than the Son of God. Dost thou sympathize with thy fellow-men? Thou canst not sympathize more than the Son of God. Dost thou long to right them, to deliver them, even at the price of thine own blood? Thou canst not long more ardently than the Son of God, who carried His longing into act, and died for them and thee. What if the end be not yet? What if evil still endure? What if the medicine have not yet conquered the disease? Have patience, have faith, have hope, as thou standest at the foot of Christ's Cross, and holdest fast to it, the anchor of the soul and reason, as well as of the heart. For however ill the world may go, or seem to go, the Cross is the everlasting token that God so loved the world, that He spared not His only-begotten Son, but freely gave Him for it. Whatsoever else is doubtful, this at least is sure,—that good must conquer, because God is good; that evil must perish, because God hates evil, even to the death.

SERMON II.

THE PERFECT LOVE.

1 JOHN IV. 10.

Herein is love, not that we loved God, but that He loved us, and
sent His Son to be the propitiation for our sins.

THIS is Passion-week; the week in which, according to
ancient and most wholesome rule, we are bidden to think
of the Passion of Jesus Christ our Lord.   To think of
that, however happy and comfortable, however busy and
eager, however covetous and ambitious, however giddy
and frivolous, however free, or at least desirous to be
free, from suffering of any kind, we are ourselves.   To
think of the sufferings of Christ, and learn how grand it
is to suffer for the Right.

And why?

Passion-week gives but one answer: but that answer
is the one best worth listening to.

It is grand and good to suffer for the Right, because
God, in Christ, has suffered for the Right.

Let us consider this awhile.

It is a first axiom in sound theology, that there is
nothing good in man, which was not first in God.

Now we all, I trust, hold God to be supremely good. We ascribe to Him, in perfection, every kind of goodness of which we can conceive in man. We say God is just; God is truthful; God is pure; God is bountiful; God is merciful; and, in one word, God is Love.

God is Love. But if we say that, do we not say that God is good with a fresh form of goodness, which is not justice, nor truthfulness, nor purity, bounty, nor mercy, though without them—never forget that—it cannot exist? And is not that fresh goodness, which we have not defined yet, the very kind of goodness which we prize most in human beings? The very kind of goodness which makes us prize and admire. love, because without it there is no true love, no love worth calling by that sacred and heavenly name? And what is that?

What—save self-sacrifice? For what is the love worth which does not shew itself in action; and more, which does not shew itself in Passion, in the true sense of that word, which this week teaches us: namely, in suffering? Not merely in acting for, but in daring, in struggling, in grieving, in agonizing, and, if need be, in dying for, the object of its love?

Every mother in this church will give but one answer to that question; for mothers give it among the very animals; and the deer who fights for her fawn, the bird who toils for her nestlings, the spider who will rather die than drop her bag of eggs, know at least that love is not worth calling love, unless it can dare and suffer for the thing it loves. The most gracious of all virtues, therefore, is self-sacrifice; and is there no like grace in

God, the fount of grace? Has God, whose name is
Love, never dared, never suffered, even to the death, in
the mightiness of a perfect Love?

We Christians say that He has. We say so, because
it has been revealed to us, not by flesh and blood, not
by brain or nerves, not by logic or emotions, but by
the Spirit of God, to whom our inmost spirits and highest
reasons have made answer—A God who has suffered for
man? That is so beautiful, that it must be true.

For otherwise we should be left—as I have argued
at length elsewhere—in this strange paradox:—that man
has fancied to himself for 1800 years a more beautiful
God, a nobler God, a better God than the God who
actually exists. It must be so, if God is not capable of
that highest virtue of self-sacrifice, while man has been
believing that He is, and that upon the first Good Friday
He sacrificed Himself for man, out of the intensity of
a boundless Love. A better God imagined by man,
than the actual God who made man? We have only to
state that absurdity, I trust, to laugh it to scorn.

Let us confess, then, that the Passion of Christ, and
the mystery of Good Friday, is as reasonable a belief
to the truly wise, as it is comfortable to the weary and
the suffering; let us agree that one of the wisest of
Englishmen, of late gone to his rest, spoke well when he
said, "As long as women and sorrow exist on earth, so
long will the gospel of Christianity find an echo in the
human heart." Let it find an echo in yours. But it
will only find one, in as far as you can enter into the
mystery of Passion-week; in as far as you can learn

from Passion-week the truest and highest theology; and see what God is like, and therefore what you must try to be like likewise.

Let us think, then, awhile of the mystery of Passion-week; the mystery of the Cross of Christ. Christ Himself was looking on the coming Cross, during this Passion-week; ay, and for many a week before. Nay rather, had He not looked on it from all eternity? For is He not the Lamb slain from the foundation of the world? Therefore we may well look on it with Him. It may seem, at first, a painful sight. But shall it cast over our minds only gloom and darkness? Or shall we not see on the Cross the full revelation of Light; of the Light which lightens every man that comes into the world: and find that painful, not because of its darkness, but as the blaze of full sunshine is painful, from unbearable intensity of warmth and light? Let us see.

On the Cross of Calvary, then, God the Father shewed His own character and the character of His co-equal and co-eternal Son, and of The Spirit which proceeds from both. For there He spared not His only-begotten Son, but freely gave Him for us. On the Cross of Calvary, not by the will of man, but by the determinate counsel and foreknowledge of God, was offered before God the one and only full, perfect, and sufficient sacrifice, oblation, and satisfaction for the sin of the whole world. God Himself did this. It was not done by any other being to alter His will; it was done to fulfil His will. It was not done to satisfy God's anger; it was done to satisfy God's love. Therefore

Good Friday was well and wisely called by our fore-fathers Good Friday; because it shews, as no other day can do, that God is good; that God's will to men, in spite of all their sins, is a good will; that so boundless, so utterly unselfish and condescending, is the eternal love of God, that when an insignificant race in a small and remote planet fell, and went wrong, and was in danger of ruin, there was nothing that God would not dare, God would not suffer, for the sake of even such as us, vile earth and miserable sinners.

Yes, this is the good news of Passion-week ; a gospel which men are too apt to forget, even to try to forget, as long as they are comfortable and prosperous, lazy and selfish. The comfortable prosperous man shrinks from the thought of Christ on His Cross. It tells him that better men than he have had to suffer; that The Son of God Himself had to suffer. And he does not like suffering; he prefers comfort. The lazy, selfish man shrinks from the sight of Christ on His Cross; for it rebukes his laziness and selfishness. Christ's Cross says to him—Thou art ignoble and base, as long as thou art lazy and selfish. Rise up, do something, dare something, suffer something, if need be, for the sake of thy fellow-creatures. Be of use. Take trouble. Face discomfort, contradiction, loss of worldly advantage, if it must be, for the sake of speaking truth and doing right. If thou wilt not do as much as that, then the simplest soldier who goes to die in battle for his duty, is a better man than thou, a nobler man than thou, more like Christ and more like God. That is what Christ's Cross preaches to the lazy, selfish man; and he feels in his heart that the sermon is true: but he does not like it. He turns from it, and says in his heart — Oh! Christ's Cross is a painful subject, and Passion-week and Good Friday a painful time. I will think of something more genial, more peaceful, more agreeable than sorrow, and shame, and agony, and death; Good Friday is too sad a day for me.

Yes, so a man says too often, as long as the fine weather lasts, and all is smooth and bright. But when the tempest comes; when poverty comes, affliction, anxiety, shame, sickness, bereavement, and still more, when persecution comes on a man; when he tries to speak truth and do right; and finds, as he will too often find, that people, instead of loving him and praising him for speaking truth and doing right, hate him and persecute him for it: then, then indeed Passion-week begins to mean something to a man; and just because it is the saddest of all times, it looks to him the brightest of all times. For in his misery and confusion he looks up to heaven and asks—Is there any one in heaven who understands all this? Does God understand my trouble? Does God feel for my trouble? Does God care for my trouble? Does God know what trouble means? Or must I fight the battle of life alone, without sympathy or help from God who made me, and has put me here? Then, then does the Cross of Christ bring a message to that man such as no other thing or being on earth can bring. For it says to him—God does understand thee utterly. For Christ understands thee. Christ feels for thee. Christ feels with thee. Christ has suffered for thee,

and suffered with thee. Thou canst go through nothing
which Christ has not gone through. He, the Son of
God, endured poverty, fear, shame, agony, death for thee,
that He might be touched with the feeling of thine in-
firmity, and help thee to endure, and bring thee safe
through all to victory and peace.

But again, Passion-week, and above all Good Friday, is a good time, because it teaches us, above all
days, what it is to be good, and what goodness means.
Therefore remember this, all of you, and take it home
with you for the year to come. He who has learnt the
lesson of Passion-week, and practises it; he and he only
is a good man.

Nay more, Passion-week tells us, I believe, what is
the law according to which the whole world of man and
of things, yea, the whole universe, sun, moon, and stars,
is made: and that is, the law of self-sacrifice; that nothing
lives merely for itself; that each thing is ordained by
God to help the things around it, even at its own expense. That is a hard saying: and yet it must be true.
The soundest Theology and the highest Reason tell us
that it must be so. For there cannot be two Holy
Spirits. Now the Spirit by which the Lord Jesus Christ
sacrificed himself upon the Cross is The Holy Spirit.
And the Spirit by which the Lord Jesus Christ made all
worlds is The Holy Spirit. But the spirit by which He
sacrificed Himself on the Cross is the spirit of self-
sacrifice. And therefore the spirit by which He made the
world is the spirit of self-sacrifice likewise; and self-
sacrifice is the law and rule on which the universe is

founded. At least, that is the true Catholic faith, as far as my poor intellect can conceive it; and in that faith I will live and die.

There are those who, now-a-days, will laugh at such a notion, and say—Self-sacrifice? It is not self-sacrifice which keeps the world going among men, or animals, or even the plants under our feet: but selfishness. Competition, they say, is the law of the universe. Everything has to take care of itself, fight for itself, compete freely and pitilessly with everything round it, till the weak are killed off, and only the strong survive; and so, out of the free play of the self-interest of each, you get the greatest possible happiness of the greatest possible number.

Do we indeed? I should have thought that unbridled selfishness, and the internecine struggle of opposing interests, had already reduced many nations, and seemed likely to reduce all mankind, if it went on, to that state of the greatest possible misery of the greatest number, from which our blessed Lord, as in this very week, died to deliver us. At all events, if that is to be the condition of man, and of society, then man is not made in the likeness of God, and has no need to be led by the Spirit of God. For what the likeness of God and the Spirit of God are, Passion-week tells us—namely, Love which knows no self-interest; Love which cares not for itself; Love which throws its own life away, that it may save those who have hated it, rebelled against it, put it to a felon's death.

My good friends, instead of believing the carnal and

selfish philosophy which cries, Every man for himself—I will not finish the proverb in this Holy place, awfully and literally true as the latter half of it is—instead of believing that, believe the message of Passion-week, which speaks rather thus: telling us that not selfishness, but unselfishness, mutual help and usefulness, is the law and will of God; and that therefore the whole universe, and all that God has made, is very good. And what does Passion-week say to men?

> "Could we but crush that ever-craving lust
>   For bliss, which kills all bliss; and lose our life,
> Our barren unit life, to find again
> A thousand lives in those for whom we die:
> So were we men and women, and should hold
> Our rightful place in God's great universe,
> Wherein, in heaven and earth, by will or nature,
> Nought lives for self. All, all, from crown to footstool.
> The Lamb, before the world's foundation slain;
> The angels, ministers to God's elect;
> The sun, who only shines to light a world;
> The clouds, whose glory is to die in showers;
> The fleeting streams, who in their ocean graves
> Flee the decay of stagnant self-content;
> The oak, ennobled by the shipwright's axe;
> The soil, which yields its marrow to the flower;
> The flower which breeds a thousand velvet worms,
> Born only to be prey to every bird—
> All spend themselves on others; and shall man,
> Whose twofold being is the mystic knot
> Which couples earth and heaven—doubly bound,
> As being both worm and angel, to that service
> By which both worms and angels hold their lives—
> Shall he, whose very breath is debt on debt,

> Refuse, forsooth, to see what God has made him?
> No, let him shew himself the creatures' lord
> By freewill gift of that self-sacrifice
> Which they, perforce, by nature's law must suffer;
> Take up his cross, and follow Christ the Lord."

And thus Passion-week tells all men in what true goodness lies. In self-sacrifice. In it Christ on His Cross shewed men what was the likeness of God, the goodness of God, the glory of God—to suffer for sinful man.

On this day Christ said—ay, and His Cross says still, and will say to all eternity—Wouldest thou be good? Wouldest thou be like God? Then work, and dare, and, if need be, suffer, for thy fellow-men. On this day Christ consecrated, and, as it were, offered up to the Father in His own body on the Cross, all loving actions, unselfish actions, merciful actions, generous actions, heroic actions, which man has done, or ever will do. From Him, from His Spirit, their strength came; and therefore He is not ashamed to call them brethren. He is the King of the noble army of martyrs; of all who suffer for love, and truth, and justice' sake; and to all such he says—Thou hast put on my likeness, and followed my footsteps; thou hast suffered for my sake, and I too have suffered for thy sake, and enabled thee to suffer in like wise; and in Me thou too art a son of God, in whom the Father is well pleased.

Oh, let us contemplate this week Christ on His Cross, sacrificing Himself for us and all mankind; and may that sight help to cast out of us all laziness and selfishness, and make us vow obedience to the spirit of self-sacrifice, the Spirit of Christ and of God, which was given to us at our baptism. And let us give, as we are most bound, in all humility and contrition of heart, thanks, praise, and adoration, to that immortal Lamb, who abideth for ever in the midst of the throne of God, the Lamb slain before the foundation of the world, by Whom all things consist; and Who in this week died on the Cross in mortal flesh and blood, that He might make this a good week to all mankind, and teach selfish man that only by being un-selfish can he too be good; and only by self-sacrifice become perfect, even as The Father in heaven is perfect.

SERMON III.

THE SPIRIT OF WHITSUNTIDE.

The spirit of the Lord shall rest upon him; the spirit of wisdom and understanding, the spirit of counsel and might, the spirit of knowledge and of the fear of the Lord.

THIS is Isaiah's description of the Spirit of Whitsuntide; the royal Spirit which was to descend, and did descend without measure, on the ideal and perfect King, even on Jesus Christ our Lord, the only-begotten Son of God.

That Spirit is the Spirit of God; and therefore the Spirit of Christ.

Let us consider a while what that Spirit is.

He is the Spirit of love. For God is love; and He is the Spirit of God. Of that there can be no doubt.

He is the Spirit of boundless love and charity, which is the Spirit of the Father, and the Spirit of the Son likewise. For when by that Spirit of love the Father sent the Son into the world that the world through Him might be saved, then the Son, by the same Spirit of love, came into the world, and humbled Himself, and took on Him the form of a slave, and was obedient unto death, even the death of the Cross.

The Spirit of God, then, is the Spirit of love.

But the text describes this Spirit in different words. According to Isaiah, the Spirit of the Lord is the spirit of wisdom and understanding, the spirit of counsel and might, the spirit of knowledge and of the fear of the Lord—in one word, that I may put it as simply as I can—the spirit of wisdom.

Now, is the spirit of wisdom the same as the spirit of love?

Sound theology, which is the highest reason, tells us that it must be so.   For consider:

If the spirit of love is the Spirit of God, and the spirit of wisdom is the Spirit of God, then they must be the same spirit.   For if they be two different spirits, then there must be two Holy Spirits; for any and every Spirit of God must be holy,—what else can He be? Unholy?   I leave you to answer that.

But two Holy Spirits there cannot be; for holiness, which is wisdom, justice, and love, is one and indivisible; and as the Athanasian Creed tells us, and as our highest reason ought to tell us, there is but one Holy Spirit, who must be at once a spirit of wisdom and a spirit of love.

To suppose anything else; to suppose that God's wisdom and God's love, or that God's justice and God's love, are different from each other, or limit each other, or oppose each other, or are anything but one and the same eternally, is to divide God's substance; to deny that God is One: which is forbidden us, rightly, and according to the highest reason, by the Athanasian Creed.

But more; experience will shew us that the spirit of love is the same as the spirit of wisdom; that if any man wishes to be truly wise and prudent, his best way—I may say his only way—is to be loving and charitable.

The experience of the apostles proves it. They were, I presume, the most perfectly loving and charitable of men; they sacrificed all for the sake of doing good; they counted not their own lives dear to them; they endured—what did they not endure?—for the one object of doing good to men; and—what is harder, still harder, for any human being, because it requires not merely enthusiasm, but charity, they made themselves (St Paul at least) all things to all men, if by any means they might save some.

But were they wise in so doing? We may judge of a man's wisdom, my friends, by his success. We English are very apt to do so. We like practical men. We say —I will tell you what a man is, by what he can do.

Now, judged by that rule, surely the apostles' method of winning men by love proved itself a wise method. What did the apostles do? They had the most enormous practical success that men ever had. They, twelve poor men, set out to convert mankind by loving them: and they succeeded.

Remember, moreover, that the text speaks of this Spirit of the Lord being given to One who was to be a King, a Ruler, a Guide, and a Judge of men; who was to exercise influence over men for their good. This prophecy was fulfilled first in the King of kings, our Lord Jesus Christ: but it was fulfilled also in His apostles, who were, in their own way and measure, kings of men, exercising a vast influence over them. And how? By the royal Spirit of love. In the apostles the Spirit of love and charity proved Himself to be also the Spirit of wisdom and understanding. He gave them such a converting, subduing, alluring power over men's hearts, as no men have had, before or since. And He will prove Himself to have the same power in us. Our own experience will be the same as the apostles' experience.

I say this deliberately. The older we grow, the more we understand our own lives and histories, the more we shall see that the spirit of wisdom is the spirit of love; that the true way to gain influence over our fellow-men, is to have charity towards them.

That is a hard lesson to learn; and those who learn it at all, generally learn it late; almost—God forgive us—too late.

Our reason, if we would let the Spirit of God enlighten it, would teach us this beforehand. But we do not usually listen to our reason, or to God's Spirit speaking to it. And therefore we have to learn the lesson by experience, often by very sad and shameful experience. And even that very experience we cannot understand, unless the Spirit of God interpret it to us: and blessed are they who, having been chastised, hearken to His interpretation.

Our reason, I say, should teach us that the spirit of wisdom is none other than the spirit of love. For consider—how does the text describe this Spirit?

As the spirit of wisdom and understanding ; that is, as the knowledge of human nature, the understanding of men and their ways. If we do not understand our fellow-creatures, we shall never love them.

But it is equally true that if we do not love them, we shall never understand them. Want of charity, want of sympathy, want of good-feeling and fellow-feeling—what does it, what can it breed, but endless mistakes and ignorances, both of men's characters and men's circumstances?

Be sure that no one knows so little of his fellow-men, as the cynical, misanthropic man, who walks in darkness, because he hates his brother. Be sure that the truly wise and understanding man is he who by sympathy puts himself in his neighbours' place ; feels with them and for them ; sees with their eyes, hears with their ears ; and therefore understands them, makes allowances for them, and is merciful to them, even as his Father in heaven is merciful.

And next ; this royal Spirit is described as " the spirit of counsel and might," that is, the spirit of prudence and practical power ; the spirit which sees how to deal with human beings, and has the practical power of making them obey.

Now that power, again, can only be got by loving human beings. There is nothing so blind as hardness, nothing so weak as violence. I, of course, can only speak from my own experience ; and my experience is this : that whensoever in my past life I have been angry and scornful, I have said or done an unwise thing ; I have more or less injured my own cause ; weakened my own influence on my fellow-men ; repelled them instead of attracting them ; made them rebel against me, rather than obey me. By patience, courtesy, and gentleness, we not only make ourselves stronger ; we not only attract our fellow-men, and make them help us and follow us willingly and joyfully : but we make ourselves wiser ; we give ourselves time and light to see what we ought to do, and how to do it.

And next; this Spirit is also " the spirit of knowledge, and of the fear of the Lord." Ay, they, indeed, both begin in love, and end in love. If you wish for knowledge, you must begin by loving knowledge for its own sake. And the more knowledge you gain, the more you will long to know, and more, and yet more for ever. You cannot succeed in a study, unless you love that study. Men of science must begin with an interest in, a love for, an enthusiasm, in the very deepest sense of the word, for the phænomena which they study. But the more they learn of them, the more their love increases ; as they see more and more of their wonder, of their beauty, of the unspeakable wisdom and power of God, shewn forth in every blade of grass which grows in the sunshine and the rain.

And if this be true of things earthly and temporary, how much more of things heavenly and eternal? We must begin by loving whatsoever things are true, whatsoever things are just, whatsoever things are pure, honest, and of good report. We must begin, I say, by loving them with a sort of child's love, without understanding them; by that simple instinct and longing after what is good and beautiful and true, which is indeed the inspiration of the Spirit of God. But as we go on, as St Paul bids us, to meditate on them; and "if there be any virtue and if there be any praise, to think on such things," and feed our minds daily with purifying, elevating, sobering, humanizing, enlightening thoughts: then we shall get to love goodness with a reasonable and manly love; to see the beauty of holiness; the strength of self-sacrifice; the glory of justice; the divineness of love; and in a word— To love God for His own sake, and to give Him thanks for His great glory, which is: That He is a good God.

This thought—remember it, I pray—brings me to the last point. This Spirit is also the spirit of the fear of the Lord. And that too, my friends, must be a spirit of love not only to God, but to our fellow-creatures. For if we but consider that God the Father loves all; that His mercy is over all His works; and that He hateth nothing that He has made: then how dare we hate anything that He has made, as long as we have any rational fear of Him, awe and respect for Him, true faith in His infinite majesty and power? If we but consider that God the Son actually came down on earth to die, and to die too on the cross, for all mankind: then how dare we hate a human being for whom He died: at least if we have true honour, gratitude, loyalty, reverence, and godly fear in our hearts toward Him, our risen Lord?

Oh let us open our eyes this Whitsuntide to the experience of our past lives. Let us see now—what we shall certainly see at the day of judgment—that whenever we have failed to be loving, we have also failed to be wise; that whenever we have been blind to our neighbours' interests, we have also been blind to our own; whenever we have hurt others, we have hurt ourselves still more. Let us, at this blessed Whitsuntide, ask forgiveness of God for all acts of malice and uncharitableness, blindness and hardness of heart; and pray for the spirit of true charity, which alone is true wisdom. And let us come to Holy Communion in charity with each other and with all; determined henceforth to feel for each other and with each other; to put ourselves in our neighbours' places; to see with their eyes, and feel with their hearts, as far as God shall give us that great grace; determined to make allowances for their mistakes and failings; to give and forgive, live and let live, even as God gives and forgives, lives and lets live for ever: that so we may be indeed the children of our Father in heaven, whose name is Love. Then we shall indeed discern the Lord's body—that it is a body of union, sympathy, mutual trust, help, affection. Then we shall, with all contrition and humility, but still in spirit and in truth, claim and obtain our share in the body and the blood, in the spirit and in the mind, of Him Who sacrificed Himself for a rebellious world.

SERMON IV.

PRAYER.

PSALM LXV. 2.

Thou that hearest prayer, unto Thee shall all flesh come.

NEXT Friday, the 20th of December, 1871, will be
marked in most churches of this province of Canter-
bury by a special ceremony. Prayers will be offered
to God for the increase of missionary labourers in the
Church of England. To many persons—I hope I may
say, to all in this congregation—this ceremony will seem
eminently rational. We shall not ask God to suspend
the laws of nature, nor alter the courses of the seasons,
for any wants, real or fancied, of our own. We shall ask
Him to make us and our countrymen wiser and better, in
order that we may make other human beings wiser and
better: and an eminently rational request I assert that
to be.

For no one will deny that it is good for heathens and
savages, even if there were no life after death, to be wiser
and better than they are. It is good, I presume, that
they should give up cannibalism, slave-trading, witchcraft,
child-murder, and a host of other abominations; and that

they should be made to give them up not from mere fear of European cannon, but of their own wills and consciences, seeing that such habits are wrong and ruinous, and loathing them accordingly; in a word, that instead of living as they do, and finding in a hundred ways that the wages of sin are death, they should be converted—that is, change their ways—and live.

Now that this is the will of God—assuming that there is a God, and a good God—is plain at least to our reason, and to our common sense; and it is equally plain to our reason and to our common sense that, as God has not taught these poor wretches to improve themselves, or sent superior beings to improve them from some other world, He therefore means their improvement to be brought about, as moral improvements are usually brought about, by the influence of their fellow-men, and specially by us who have put ourselves in contact with them in our world-wide search for wealth; and who are certain, as we know by sad experience, to make the heathen worse, if we do not make them better. And as we find from experience that our missionaries, wherever they are brought in contact with these savages, do make them wiser and happier, we ask God to inspire more persons with the desire of improving the heathen, and to teach them how to improve them. I say, how to improve them. All sneers, whether at the failure of missionary labours, or at the small results in return for the vast sums spent on missions—all such sneers, I say, instead of deterring us from praying to God on this matter, ought to make us pray the more earnestly in proportion as they are deserved. For they ought to remind us that we possibly may not have gone to work as yet altogether in the right way; that there may be mistakes and deficiencies in our method of dealing with the heathen. And if so, it seems all the more reason for asking God to set us and others right, in case we should be wrong; and to make us and others strong, in case we should be weak.

We thus commit the matter to God. We do not ask God to raise up such missionary labourers as we think fit: but such as He thinks fit. We do not pray Him to alter His will concerning the heathen: but to enable us to do what we know already to be His will. And this course seems to me eminently rational; provided always, of course, that it is rational to believe that there is a God who answers prayer; and that if we ask anything according to His will, He hears us.

Now the older I grow, and the more I see of the chances and changes of this mortal life, and of the needs and longings of the human heart, the more important seems this question, and all words concerning it, whether in the Bible or out of the Bible—

Is there anywhere in the universe any being who can hear our prayers? Is prayer a superfluous folly, or the highest prudence?

I say—Is there a being who can even hear our prayers? I do not say, a being who will always answer them, and give us all we ask: but one who will at least hear, who will listen; consider whether what we ask is fit to be granted or not; and grant or refuse accordingly.

K. S.   5

You say What is the need of asking such a question? Of course we believe that. Of course we pray, else why are we in church to-day?

Well, my friends, God grant that you may all believe it in spirit and in truth. But you must remember that if so, you are in the minority; that the majority of civilized men, like the majority of mere savages, do not pray, whatever the women may do; and that prayer among thinking and civilized white men has been becoming, for the last 100 years at least, more and more unfashionable; and is likely, to judge from the signs of the times, to become more unfashionable still: after which reign of degrading ungodliness, I presume—from the experience of all history—that our children or grand-children will see a revulsion to some degrading superstition, and the latter end be worse than the beginning. But it is notorious that men are doubting more and more of the efficacy of prayer; that philosophers so-called, for true philosophers they are not—even though they may be true, able, and worthy students of merely physical science—are getting a hearing more and more readily, when they tell men they need not pray.

They say; and here they say rightly—The world is ruled by laws. But some say further; and there they say wrongly;—For that reason prayer is of no use; the laws will not be altered to please you. You yourself are but tiny parts of a great machine, which will grind on in spite of you, though it grind you to powder; and there is no use in asking the machine to stop. So, they say, prayer is an impertinence. I would that they stopped there. For then we who deny that the world is a machine, or anything like a machine, might argue fairly with them on the common ground of a common belief in God.

But some go further still, and say—A God? We do not deny that there may be a God: but we do not deny that there may not be one. This we say—If He exists, we know nothing of Him: and what is more, you know nothing of Him. No man can know aught of Him. No man can know whether there be a God or not. A living God, an acting God, a God of providence, a God who hears prayer, a God such as your Bible tells you of, is an inconceivable Being; and what you cannot conceive, that you must not believe: and therefore prayer is not merely an impertinence, it is a mistake; for it is speaking to a Being who only exists in your own imagination. I need not say, my friends, that all this, to my mind, is only a train of sophistry and false reasoning, which—so I at least hold—has been answered and refuted again and again. And I trust in God and in Christ sufficiently to believe that He will raise up sound divines and true philosophers in His Church, who will refute it once more. But meanwhile I can only appeal to your common sense; to the true and higher reason, which lies in men's hearts, not in their heads; and ask—And is it come to this? Is this the last outcome of civilization, the last discovery of the human intellect, the last good news for man? That the soundest thinkers—they who have the truest and clearest notion of the universe—are the savage who knows nothing but what his five senses teach him, and the ungodly who makes boast of his own desire, and speaks good of the covetous whom God abhorreth, while he says, "Tush, God hath forgotten. He hideth away his face, and God will never see it"?

True: these so-called philosophers would say that the savage makes a mistake in his sensuality, and the worldling in his covetousness and his tyranny; that from an imperfect conception of their own true self-interest, they carry their philosophy to conclusions which the philosopher in his study must regret. But as to their philosophy being correct: there can be no question that if providence, and prayer, and the living God, be phantoms of man's imagination, then the cynical worldling at one end of the social scale, and the brutal savage at the other, are wiser than apostles and prophets, and sages and divines.

These men talk of facts, the facts of human nature. Why do they ask us to ignore the most striking fact of human nature, that man, even if he were a mere animal, is alone of all animals—a praying animal? Is that strange instinct of worship, which rises in the heart of man as soon as he begins to think, to become a civilized being and not a savage, to be disregarded as a childish dream when he rises to a higher civilization still? Is the experience of men, heathen as well as Christian, for all these ages to go for nought? Has it mattered nought whether men cried to Baal or to God; for with both alike there has been neither sound nor voice, nor any that answered? Has every utterance that has ever gone up from suffering and doubting humanity, gone up in vain? Have the prayers of saints, the hymns of psalmists, the agonies of martyrs, the aspirations of poets, the thoughts of sages, the cries of the oppressed, the pleadings of the mother for her child, the maiden praying in her chamber for her lover upon the distant battle-field, the soldier answering her prayer from afar off with, " Sleep quiet, I am in God's hands "—those very utterances of humanity which seemed to us most noble, most pure, most beautiful, most divine, been all in vain ?—impertinences ; the babblings of fair dreams, poured forth into nowhere, to no thing, and in vain ? Has every suffering, searching soul which ever gazed up into the darkness of the unknown, in hopes of catching even a glimpse of a divine eye, beholding all, and ordering all, and pitying all, gazed up in vain ? For at the ground of the universe is "*not a divine eye, but only a blank bottomless eye-socket*[1];" and man has no Father in heaven; and Christ revealed Him not, because He was not there to reveal ; and there was no hope, no remedy, no deliverance, for the miserable among the sons of men ?

Oh, my friends, those who believe, or fancy that they believe such things, must be able to do so only through some peculiar conformation either of brain or heart. Only want of imagination to conceive the consequences of such doctrines can enable them, if they have any love and pity for their fellow-men, to preach those doctrines without pity and horror. They know not, they know not, of what they rob a mankind already but too miserable by its own folly and its own sin ; a mankind which, if it have not hope in God and in Christ, is truly—as Homer

---

[1] J. P. Richter.

said of old—more miserable than the beasts of the field. If their unconscious conceit did not make them unintentionally cruel, they would surely be silent for pity's sake; they would let men go on in the pleasant delusion that there is a living God, and a Word of God who has revealed Him to men; and would hide from their fellow-creatures the dreadful secret which they think they have discovered—That there is none that heareth prayer, and therefore to Him need no flesh come.

Men take up with such notions, I believe, most generally in days of comfort, ease, safety. They find the world so well ordered outwardly, that it seems able enough to go on its way without a God. They have themselves so few sorrows, struggles, doubts, that they never feel that sense of helplessness, of danger, of ignorance, which has made the hearts of men, in every age, yearn for an unseen helper, an unseen deliverer, an unseen teacher.

And so it is—and shameful it is that so it should be—that the more God gives to men, the less they thank Him, the less they fancy that they need Him: but take His bounties, as they take the air they breathe, unconsciously, and as a matter of course.

And therefore adversity is wholesome, danger is wholesome; so wholesome, that in all ages, as far as I can find, the godliest, the most moral, the most manful, and therefore the really happiest and most successful nations or communities of men, have been those who were in perpetual danger, difficulty, struggle; and who have thereby had their faith in God called out; who have

learned in the depth, to cry out of the depth to God; to
lift up their eyes unto the Lord, and know that their help
comes from Him.

I know a village down in the far West, where the
121st Psalm which I just quoted, was a favourite, and
more than a favourite. Whenever it was given out in
church—and the congregation used often to ask for it—
all joined in singing it, young and old, men and maidens,
with an earnestness, a fervour, a passion, such as I never
heard elsewhere; such as shewed how intensely they felt
that the psalm was true, and true for them. Of all con-
gregational singing I ever heard, never have I heard any
so touching as those voices, when they joined in the old
words they loved so well.

> Sheltered beneath the Almighty wings
> Thou shalt securely rest,
> Where neither sun nor moon shall thee
> By day or night molest.
> At home, abroad, in peace, in war,
> Thy God shall thee defend;
> Conduct thee through life's pilgrimage
> Safe to thy journey's end.

Do you fancy these people were specially comfortable, prosperous folk, who had no sorrows, and lived
safe from all danger, and therefore knew that God protected them from all ill?

Nothing less, my friends, nothing less. There was
hardly a man who joined in that psalm, but knew that
he carried his life in his hand from year to year, that any
day might see him a corpse—drowned at sea. Hardly

a woman who sang that psalm but had lost a husband, a father, a brother, a kinsman—drowned at sea. And yet they believed that God preserved them. They were fishers and sailors, earning an uncertain livelihood, on a wild and rocky coast. A sudden shift of wind might make, as I knew it once to make, 60 widows and orphans in a single night. The fishery for the year might fail, and all the expense of boats and nets be thrown away. Or in default of work at home, the young men would go out on voyages to foreign parts: and often never came back again, dying far from home, of fever, of wreck, of some of the hundred accidents which befal seafaring men. And yet they believed that God preserved them. Surely their faith was tried, if ever faith was tried. But as surely their faith failed not, for—if I may so say— they dared not let it fail. If they ceased to trust God, what had they to trust in? Not in their own skill in seamanship, though it was great : they knew how weak it was, on which to lean. Not in the so-called laws of nature ; the treacherous sea, the wild wind, the uncertain shoals of fish, the chances and changes of a long foreign voyage. Without trust in God, their lives must have been lives of doubt and of terror, for ever anxious about the morrow : or else of blind recklessness, saying, " Let us eat and drink, for to-morrow we die." Because they kept their faith in God, their lives were for the most part lives of hardy and hopeful enterprise ; cheerful always, in bad luck as in good ; thankful when their labours were blest with success ; and when calamity and failure came, saying with noble resignation—" I have received good from the hand of the Lord, and shall I not receive evil? Though He slay me, yet will I trust in Him."

It is a life like theirs, mixed with danger and uncertainty, which most calls out faith in God. It is the life of safety and comfort, in which our wants are all supplied ready to our hand, which calls it out least. And therefore it is that life in cities, just because it is most safe and most comfortable, is so often, alas, most ungodly, at least among the men. Less common, thank God, is this ungodliness among the women. The nursing of the sick ; the cares of a family, often too sorrows, manifold and bitter, put them continually in mind of human weakness, and of their own weakness likewise. Yes. It is sorrow, my friends, sorrow and failure, which forces men to believe that there is One who heareth prayer, forces them to lift up their eyes to One from whom cometh their help. Before the terrible realities of danger, death, bereavement, disappointment, shame, ruin—and most of all before deserved shame, deserved ruin—all the arguments of the conceited sophist melt away like the maxims of the comfortable worldling ; and the man or woman who was but too ready a day before to say, " Tush, God will never see, and will never hear," begins to hope passionately that God does see, that God does hear. In the hour of darkness ; when there is no comfort in man nor help in man, when he has no place to flee unto, and no man careth for his soul : then the most awful, the most blessed of all questions is: But is there no one higher than man to whom I can flee? No one higher than man who cares for my soul and for the souls of those who are dearer to me than my own soul? No friend? No helper? No deliverer? No counsellor? Even no judge? No punisher? No God, even though He be a consuming fire? Am I and my misery alone together in the universe? Is my misery without any meaning, and I without hope? If there be no God: then all that is left for me is despair and death. But if there be, then I can hope that there is a meaning in my misery; that it comes to me not without cause, even though that cause be my own fault. I can plead with God like poor Job of old, even though in wild words like Job; and ask— What is the meaning of this sorrow? What have I done? What should I do? "I will say unto God, Do not condemn me; shew me wherefore thou contendest with me. Surely I would speak unto the Almighty, and desire to reason with God."

"I would speak unto the Almighty, and desire to reason with God." Oh my friends, a man, I believe, can gain courage and wisdom to say that, only by the inspiration of the Spirit of God.

But when once he has said that from his heart, he begins to be justified by faith. For he has had faith in God; he has trusted God enough to speak to God who made him; and so he has put himself, so far at least, into his just and right place, as a spiritual and rational being, made in the image of God.

But more, he has justified God. He has confessed that God is not a mere force or law of nature; nor a mere tyrant and tormentor: but a reasonable being, who will hear reason, and a just being, who will do justice by the creatures whom He has made.

And so the very act of prayer justifies God, and honours God, and gives glory to God; for it confesses that God is what He is, a good God, to whom the humblest and the most fallen of His creatures dare speak out the depths of their abasement, and acknowledge that His glory is this—That in spite of all His majesty, He is one who heareth prayer; a being as magnificent in His justice, as He is magnificent in His majesty and His might.

All this is argued out, as it never has been argued out before or since, in the book of Job: and for seeing so much as this, was Job approved by God. But there is a further question, to which the book of Job gives no answer; and to which indeed all the Old Testament gives but a partial answer. And that is this—This just and magnificent God, has He also human pity, tenderness, charity, condescension, love? In one word, have we not only a God in heaven, but a Father in heaven?

That question could only be answered by the coming of our Lord Jesus Christ. Truly He said—No one cometh to the Father, but by me. No man hath seen God at any time: but the only-begotten Son, who is in the bosom of the Father, He hath revealed Him. He revealed Him in part to Abraham, in part to Moses, to Job, to David, to the prophets. But He revealed Him perfectly when He said—I and the Father are one. He that hath seen me hath seen the Father. Yes. Now we can find boundless comfort in the words, "Such as the Father is, such is the Son, and such is the Holy Ghost"—Love and condescension without bounds. Now we know that there is A Man in the midst of the throne of God, who is the brightness of God's glory and the express image of His character; a high priest who can be touched with the feeling of our infirmities, seeing that He was tempted in all things like as we are, yet without sin.

To Him we can cry, with human passion and in human words; because we know that His human heart will respond to our human hearts, and that His human heart again will respond to His divine Spirit, and that His divine Spirit is the same as the divine Spirit of His Father; for their wills and minds are one; and their will and their mind is—boundless love to sinful man.

Yes, we can look up by faith into the sacred face of Christ, and take refuge by faith within His sacred heart, saying—If it be good for me, He will give what I ask: and if He gives it not, it is because that too is good for me, and for others beside me. In all the chances and changes of this mortal life we can say to Him, as He said in that supreme hour—" If it be possible, let this cup pass from me; nevertheless not my will, but thine, be done," sure that He will present that prayer to His Father, and to our Father, and to His God and to our God; and that whatsoever be the answer vouchsafed by Him whose ways are not as our ways, nor His thoughts as our thoughts, the prayer will not have gone up to Christ in vain.

And in such a case as this of missions to the heathen

—If we believe that Christ died for these poor heathen; if we believe that Christ loves these poor heathen infinitely more than we, or than the most devoted missionary who ever lived or died for them: shall we say—Then we may leave them in Christ's hands to follow their own nature. If He is satisfied with their degradation, so may we be? Shall we not rather say—Their misery and degradation must pain His sacred heart, far more than our sinful hearts; and if He does not come down again on earth to help them Himself, it must be because He means to help them through us, His disciples? Let us ask Him to teach us and others how to help them; to enable us and others to help them. Let us pray to Him the one prayer which, unless prayer be a dream, is certain to be answered, because it is certainly according to God's will; the prayer to be taught and helped to do our duty by our fellow-men. And for the rest: let us pray in the words of that most noble of all collects, to pray which is to take refuge from our own ignorance in the boundless wisdom of God's love—" Thou who knowest our necessities before we ask, and our ignorance in asking: Have compassion on our infirmities, and those things which for our unworthiness we dare not, and for our blindness we cannot ask, condescend to give us, for the worthiness of Jesus Christ our Lord. Amen."

SERMON V.

THE DEAF AND DUMB.

St Mark VII. 32—37.

And they bring unto Jesus one that was deaf, and had an impediment in his speech ; and they beseech Him to put His hand
upon him.   And He took him aside from the multitude, and put
His fingers into his ears, and He spit, and touched his tongue ;
and looking up to heaven, He sighed, and said, Ephphatha,
that is, Be opened.   And straightway his ears were opened, and
the string of his tongue was loosed, and he spake plain............
And they were beyond measure astonished, saying, He hath
done all things well : He maketh both the deaf to hear, and the
dumb to speak.

Our greatest living philologer has said, and said truly—
"If wonder arises from ignorance, it is from that conscious ignorance which, if we look back at the history of
most of our sciences, has been the mother of all human
knowledge.   Till men began to wonder at the stratifica-
tion of rocks, and the fossilization of shells, there was no
science of Geology.   Till they began to wonder at the
words which were perpetually in their mouths, there was
no science of Language."

He might have added, that till men began to wonder
at the organization of their own bodies, there was no

science of healing; that in proportion as the common fact of health became mysterious and marvellous in their eyes, just in that proportion did they become able to explain and to conquer disease. For there is a deep difference between the wonder of the uneducated or half-educated man, and the wonder of the educated man. The ignorant in all ages have wondered at the exception; the wise, in proportion as they have become wise, have wondered at the rule. Pestilences, prodigies, portents, the results of seeming accidents, excite the vulgar mind. Only the abnormal or casual is worthy of their attention. The man of science finds a deeper and more awful charm in contemplating the results of law; in watching, not what seem to be occasional failures in nature: but what is a perpetual and calm success.

The savage knows not, I am told, what wonder means, save from some prodigy. Seeing no marvel in the daily glory of the sunlight, he is startled out of his usual stupidity and carelessness by the occurrence of an eclipse, an earthquake, a thunderbolt. The uneducated, whatever their rank may be, are apt to be more interested by the sight of deformities, and defects or excesses in nature, than by that of the most perfect normal and natural beauty.

Those, in the same way, who in the infancy of European science, thought it worth while to register natural phenomena, registered exclusively the exceptions. Eclipses, meteors, auroras, earthquakes, storms, and especially monstrosities, animal or vegetable, exercised their barbaric wonder. The mystery and miracle which underlies the unfolding of every bud, the development of every embryo, the growth of every atom of tissue, in any organism, animal or vegetable—to all this their intellectual eye was blind. How different from such a state of mind, that calm and constant wonder, humbling and yet inspiring, with which the modern man of science searches into the "open mystery" of the universe; and sees that the true marvel lies, not in the infringement of law, but in its permanence; not in the imperfect, but in the perfect; not in disease, but in health; not in deformity, but in beauty.

These words are true of all nature; and specially true, it seems to me, of our outward senses and faculties; true of sight, hearing, speech. The wonder, I think, with the wise man will be, not that there are deaf and dumb persons to be found here and there among us: but that the average, nay, the majority of mankind, are not deaf and dumb. Paradoxical as this assertion may seem at first, a little thought I believe will prove it to be reasonable.

Whatever view you take of the origin of sight, hearing, voice, the wonder to a thoughtful mind is just the same; how, under the storm of circumstances, and through the lapse of ages, those faculties have not been lost again and again, by countless individuals, nay, by the whole species. For we must confess that those faculties are gradually developed in each individual; that every animal and every human being which is born into the world, has built up, unconsciously, involuntarily, and as it were out of nothing, those delicate and complex organs, by which he afterwards learns to see, hear, and utter sounds. Is not the wonder, that he should, in the majority of cases, succeed without any effort of his own?

And if I am answered, that the success is owing to hereditary tendencies, and to the laws by which the off-spring resembles the parents, I answer: Is not that a greater wonder still? A wonder which all the discoveries of the scalpel and the microscope have been as yet unable, and will be, I believe, to the last unable, to unravel, even to touch? A wonder which can be explained by no theories of vibratory atoms, vital forces, plastic powers of nature, or other such phrases, which are but metaphysical abstractions, having no counterpart in fact, and only hiding from us our ignorance of the vast and venerable unknown. The physiologist, when he considers the manifold combination of innumerable microscopic circumstances which are required to bring any one creature into the world with a perfectly hearing ear, ought to confess that the chances—if the world were governed by chance—are infinitely greater in favour of a child's being born with an imperfect ear rather than with a perfect one. And if he should evade the difficulty; and try to explain the usual success by saying that nature is governed by law: I answer—What is nature? What is law? You never saw nature nor law either under the microscope. They too are metaphysical abstractions, necessary notions and conceptions of your own brain. You have seen nothing but the fact and the custom; and all you can do, if you be strictly rational, is with a certain modern school to say, with a despairing humility, which I deplore while I respect—deploring it because it is needless despair, and yet respecting it because it is humility, which is the path out of despair and darkness into hope and light—to say with them, "Man can know nothing of causes, he can only register positive facts." This, I say, is one path—one which I trust none here will tread. The only other path, I believe, is, to go back to the lessons which we ought to have learnt in our childhood, for those to whom the human race owes most learnt them thousands of years ago; and to ascribe the ever successful miracles of nature to a Will, to a Mind, to a Providence so like that which each of us exercises in his own petty sphere, that we are not only able to understand in part the works of God, but to know from the very fact of being able to understand them—as one of our greatest astronomers has so well said lately—that we are made in the image of God. To say with the old Psalmist, that the universe is governed by "a law which cannot be broken :" but why? Because God has given it that law. To say "All things continue as they were at the beginning :" but why? Because all things serve Him in whom we live and move and have our being. To confess the mystery and miracle of our mortal bodies, and say with David, "I am fearfully and wonderfully made; such knowledge is too wonderful and excellent for me, I cannot attain unto it :" but to add the one only rational explanation of the mystery which, thank God, common sense has taught, though it may be often in confused and defective forms, to the vast majority of the human race in all times and all lands—that He who grasps the mystery and works the miracle is God; that "His eye sees our substances yet being imperfect; and in His book are all our members written, which day by day were fashioned, when as yet there were none of them."

And then to go forward with the Psalmist, and with the common sense of humanity; to conclude that if there be a Creator, there must also be a Providence; that that life-giving Spirit which presided over the creation of each organism presides also over its growth, its circumstances, its fortunes; and to say with David, "Whither shall I go then from Thy Spirit, or whither shall I flee from Thy presence? If I climb up to heaven, Thou art there. If I go down to hell, Thou art there also. If I take the wings of the morning, and remain in the uttermost parts of the sea; even there Thy hand shall lead me; Thy right hand shall hold me still."

Yes. To this—to faith and adoration—ought right and reason to lead the physical philosopher. And to what ought it to lead us, who are most of us, I presume, not physical philosophers? To gratitude, surely, not unmixed with fear and trembling; till we say to ourselves—Who am I, to boast? Who am I, to pride myself on possessing a single faculty which one of my neighbours may want? What have I, that I did not receive? Considering the endless chances of failure, if the world were left to chance; and I may say, the absolute certainty of failures, if the world were left to the blind competition of merely physical laws, is it not only of the Lord's mercies that we are not failures too? that we have not been born crippled, blind, deaf, dumb— what not?—by the effect of circumstances over which

we have had no control; which have been working, it
may be, for generations past, in the organizations of our
ancestors?

But what shall we say of those who have not received
what we have received? What shall we say of those
who, like the deaf and dumb, are, in some respects at
least, failures—instances in which the laws which regu-
late our organization have not succeeded in effecting a
full development?

We can say this, at least, without entangling and
dazzling ourselves in speculations about final causes;
without attempting to pry into the mystery of evil.

We can say this: That if there be a God—as there
is a God—these failures are not according to His
will. The highest reason should teach us that; for
it must tell us that in the work of the Divine Artist,
as in the work of the human, imperfection, impo-
tence, disorder of any kind, must be contrary to the
mind and will of the Creator. The highest reason,
I say, teaches us this. And Scripture teaches it likewise. For if we believe our Lord to have been—as
He was—the express image of the Almighty Father;
if we believe that He came—as He did come—to reveal
to men His Father's will, His Father's mind, His Father's
character: then we must believe that He acted according
to that will and according to that character, when He
made the healing of disease, and the curing of imper-
fections of this very kind, an important and an integral
part of His work on earth.

"And they brought unto Jesus one that was deaf,

and had an impediment in his speech, and besought Him to put His hand upon him. And Jesus took him aside from the multitude, and put His fingers into his ears; and He spit, and touched his tongue; and looking up to heaven, He sighed, and said unto him, Ephphatha, that is, Be opened. And straightway his ears were opened, and the string of his tongue was loosed, and he spake plain...... And they were beyond measure astonished, saying, He hath done all things well: He maketh both the deaf to hear, and the dumb to speak."

Consider this story awhile. He healed the man miraculously, by means at which we cannot guess, which we cannot even conceive. But the healing signified at least two things—that the man could be healed, and that the man ought to be healed; that his bodily defect—the retribution of no sin of his own—was contrary to the will of that Father in Heaven, who willeth not that one little one should perish.

But Jesus sighed likewise. There was in Him a sorrow, a compassion, most human and most divine. It may have been—may He forgive me if I dare rashly to impute motives or thoughts to Him—that there was something too of a divine weariness—I dare not say impatience, seeing how patient He was then and how patient He has been since for more than 1800 years—of the folly and ignorance of man, who brings on himself and on his descendants these and a hundred other preventible miseries, simply because he will not study and obey the physical laws of the universe; simply because he will not see that those laws which concern the welfare of his body, are as surely the will of God as those which concern the welfare of his soul; and that therefore it is not merely his interest but his solemn duty to study and to obey them, lest he bear the punishment of his own neglect and disobedience.

It is not for man even to guess what thoughts may have passed through the mind of Christ when He sighed over the very defect which He was healing. But it is surely not irreverent in us to say that our Lord had cause enough to sigh, if He foresaw the follies of mankind during an age which was too soon to come.—How men, instead of taking the spirit of His miracles and acting on it, would counterfeit the mere outward signs of them, to feed the vanity or the superstition of a few devotees. How, instead of looking on His miracles as rebukes to their own ignorance and imbecility; instead of perceiving that their bodily afflictions were contrary to the will of God, and therefore curable; instead of setting themselves to work manfully, in the light of God, and by the help of God, to discover and correct the errors which produced them, mankind would idle away precious centuries in barbaric wonder at seeming prodigies and seeming miracles, and would neglect utterly the study of those far more wondrous laws of nature which Christ had proved to be under His government and His guidance, and had therefore proved to be working for the good of those for whom He came to die. Christ had indeed sown good seed in His field. He had taught men by His miracles, as He had taught them by His parables, to Whom nature belonged, and Whose laws nature obeyed.

And the cessation of miracles after the time of Christ and His Apostles had taught, or ought to have taught, mankind a further lesson; the lesson that henceforth they were to carry on for themselves, by the faculties which God had given them, that work of healing and deliverance which He had begun. Miracles, like prophecies, like tongues, like supernatural knowledge, were to cease and vanish away: but charity, charity which devotes itself for the welfare of the human race, was to abide for ever.

Christ, as I said, had sown good seed: but an enemy —we know not whence or when—certainly within the three first centuries of the Church—came and sowed tares among that wheat. Then began men to believe that devils, and not their Father in Heaven, were, to all practical intents, the lords of nature. Then began they to believe that man's body was the property of Satan, and his soul only the property of God. Then began they to fancy that man was to be delivered from his manifold earthly miseries, not by purity and virtue, reason and knowledge, but by magic, masked under the sacred name of religion. No wonder if, in such a temper of mind, the physical amelioration of the human race stood still. How could it be otherwise, while men refused to see in facts the acted will of God; and sought not in God's universe, but in the dreams of their own brains, for glimpses of that divine and wonderful order by which The eternal Father and The eternal Son are working together for ever through The eternal Spirit for the welfare of the universe?

We boast, my friends, at times, of the rapid triumphs of modern science. Were we but aware of the vast amount of preventible misery around us, and of the vast possibility of removing it, which lies in the little science which we know already, we should rather bewail the slow departure of modern barbarism.

There has been no period of the world for centuries back, I believe, in which man might not have been infinitely healthier, happier, more prosperous, more long-lived than he has been, if he had only believed that disease, misery, and premature death were not the will of God and of Christ; and that God had endowed him with an intellect which could understand the laws of the universe, in order that he might use those laws for his own health, wealth, and life. Very late is society in commencing that rational course on which it ought to have entered centuries ago; and therefore very culpable. And it is not too much to say, that to the average of persons suffering under preventible disease or defect, even though it be hereditary, society owes a sacred debt, which it is bound to pay by making those innocent sufferers from other's sins as happy as possible; where it has not yet learnt—as it will learn, please God, some day—to cure them.

There is, thank God, a healthier feeling than of old abroad of late upon this point. Men are learning more and more to regard such sufferers not as the victims of God's wrath, but of human ignorance, vice, or folly. And it was with deep satisfaction that I read in the last Report of the Schools for the Deaf and Dumb a statement of what were considered the most probable physical causes of deafness and dumbness, and a hope that it would be possible, hereafter, to prevent as well as cure those diseases.

Whether the causes assigned in that Report are the true ones, is a point of inferior importance for the moment. The really important point is, that the principle should be allowed, the question raised, by a society, composed of religious men, and teaching to those poor deaf and dumb as almost their primary work that true religion which they are just as capable of receiving as we. The right path has been entered—the path which is certain in due time to lead to success. And meanwhile our duty is, while we confess that it is the fault of society and not of God, that these afflicted ones exist among us—it is our duty, I say, to cultivate and to develop to the highest every faculty, instinct, and power, in them which God's order has preserved from the effects of man's disorder; to feed the eye with fair and noble sights, though the ear be shut to soothing and inspiring sounds; to cultivate the intellect to such a pitch that it may be able to perform practical work, and if possible to earn a sufficient livelihood, even though the want of speech makes it impossible for them, deaf and dumb, to compete on equal terms with their fellow-men; to awaken in them, by religious training, teaching and worship, those purer and more unselfish emotions by which their hearts may become a field ready and prepared for God's grace. To do this; and to regard them, whenever we come in contact with them; not merely

with pity, while we remember how much their intellects
lose, in losing the whole world of sound; but with hope,
when we see that through the one sense which is left
they take in fully not only the meaning of the voluble
hands which teach them, but more, the meaning of that
meaning—the spiritual truths and feelings which signs
express; with wonder, not at the defect, but at the
innate health which almost compensates for the want of
hearing by concentrating its powers upon the sight; and
lastly, with admiration for that humanity which, as it
were imprisoned, fettered, maimed, yet can, by the God-
given force of the immortal spirit, so burst its prison-
bars, and rise, through hindrances which seem to us im-
passable, to the tenderest, the noblest, the purest, and
most devout emotions.

SERMON VI.

THE FRUITS OF THE SPIRIT.

St John iii. 8.

*The wind bloweth whither it listeth, and thou hearest the sound
thereof, but canst not tell whence it cometh, or whither it goeth:
so is every one that is born of the Spirit.*

It is often asked—men have a right to ask—what would
the world have been by now without Christianity? without
the Christian religion? without the Church?

But before these questions can be answered, we must
define, it is discovered, what we mean by Christianity,
the Christian religion, the Church.

And it is found—or I at least believe it will be found
—more safe and wise to ask a deeper and yet a simpler
question still: What would the world have been without
that influence on which Christianity, and religion, and
the Church depend? What would the world have been
without the Holy Spirit of God?

But some will say: This is a more abstruse question
still. How can you define, how can you analyse, the
Spirit of God? Nay, more, how can you prove its

existence ?—Such questioners have been, as it were, baptized unto John's baptism. They are very glad to see people do right, and not do wrong, from any well-calculated motives, or wholesome and pleasant emotions. But they have not as yet heard whether there be any Holy Spirit.

We can only answer, Just so. This Holy Spirit in Whom we believe defies all analysis, all definition whatsoever. His nature can be brought under no terms derived from human emotions or motives. He is literally invisible; as invisible to the conception of the brain as He is to the bodily eye. His presence is proved only by its effects. The Spirit bloweth whither it listeth, and thou hearest the sound thereof, but thou canst not tell whence it cometh, nor whither it goeth.

Such words must sound as dreams to those analytical philosophers who allow nothing in man below the sphere of consciousness, actual or possible; who have dissected the human mind till they find in it no personal will, no indestructible and spiritual self, but a character which is only the net result of innumerable states of consciousness; who hold that man's outward actions, and also his inmost instincts, are all the result either of calculations about profit and loss, pleasure and pain, or of emotions, whether hereditary or acquired. Ignoring the deep and ancient distinction, which no one ever brought out so clearly as St Paul, between the flesh and the spirit, they hold that man is flesh, and can be nothing more; that each person is not really a person, but is the consequence of his brain and nerves; and having thus, by logical analysis, got rid of the spirit of man, their reason and their conscience quite honestly and consistently see no need for, or possibility of, a Spirit of God, to ennoble and enable the human spirit. Why need there be, if the difference between an animal and a man be one of degree alone, and not of kind?

We answer: That there is a flesh in man, brain and nerves, emotions and passions, identical with that of animals, we do not deny. We should be fools if we did deny it; for the fact is hideously and shamefully patent. None knew that better than St Paul, who gave a list of the works of the flesh, the things which a man does who is the slave of his own brain and nerves—and a very ugly list it is—beginning with adultery and ending with drunkenness, after passing through all the seven deadly sins. And neither St Paul nor we deny, that in this fleshly, carnal and animal state the vast majority of the human race has lived, and lives still, to its own infinite misery and confusion; and that it has a per-petual tendency, whenever lifted out of that state, to fall back into it again, and perish.

But St Paul says, and we say: That crushed under this animal nature there is in man a spirit. We say: That below all his consciousness lies a nobler element; a divine spark, or at least a divine fuel, which must be kindled into life by the divine Spirit, the Spirit of God. And we say that in proportion as that Spirit of God kindles the spirit of man, he begins to act after a fashion for which he can give no logical reason; that by instinct, and without calculation of profit or loss, pleasure or pain, he begins to act on what he calls duty, honour, love, self sacrifice. But what these are he cannot analyse. Mere words cannot define them. He can only obey that which prompts him, he knows not what nor whence; and say with Luther of old: "I can do no otherwise. God help me."

And we say that such men and women are the salt of the earth, who keep society from rotting; that by such men and women, and by their example and influence, direct and indirect, has Christendom been raised up out of the accursed slough into which Europe and, indeed, the whole known world, had fallen during the early Roman Empire; and that to this influence, and therefore to the Holy Spirit of God alone, and not to any prudential calculations, combined experiences, or so-called philosophies of men, is owing all which keeps Europe from being a hell on earth. And we say, moreover, that those who deny this, and dream of a morality and a civilization without The Spirit of God, are unconsciously throwing down the ladder by which they themselves have climbed, and sawing off the very bough to which they cling.

Duty, honour, love, self-sacrifice—these are the fruits of The Spirit; unknown to, and unobeyed by, the savage, or by the civilized man who—as has too often happened—as is happening now in too many lands, on both sides of the Atlantic, is sinking back into inward savagery, amid an outward and material civilization.

Moreover—and this appears to us a fair experimental proof that our old-fashioned belief in A Spirit of God, which acts upon the spirit of man, is a true belief—moreover, I say: It is a patent fact, that wherever and whenever there has been a revival of the Christian religion; whenever, that is, amid whatsoever confusions and errors, men have begun to feel the need of the Holy Spirit of God, and to pray for that Spirit, a moral revival has accompanied the religious one. Men and women have not only become better themselves; and that often suddenly and in very truth miraculously better: but the yearning has awoke in them to make others better likewise. The grace of God, as they have called it, has made them gracious to their fellow-creatures; and duty, honour, love, self-sacrifice, call it by what name we will, has said to them, with a still small voice more potent than all the thunders of the law: Go, and seek and save that which is lost.

In no case has this instinctive tendency to practical benevolence been more striking, than in the case of that great religious revival throughout England at the beginning of this century, which issued in the rise of the Evangelical school: a school rightly so called, because its members did try to obey the precepts of the Gospel, according to their understanding of them, in spirit and in truth.

The doctrines which they held are a matter not for us, but for God and their own souls. The deeds which they did are matter for us, and for all England; for they have left their mark on the length and breadth of the land. They were inspired—cultivated, highborn, and wealthy folk many of them—with a strange new instinct that God had bidden them to feed the hungry, to clothe the naked, to visit the prisoner and the sick, to bind up the broken-hearted, to proclaim liberty to the captives, and to preach good tidings to the meek. A strange new instinct: and from what cause, save from the same cause as that which Isaiah assigned to his own like deeds?— Because "The Spirit of the Lord was upon him."

Yes, if those gracious men, those gracious women, did not shew forth the Spirit and grace of God with power, then there is either no Spirit of God, no grace of God; or those who deny to them the name of saints forget the words of Him Who said: By their fruits ye shall know them; of Him Who said, too: That the unpardonable sin, the sin which shewed complete moral perversion, the sin against the Holy Spirit of God, was to attribute good deeds to bad motives, and say: He casteth out devils by Beelzebub, the prince of the devils.

Yes, that old Evangelical School may now have passed its prime. It may now be verging toward old age; and other schools, younger and stronger, with broader and clearer knowledge of dogma, of history, civil and ecclesiastical, of the value of ceremonial, of the needs of the human intellect and emotions, may have passed it in a noble rivalry, and snatched, as it were, from the hands of the old Evangelical School the lamp of truth, to bear it further forward in the race. But God forbid that the spiritual children should be ungrateful to their spiritual parents, though God may have taught them things which their parents did not know.

And they were our spiritual parents, those old Evangelicals. No just and well-informed man who has passed middle age, but must confess, that to them we owe whatsoever vital religion exists at this moment in any school or party of the Church of England; that to them we owe the germs at least, and in many cases the full organization and the final success, of a hundred schemes of practical benevolence and practical justice, without which this country, in its haste to grow rich at all risks and by all means, might have plunged itself ere now into anarchy and revolution. And he must confess, too, if he is one who has seen much of his fellow-creatures and their characters, that that school numbered among its disciples —and, thank God, they are not all yet gone home to their rest—some of the loveliest human souls, whose converse has chastened and ennobled his own soul.

Ah, well—

> The old order changeth, giving place to the new;
> And God fulfils Himself in many ways,
> Lest one good custom should corrupt the world.

And new methods and new institutions have arisen, and will yet arise, for seeking and saving that which is lost. God's blessing on them all, to whatsoever party, church, or sect they may belong! Whosoever cast out devils in Christ's name, Christ has forbidden us to forbid them, whether they follow us or not. But yet shall we not still honour and love the old Evangelical School, and many an Institution which it has left behind, as heirlooms to some of us, at least, from our mothers, or from women to whom we owed, in long past years, our earliest influences for good, our earliest examples of a practical Christian life, our earliest proofs that there was indeed a Spirit of God, a gracious Spirit, Who gave grace to the hearts, the deeds, the very looks and voices of those in whom He dwelt; Institutions, which are too likely some of them to die, simply from the loss of old friends?

The loss of old friends. Yes, so it is always in this world. The old earnest hearts go home one by one to their rest; and the young earnest hearts—and who shall blame them?—go elsewhere; and try new fashions of doing good, which are more graceful and more agreeable to them. For the religious world, like all other forms of the world, has its fashions; and of them too stands true the saying of the apostle: That this world and the fashion thereof pass away. Many a good work, which once was somewhat fashionable in its way, has become somewhat unfashionable, and something else is fashionable in its place; and five-and-twenty years hence something else will have become fashionable; and our children will look back on our ways of doing good with pity, if not with contempt, as narrow and unenlightened, just as we are too apt to look back on our fathers' ways. And all the while, what can they teach worth teaching, what can we teach worth teaching, save what our fathers and mothers taught, what the Spirit of God taught them, and has taught to all who would listen since the foundation of the world, "shewing man what was good:" and what was that—"What doth the Lord require of thee, but to do justly, and to love mercy, and to walk humbly with thy God?"

Ah! why do we, even in religious and moral matters, even in the doing. good to the souls and bodies of our fellow-creatures, allow ourselves to be the puppets of fashions? Of fashions which even when harmless, even beautiful, are but the garments, or rather stage-properties, in which we dress up the high instincts which God's Spirit bestows on us, in order to make them agreeable enough for our own prejudices, or pretty enough for our own tastes. How little do we perceive our own danger—so little that we yield to it every day—the danger of mistaking our fashion of doing good for the good done; aye, for the very Spirit of God Who inspires that good; mistaking the garment for the person who wears it, the outward and visible sign for the inward and spiritual grace; and so in our hearts falling actually into that very error of transubstantiation, of which we repudiate the name!

Why, ah why, will we not take refuge from fashions in Him in Whom are no fashions—even in the Holy Spirit of God, Who is unchangeable and eternal as the Father and the Son from Whom He proceeds; Who has spoken words in sundry and divers manners to all the elect of God; Who has inspired every good thought and feeling which was ever thought or felt in earth or heaven; but Whose message of inspiration has been, and will be, for ever the same—"Do justly, love mercy, walk humbly with thy God"?

Could we but utterly trust Him, and utterly believe in His presence: then we should welcome all truth, under whatever outward forms of the mere intellect it was uttered; then we should bless every good deed, by whomsoever and howsoever it was done; then we should rise above all party strifes, party cries, party fashions and shibboleths, to the contemplation of the One supreme good Spirit—the Spirit of Jesus Christ, the same yesterday, to-day, and for ever; and hold to the One Fashion of Almighty God, which never changes, for it is eternal by the necessity of His own eternal character; namely,—To be perfect, even as our Father in Heaven is perfect; because He causes His sun to shine on the evil and on the good, and His rain to fall on the just and on the unjust.

SERMON VII.

CONFUSION.

PSALM CXIX. 31.

I have stuck unto thy testimonies : O Lord, confound me not.

WHAT is the meaning of this text? What is this which
the Psalmist and prophets call being confounded ; being
put to shame and confusion of face? What is it? It is
something which they dread more than death; which
they dread as much as hell. Nay, it seems in the mind
of some of them to be part and parcel of hell itself; one
of the very worst things which could happen to them
after death: for what is written in the Book of the Prophet Daniel?—" Many of them that sleep in the dust of
the earth shall awake, some to everlasting life, and some
to shame and everlasting contempt."

And we Christians are excusable if we dread it likewise. How often does St Paul speak of shame as an evil
to be dreaded ; just as he speaks, even more often, of
glory and honour as a thing to be longed for and striven
after. That one word, "ashamed," occurs twelve times
and more in the New Testament, beside St John's warning, which alone is enough to prove what I allege,

"that we have not to be ashamed before Christ at his coming."

And how does the Te Deum—the noblest hymn written by man since St John finished his Book of Revelations—how does that end, but with the same old cry as that of the Psalmist in the 119th Psalm—

"O Lord, in thee have I trusted, let me never be confounded"?

Now it is difficult to tell men what being confounded means; difficult and almost needless; for there are those who know what it means without being told; and those who do not know what it means without being told, are not likely to know by my telling, or any man's telling. No, not if an angel from heaven came and told them what being confounded meant would they understand him, at least till they were confounded themselves; and then they would know by bitter experience—perhaps when it was too late.

And who are they? What sort of people are they?

First, silly persons; whom Solomon calls fools—though they often think themselves refined and clever enough—luxurious and "fashionable" people, who do not care to learn, who think nothing worth learning save how to enjoy themselves; who call it "bad form" to be earnest, and turn off all serious questions with a jest. These are they of whom Wisdom says—"How long, ye simple ones, will ye love simplicity, and the scorners delight in their scorning, and fools hate knowledge? I also will laugh at your calamity, and mock when your fear cometh."

Next, mean and truly vulgar persons; who are shame-less; who do not care if they are caught out in a lie or in a trick. These are they of whom it is written that out-side of God's kingdom, in the outer darkness wherein are weeping and gnashing of teeth, are dogs, and whosoever loveth and maketh a lie.

And next, and worst of all, self-conceited people. These are they of whom Solomon says, "Seest thou a man who is wise in his own conceit? There is more hope of a fool than of him." They are the people who will not see when they are going wrong ; who will not hear reason, nor take advice, no, nor even take scorn and contempt; who will not see that they are making fools of themselves, but, while all the world is laughing at them, walk on serenely self-satisfied, certain that they, and they only, know what the world is made of, and how to manage the world. These are they of whom it is written—"He that being often reproved, hardeneth his neck, shall suddenly be destroyed, and that without remedy." Then they will learn, and with a vengeance, what being confounded means by being confounded themselves, and finding themselves utterly wrong, where they thought themselves utterly right. Yet no. I do not think that even that would cure some people. There are those, I verily believe, who would not confess that they were in the wrong even in the bottomless pit, but, like Satan and his fallen angels in Milton's poem, would have excellent arguments to prove that they were injured and ill-used, deceived and betrayed, and lay the blame of their misery on God, on man, on anything but their own infallible selves.

Who, then, are the people who know what being confounded means; who are afraid, and terribly afraid, of being brought to shame and confusion of face?

I should say, all human beings in proportion as they are truly human beings, are not brutal; in proportion, that is, as they are good or have the capacity of goodness in them; that is, in proportion as the Spirit of God is working in them, giving them the tender heart, the quick feelings, the earnestness, the modesty, the conscientiousness, the reverence for the good opinion of their fellow-men, which is the beginning of eternal life. Do you not see it in the young? Modesty, bashfulness, shame-facedness—as the good old English word was—that is the very beginning of all goodness in boys and girls. It is the very material out of which all other goodness is made; and those who laugh at, or torment, young people for being modest and bashful, are doing the devil's work, and putting themselves under the curse which God, by the mouth of Solomon the wise, pronounced against the scorners who love scorning, and the fools who hate knowledge.

This is the rule with dumb animals likewise. The more intelligent, the more high-bred they are, the more they are capable of feeling shame; and the more they are liable to be confounded, to lose their heads, and become frantic with doubt and fear. Who that has watched dogs does not know that the cleverer they are, the more they are capable of being actually ashamed of themselves, as

human beings are, or ought to be? Who that has trained
horses does not know that the stupid horse is never
vicious, never takes fright? The failing which high-bred
horses have of becoming utterly unmanageable, not so
much from bodily fear, as from being confounded, not
knowing what people want them to do—that is the very
sign, the very effect, of their superior organization: and
more shame to those who ill-use such horses. If God,
my friends, dealt with us as cruelly and as clumsily as too
many men deal with their horses, He would not be long
in driving us mad with terror and shame and confusion.
But He remembers our frame; He knoweth whereof we
are made, and remembereth that we are but dust: else
the spirit would fail before Him, and the souls which He
hath made. And to Him we can cry, even when we
know that we have made fools of ourselves—Father who
made me, Christ who died for me, Holy Spirit who teach-
est me, have patience with my stupidity and my ignorance. Lord, in thee have I trusted, let me never be
confounded.

But some will tell us—It is a sign of weakness to feel
shame. Why should you care for the opinion of your
fellow-men? If you are doing right, what matter what
they say of you?

Yes, my friends, if you are doing right. But if you
are not doing right—What then?

If you have only been fancying that you are doing
right, and suspect suddenly that you have been very likely
doing wrong—What then?

When a man tells me that he does not care what

people think of him; that they cannot shame him: in the first place, I do not quite believe that he is speaking truth; and in the next place, I hope he is *not* speaking truth. I hope—for his own sake—that he does care what people think of him: or else I must suspect him of being very dull or very conceited.

And if he tells me that the old prophets, and holy, and just, and heroic men in all ages, never cared for people's laughing at them and despising them, provided they were doing right according to their own conscience: I answer—That he knows nothing about the matter; that he has not honestly read the writings of these men. I say that the Psalmist who wrote Ps. 119, was a man, on his own shewing, intensely open to the feeling of shame, and felt intensely what men said of him; felt intensely slander and insult. We talk of independent and true patriots now-a-days. I will tell you of four of the noblest patriots the world ever saw, who were men of that stamp. I say that Isaiah was such a man; that Jeremiah was such a man; that Ezekiel was such a man; that their writings shew that they felt intensely the rebukes and the contempt which they had to endure from those whom they tried to warn and save. I say again that St Paul, as may be seen from his own epistles, was such a man; a man who was intensely sensitive of what men thought and said of him; yearning after the love and approbation of his fellow-men, and above all of his fellow-countrymen, his own flesh and blood; and that that feeling in him, which may have been hurtful to him before he was converted, was of the greatest use to him after his conversion; that it enabled him to win all hearts, because he felt with men and for men; and gained him over the hearts of men such a power as no mere human being ever had before or since.

And I say that of all men the Lord Jesus Christ, the Son of Man, had that feeling; that longing for the love and appreciation of men—and above all, for the love and appreciation of His countrymen according to the flesh, the Jews, He had—strange as it may seem, yet there it is in the Gospels, written for ever and undeniable—that capacity of shame which is the mark of true nobleness of soul.

He endured the cross, despising the shame. Yes: but there are too many on earth who endure shame with brazen faces, just because they do not feel it. If He had not felt the shame, what merit in despising it? It was His glory that He felt the shame; and yet conquered the shame, and crushed it down by the might of His love for fallen man.

Do you fancy that in His agony in the garden, when His sweat was as great drops of blood, that it was only bodily fear of pain and death which crushed Him for the moment? He felt that, I doubt not; as He had to taste death for every man, and feel all human weakness, yet without sin. But it was a deeper, more painful, and yet more noble feeling than mere fear which then convulsed His sacred heart; even the feeling of shame—the mockery of the crowd—the— But I dare not enlarge on anything so awful; at least I will say this—That he had to cry as none ever cried before or since, "O God, in thee have I trusted, let me never be confounded;" for he had, it seems, actually, at one supreme moment, to feel confounded; and to say, "My God, my God, why hast thou forsaken me?" That was the highest and most precious jewel of all his self-sacrifice. Of it let us only say—

Our Lord and Saviour stooped to be confounded for a moment, that we might not be confounded to all eternity.

And therefore our blessed Lord is to us an example. As he did, so must we try to do. He entered into glory, by suffering shame, and yet despising it. He submitted to be confounded before men, that He might not be confounded in the sight of God His Father. And so must we, sometimes, at least. Every man who makes up his mind to do right and to be good, must expect ridicule now and then. Rich or poor, boy or man, if you try to keep your hands clean, and your path straight, the world will think you a fool, and will be ready enough to tell you so; for it is cruel and insolent enough. And the more tender your heart; the more you wish for the love and approbation of your fellow-men; the more of noble and modest self-distrust there is in you, the more painful will that be to you; the more you will be tempted to obey man, and not God, and to follow after the multitude to do evil, merely to keep the peace, and live a quiet life, and not be laughed at and tormented. And thus the fear of man brings a snare; and naught can deliver you out of that snare, save the opposite fear— the fear of God, which is the same as trust in God.

Joseph of old feared God when he was tempted; and said, "How can I do this great wickedness, and sin against God?" But I doubt not there were plenty in Egypt who would have called him a fool for his pains. There are hundreds of gay youths in any great city—there may be a few in this Abbey now for aught I know—who would have laughed loudly enough at Joseph for throwing away the opportunity of what certain foolish French have learnt to call, as its proper name, a "bonne fortune"—a piece of good luck.—As if breaking the 7th Commandment could be aught but bad fortune, and the cause of endless miseries in this life and the life to come.

And it may be, as Joseph was all but confounded and brought to shame, at least from man, when he found that all that he gained by fearing God was—a false accusation, the very shame and contempt from which he most shrank, danger of death, imprisonment in a dungeon.

But he was true to God, and God was true to him. He trusted in God; and therefore he feared God: for he trusted that God's laws were just and good, and worth obeying; and therefore he was afraid to break them. He trusted in God; and therefore he hoped in God; for he trusted that God was strong enough and good enough to deliver him out of prison, and make his righteousness as clear as the light and his just dealing as the noonday. He cried out of his prison, doubt it not, many a time and oft—"O God, in thee have I trusted; let me never be confounded."

And he was not confounded. He came into Egypt a slave. He was cast into prison on a shameful accusation : but he came out of prison to be a ruler and a prince, honoured and obeyed by the greatest nation of the old world. He trusted in God, and he was not confounded for ever ; even as the Lord Christ trusted in God and was not confounded for ever ; even as we, if we do not wish to be confounded for ever, must trust in God ; and instead of being scornful, careless, conceited, must fear Him, and say, " My flesh trembleth because of Thy righteous judgments." And then the laughter of fools will end, where it began, in harmless noise, like (says Solomon) the crackling of thorns under a pot. Then, whosoever may scorn you on earth, the great God in heaven will not scorn you. You may be confounded for a moment here on earth. Worldly people may take advantage of your misfortunes, and cry over you—There, there, so would we have it. Take him and persecute him, for there is none to deliver him ; where is now his God ? So it may be with you ; for as surely as you fall, many a cur will spring up and bark at you, who dared not open his mouth at you while you stood safe. Or—worse by far than that—the world may take hold of your really weak points, of your inconsistencies, of your faults and failings ; and cry—Fie on thee, fie on thee. We saw it with our eyes. For all his high professions, for all his talk of truth and justice, he is no better than the rest of the world. And that scoff does go very near to confound a man ; because he feels that it is half true, half deserved, and is afraid that it may be quite true and quite deserved: and then confounded indeed he would be, by his own conscience and by God, as well as by man.   All he can do is, to cry to God, like him who wrote the 119th Psalm,—I have stuck unto thy testimonies: O Lord, confound me not.   I know I am weak, ignorant, unsuccessful; full of faults too, and failings, which make me ashamed of myself every day of my life.   I have gone astray like a sheep that is lost. But seek thy servant, O Lord, for I do not forget thy commandments.   I am trying to learn my duty.   I am trying to do my duty.   I have stuck unto thy testimonies: O Lord, confound me not.   Man may confound me. But do not thou, of thy mercy and pity, O Lord.   Do not let me find, when I die, or before I die, that all my labour has been in vain; that I am not a better man, not a wiser man, not a more useful man after all. Do not let my grey hairs go down with sorrow to the grave.   Do not let me die with the miserable thought that, in spite of all my struggles to do my duty, my life has been a failure, and I a fool.   Do not let me wake in the next life, like Dives in the torment, to be utterly confounded; to find that I was all wrong, and have nothing left but everlasting disappointment and confusion of face.   O Lord, who didst endure all shame for me, save me from that most utter shame.   O God, in thee have I trusted; let me never be confounded.

Wake in the next life to find oneself confounded? Alas! alas!   Many a man wakes in this life to find himself that; and really sometimes by no fault, seemingly, of his own: so that all he can do is to be dumb, and not to open his mouth, for it is God's doing.   For a man's worst miseries and sorrows are, too often, caused not by himself, but by those whom he loves.

Consider the one case of vice, or even of mere ingratitude, in those nearest and dearest to a man's heart; and of being so confounded through them, and by them, in spite of all love, care, strictness, tenderness, teaching, prayers—what not—and all in vain.

No wonder that, under that bitterest blow, valiant and virtuous men, ere now, have never lifted up their heads again, but turned their faces to the wall, and died: and may the Lord have mercy on them.   Confounded they have been in this world; confounded they will not be, we must trust, in the world to come.   The Lord of all pity will pity them, and pour His oil and wine into their aching wounds, and bring them to His own inn, and to His secret dwelling-place, where the wicked cease from troubling, and the weary are at rest.

One word more, and I have done.   Do you wish to pray, with hope that you may be heard,—O Lord, confound me not, and bring me not to shame?   Then hold to one commandment of Christ's.   Do to others as you would they should do to you.   For with what measure you measure to your fellow-men, it shall be measured to you again.   Have charity, have patience, have mercy. Never bring a human being, however silly, ignorant, or weak, above all any little child, to shame and confusion of face.   Never, by cruelty, by petulance, by suspicion, by ridicule, even by selfish and silly haste; never, above all, by indulging in the devilish pleasure of a sneer, crush what is finest, and rouse up what is coarsest in the heart of any fellow-creature. Never confound any human soul in the hour of its weakness. For then, it may be, in the hour of thy weakness, Christ will not confound thee.

SERMON VIII.

THE SHAKING OF THE HEAVENS AND THE EARTH.

HEBREWS XII. 26—29.

Yet once more I shake not the earth only, but also heaven. And
this word, Yet once more, signifieth the removing of those
things that are shaken, as of things that are made, that those
things which cannot be shaken may remain. Wherefore we
receiving a kingdom which cannot be moved, let us have grace,
whereby we may serve God acceptably with reverence and godly
fear: for our God is a consuming fire.

THIS is one of the Royal texts of Scripture. It is inex-
haustible, like the God who inspired it. It has fulfilled
itself again and again, at different epochs. It fulfilled
itself specially and notoriously in the first century. But
it fulfilled itself again in the fifth century; and again at
the Crusades; and again at the Reformation in the sixteenth century. And it may be that it is fulfilling itself
at this very day; that in this century, both in the time of
our fathers and in our own, the Lord has been shaking
the heavens and the earth, that those things which can
be shaken may be removed, as things that are made,
while those things which cannot be shaken may remain.

All confess this to be true, each in his own words.
They talk of this age as one of change; of rapid progress, for good or evil; of unexpected discoveries; of
revolutions, intellectual, moral, social, as well as political.

Our notions of the physical universe are rapidly altering, with the new discoveries of science; and our notions of ethics and theology are altering as rapidly. The era assumes a different aspect to different minds, just as did the first century after Christ, according as men look forward to the future with hope, or back to the past with regret. Some glory in the nineteenth century as one of rapid progress for good; as the commencement of a new era for humanity; as the inauguration of a Reformation as grand as that of the sixteenth century. Others bewail it as an age of rapid decay; in which the old landmarks are being removed, the old paths lost; in which we are rushing headlong into scepticism and atheism; in which the world and the Church are both in danger; and the last day is at hand.

Both parties may be right; and yet both may be wrong. Men have always talked thus, at great crises in the world's life. They talked thus in the first century; and in the fifth, and in the eleventh; and again in the sixteenth; and then both parties were partially right and partially wrong; and so they may be now. What they meant to say, what they wanted to say, what we mean and want to say, has been said already for us in far deeper, wider, and more accurate words, by him who wrote this wonderful Epistle to the Hebrews, when he told the Jews of his time that the Lord was shaking the heavens and the earth, that those things which were shaken might be removed, as things that are made—cosmogonies, systems, theories, prejudices, fashions, of man's invention: while those things which could not be shaken might remain, because they were according to the mind and will of God, eternal as that source from whence they came forth, even the bosom of God the Father.

"Yet once more I shake, not the earth only, but also heaven."

How has the earth been shaken in our days; and the heaven likewise. How rapidly have our conceptions of both altered. How easy, simple, certain, it all looked to our forefathers in the middle age. How difficult, complex, uncertain, it all looks to us. With increased knowledge has come—not increased doubt: that I deny utterly. I deny, once and for all, that this age is an irreverent age. I say that an irreverent age is one like the age of the Schoolmen; when men defined and explained all heaven and earth by à priori theories, and cosmogonies invented in the cloister; and dared, poor, simple, ignorant mortals, to fancy that they could comprehend and gauge the ways of Him Whom the heaven and the heaven of heavens could not contain. This, this is irreverence: but it is neither irreverence nor want of faith, if a man, awed by the mystery which encompasses him from the cradle to the grave, shall lay his hand upon his mouth, with Job, and obey the voice which cries to him from earth and heaven—"Be still, and know that as the heavens are higher than the earth, so are my ways higher than thy ways, and my thoughts higher than thine."

But it was all easy, and simple, and certain enough to our forefathers. The earth, according to the popular notion, was a flat plane; or, if it were, as the wiser held, a sphere, yet antipodes were an unscriptural heresy.

Above it were the heavens, in which the stars were fixed, or wandered; and above them heaven after heaven, each tenanted by its own orders of beings, up to that heaven of heavens in which Deity—and by Him, be it always remembered, the mother of Deity—was enthroned.

And if above the earth was the kingdom of light, and purity, and holiness, what could be more plain, than that below it was the kingdom of darkness, and impurity, and sin? That was no theory to our forefathers: it was a physical fact. Had not even the heathens believed as much, and said so, by the mouth of the poet Virgil? He had declared that the mouth of Tartarus lay in Italy, hard by the volcanic lake Avernus; and after the unexpected eruption of Vesuvius in the first century, nothing seemed more clear than that Virgil was right; and that men were justified in talking of Tartarus, Styx, and Phlegethon as indisputable Christian entities. Etna, Stromboli, Hecla, were (according to this cosmogony) in like wise mouths of hell; and there were not wanting holy hermits, who had heard, from within those craters, shrieks, and clanking chains, and the howls of demons tormenting the souls of the endlessly lost.

Our forefathers were not aware that, centuries before the Incarnation of our Lord, the Buddhist priests had held exactly the same theory of moral retribution; and that, painted on the walls of Buddhist temples, might be seen horrors identical with those which adorned the walls of many a Christian Church, in the days when men believed in this Tartarology as firmly as they now believe in the results of chemistry or of astronomy.

And now—How is the earth shaken, and the heavens likewise, in that very sense in which the expression is used by him who wrote to the Hebrews? Our conceptions of them are shaken. How much of that mediæval cosmogony do educated men believe, in the sense in which they believe that the three angles of a triangle are equal to two right angles, or that if they steal their neighbour's goods they commit a sin?

The earth has been shaken for us, more and more violently, as the years have rolled on. It was shaken when Astronomy told us that the earth was not the centre of the universe, but a tiny planet revolving round a sun in a remote region thereof.

It was shaken when Geology told us that the earth had endured for countless ages, during which continents had become oceans, and oceans continents, again and again. And even now, it is being shaken by researches into the antiquity of man, into the origin and permanence of species, which—let the result be what it will— must in the meanwhile shake for us theories and dogmas which have been undisputed for 1500 years.

And with the rest of our cosmogony, that conception of a physical Tartarus below the earth has been shaken likewise, till good men have been fain to find a fresh place for it in the sun, or in a comet; or to patronize the probable, but as yet unproved theory of a central fire within the earth; not on any scientific grounds, but simply if by any means they can assign a region in space, wherein material torment can be inflicted on the spirits of the lost.

And meanwhile the heavens, the spiritual world, is being shaken no less. More and more frequently, more and more loudly, men are asking—not sceptics merely, but pious men, men who wish to be, and who believe themselves to be, orthodox Christians—more and more loudly are such men asking questions which demand an answer, with a learning and an eloquence, as well as with a devoutness and a reverence for Scripture, which—whether rightly or wrongly employed—is certain to com mand attention.

Rightly or wrongly, these men are asking, whether the actual and literal words of Scripture really involve the mediæval theory of an endless Tartarus.

They are saying, "It is not we who deny, but you who assert, endless torments, who are playing fast and loose with the letter of Scripture. You are reading into it conceptions borrowed from Virgil, Dante, Milton, when you translate into the formula 'endless torment' such phrases as 'the outer darkness,' 'the fire of Gehenna,' 'the worm that dieth not;' which, according to all just laws of interpretation, refer not to the next life, but to this life, and specially to the approaching cata-strophe of the Jewish nation; or when you say that eternal death really means eternal life—only life in torture."

Rightly or wrongly, they are saying this; and then they add, "We do not yield to you in love and esteem for Scripture. We demand not a looser, but a stricter; not a more metaphoric, but a more literal; not a more contemptuous, but a more reverent interpretation there-of."

So these men speak, rightly or wrongly. And for good or for evil, they will be heard.

And with these questions others have arisen, not new at all—say these men—but to be found, amid many contradictions, in the writings of all the best divines, when they have given up for a moment systems and theories, and listened to the voice of their own hearts; questions natural enough to an age which abhors cruelty, has abolished torture, labours for the reformation of criminals, and debates—rightly or wrongly—about abolishing capital punishment. Men are asking questions about the heaven—the spiritual world—and saying—"The spiritual world? Is it only another material world which happens to be invisible now, but which may become visible hereafter: or is it not rather the moral world—the world of right and wrong? Heaven? Is not the true and real heaven the kingdom of love, justice, purity, beneficence? Is not that the eternal heaven wherein God abides for ever, and with Him those who are like God? And hell? Is it not rather the anarchy of hate, injustice, impurity, uselessness; wherein abides all that is opposed to God?"

And with those thoughts come others about moral retribution—"What is its purpose? Can it—can any punishment have any right purpose save the correction, or the annihilation, of the criminal? Can God, in this respect, be at once less merciful and less powerful than man? Is He so controlled by necessity that He is forced to bring into the world beings whom He knows to be incorrigible, and doomed to endless misery? And if not so controlled, is not the alternative as to His character even more fearful? He bids us copy His justice, His love. Is that His justice, that His love, which if we copied, we should call each other, and deservedly, utterly unjust and unloving? Can there be one morality for God, and another for man, made in the image of God? Are these dark dogmas worthy of a Father who hateth nothing that He hath made, and is perfect in this—that He makes His sun shine on the evil and on the good, and His rain fall on the just and on the unjust, and is good to the unthankful and to the evil? Are they worthy of a Son who, in the fire of His divine charity, stooped from heaven to earth, to toil, to suffer, to die on the Cross, that the world by Him might be saved? Are they worthy of that Spirit which proceeds from the Father and the Son, even that Spirit of boundless charity, and fervent love, by which the Son offered Himself to the Father, a sacrifice for the sins of the whole world—and surely not in vain?"

So men are asking—rightly or wrongly; and they are guarding themselves, at the same time, from the imputation of disbelief in moral retribution; of fancying God to be a careless, epicurean deity, cruelly indulgent to sin, and therefore, in so far, immoral.

They say—"We believe firmly enough in moral retribution. How can we help believing in it, while we see it working around us, in many a fearful shape, here, now, in this life? And we believe that it may work on, in still more fearful shapes, in the life to come. We believe that as long as a sinner is impenitent, he must be miserable; that if he goes on impenitent for ever, he must go on making himself miserable—ay, it may be more and more miserable for ever. Only do not tell us that he must go on. That his impenitence, and therefore his punishment, is irremediable, necessary, endless; and thereby destroy the whole purpose, and we should say, the whole morality, of his punishment. If that punishment be corrective, our moral sense is not shocked by any severity, by any duration: but if it is irremediable, it cannot be corrective; and then, what it is, or why it is, we cannot—or rather dare not—say. We, too, believe in an eternal fire. But because we believe also the Athanasian Creed, which tells us that there is but One Eternal, we believe that that fire must be the fire of God, and therefore, like all that is in God and of God, good and not evil, a blessing and not a curse. We believe that that fire is for ever burning, though men are for ever trying to quench it all day long; and that it has been and will be in every age burning up all the chaff and stubble of man's inventions; the folly, the falsehood, the ignorance, the vice of this sinful world; and we praise God for it; and give thanks to Him for His great glory, that He is the everlasting and triumphant foe of evil and misery, of whom it is written, that our God is a consuming fire."

Such words are being spoken, right or wrong. Such words will bear their fruit, for good or evil. I do not pronounce how much of them is true or false. It is not my place to dogmatize and define, where the Church of England, as by law established, has declined to do so. Neither is it for you to settle these questions. It is rather a matter for your children. A generation more, it may be, of earnest thought will be required, ere the true answer has been found. But it is your duty, if you be educated and thoughtful persons, to face these questions; to consider seriously what these men would have you consider—whether you are believing the exact words of the Bible, and the conclusions of your own reason and moral sense; or whether you are merely believing that cosmogony elaborated in the cloister, that theory of moral retribution pardonable in the middle age, which Dante and Milton sang.

But this I do not hesitate to say—That if we of the clergy can find no other answers to these doubts than those which were reasonable and popular in an age when men racked women, burned heretics, and believed that every Mussulman killed in a crusade went straight to Tartarus—then very serious times are at hand, both for the Christian clergy and for Christianity itself.

What, then, are we to believe and do? Shall we degenerate into a lazy scepticism, which believes that everything is a little true, and everything a little false—in plain words, believes nothing at all? Or shall we degenerate into faithless fears, and unmanly wailings that the flood of infidelity is irresistible, and that Christ has left His Church?

We shall do neither, if we believe the text. That tells us of a firm standing-ground amid the wreck of fashions and opinions. Of a kingdom which cannot be moved, though the heavens pass away like a scroll, and the earth be burnt up with fervent heat.

And it tells us that the King of that kingdom is He, who is called Jesus Christ—the same yesterday, to-day, and for ever.

An eternal and changeless kingdom, and an eternal and changeless King. These the Epistle to the Hebrews preaches to all generations.

It does not say that we have an unchangeable cosmogony, an unchangeable eschatology, an unchangeable theory of moral retribution, an unchangeable dogmatic system: not to these does it point the Jews, while their own nation and worship were in their very death-agony, and the world was rocking and reeling round them, decay and birth going on side by side, in a chaos such as man had never seen before. Not to these does the Epistle point the Hebrews: but to the changeless kingdom and to the changeless King.

My friends, do you really believe in that kingdom, and in that King? Do you believe that you are now actually in a kingdom of heaven, which cannot be moved; and that the living, acting, guiding, practical, real King thereof is Christ who died on the Cross?

These are days in which a preacher is bound to ask his congregation—and still more to ask himself—whether he really believes in that kingdom, and in that King; and to bid himself and them, if they have not believed earnestly enough therein, to repent, in this time of Lent, of that at least; to repent of having neglected that most cardinal doctrine of Scripture and of the Christian faith.

But if we really believe in that changeless kingdom and in that changeless King, shall we not—considering

who Christ is, the co-equal and co-eternal Son of God—
believe also, that if the heavens and the earth are being
shaken, then Christ Himself may be shaking them? That
if opinions be changing, then Christ Himself may be
changing them? That if new truths are being discovered, Christ Himself may be revealing them? That
if some of those truths seem to contradict those which
He has revealed already, they do not really contradict
them? That, as in the sixteenth century, Christ is
burning up the wood and stubble with which men have
built on His foundation, that the pure gold of His truth
may alone be left? It is at least possible; it is probable,
if we believe that Christ is a living, acting King, to
whom all power is given in heaven and earth, and
who is actually exercising that power; and educating
Christendom, and through Christendom the whole human
race, to a knowledge of Himself, and through Himself
of God their Father in heaven.

Should we not say—We know that Christ has been
so doing, for centuries and for ages? Through Abraham,
through Moses, through the prophets, through the Greeks,
through the Romans, and at last through Himself, He gave
men juster and wider views of themselves, of the universe,
and of God. And even then He did not stop. How could
He, who said of Himself, " My Father worketh hitherto,
and I work"? How could He, if He be the same yesterday, to-day, and for ever? Through the Apostles, and
specially through St Paul, He enlarged, while He con-
firmed, His own teaching. And did He not do the same in
the sixteenth century? Did He not then sweep from the

minds and hearts of half Christendom beliefs which had been held sacred and indubitable for a thousand years? Why should He not be doing so now? If it be answered, that the Reformation of the sixteenth century was only a return to simpler and purer Apostolic truth—why, again, should it not be so now? Why should He not be perfecting His work one step more, and sweeping away more of man's inventions, which are not integral and necessary elements of the one Catholic faith, but have been left behind, in pardonable human weakness, by our great Reformers? Great they were, and good: giants on the earth, while we are but as dwarfs beside them. But, as the hackneyed proverb says, the dwarf on the giant's shoulders may see further than the giant himself: and so may we.

Oh! that men would approach new truth in something of that spirit; in the spirit of reverence and Godly fear, which springs from a living belief in Christ the living King, which is—as the text tells us—the spirit in which we can serve God acceptably. Oh! that they would serve God; waiting reverently and anxiously, as servants standing in the presence of their Lord, for the slightest sign or hint of His will. Then they would have grace; by which they would receive new thought with grace; gracefully, courteously, fairly, charitably, reverently; believing that, however strange or startling, it may come from Him whose ways are not as our ways, nor His thoughts as our thoughts; and that he who fights against it, may haply be fighting against God.

True, they would receive all new thought with caution,

that conservative spirit, which is the duty of every Christian; which is the peculiar strength of the Englishman, because it enables him calmly and slowly to take in the new, without losing the old which his forefathers have already won for him. So they would be cautious, even anxious, lest in grasping too greedily at seeming improvements, they let go some precious knowledge which they had already attained: but they would be on the look out for improvements; because they would consider themselves, and their generation, as under a divine education. They would prove all things fairly and boldly, and hold fast that which is good; all that which is beautiful, noble, improving and elevating to human souls, minds, or bodies; all that increases the amount of justice, mercy, knowledge, refinement; all that lessens the amount of vice, cruelty, ignorance, barbarism. That at least must come from Christ. That at least must be the inspiration of the Spirit of God: unless the Pharisees were right after all when they said, that evil spirits could be cast out by the prince of the devils.

Be these things as they may, one comfort it will give us, to believe firmly and actively in the changeless kingdom, and in the changeless King. It will give us calm, patience, faith and hope, though the heavens and the earth be shaken around us. For then we shall see that the Kingdom, of which we are citizens, is a kingdom of light, and not of darkness; of truth, and not of falsehood; of freedom, and not of slavery; of bounty and mercy, and not of wrath and fear; that we live and move and have our being not in a "Deus quidam deceptor" who grudges his children wisdom, but in a Father of Light, from whom comes every good and perfect gift; who willeth that all men should be saved, and come to the knowledge of the truth.   In His kingdom we are; and in the King whom He has set over it we can have the most perfect trust.   For us that King stooped from heaven to earth; for us He was born, for us He toiled, for us He suffered, for us He died, for us He rose, for us He sits for ever at God's right hand.   And can we not trust Him? Let Him do what He will.   Let Him lead us whither He will. Wheresoever He leads must be the way of truth and life.   Whatsoever He does, must be in harmony with that infinite love which He displayed for us upon the Cross.   Whatsoever He does, must be in harmony with that eternal purpose by which He reveals to men God their Father.   Therefore, though the heaven and the earth be shaken around us, we will trust in Him.   For we know that He is the same yesterday, to-day, and for ever; and that His will and promise is, to lead those who trust in Him into all truth.

SERMON IX.

THE KINGDOM OF GOD.

LUKE XXI. 29—33.

And Jesus spake to them a parable; Behold the fig tree, and all the trees; when they now shoot forth, ye see and know of your own selves that summer is now nigh at hand. So likewise ye, when ye see these things come to pass, know ye that the kingdom of God is nigh at hand. Verily I say unto you, This generation shall not pass away, till all be fulfilled. Heaven and earth shall pass away: but my words shall not pass away.

THE question which naturally suggests itself when we hear these words, is—When were these things to take place?

If we heard one whom we regarded as at least a person of perfect virtue, truthfulness, and earnestness, foretell that the city in which we now stand should be destroyed. If he told us, that when we saw it encompassed with armies, we were to know that its desolation was at hand. If he told us that then those who were in the surrounding country were to flee to the mountains, and those in the city to come out of it. If he pronounced woe in that day on mothers and weak women who could not escape. If he told us, nevertheless, that when these things came to pass we were to rejoice and lift up our heads, for our redemption was drawing nigh. If he told us to look at the trees in spring; for, as surely as their budding was a sign that summer was nigh, so was the coming to pass of these terrible woes a sign that something was nigh, which he called the Kingdom of God. If he told us, with a solemn asseveration, that this generation should not pass away till all had happened. If he went on to warn us against profligacy, frivolity, worldliness, lest that day should come upon us unaware. If he bade us keep awake always, that we might be found worthy to escape all that was coming, and to stand before Him, The Son of Man. If he used throughout his address the second person, speaking to us, but never mentioning our descendants; giving the signs, the warnings, the counsels to us only, should we not, even if he had not solemnly told us that the present generation should not pass away till all was fulfilled—should we not, I say, suppose naturally that he spoke of events which in his opinion our own eyes would see; which would, in his opinion, occur during our lifetime?

Whether he were right in his expectation, or wrong, still it would be clear that such was his expectation; that he considered the danger as imminent, the warning as addressed personally to us who heard him speak.

We should leave his presence with that impression, in fear and anxiety. But if we afterwards discovered that our fear and anxiety were superfluous; that the events of which he spoke—the most awful and wonderful of them at least—were not to occur for many centuries to come; that, even if some calamity were imminent, the immediate future and the very distant future were so intermingled in his discourse, that it would require the labours of commentator after commentator, for many hundred years, to disentangle them, and that their labours would be in vain; that the coming of the Son of Man, and of the Kingdom of God, of which he had spoken, were to be referred to a time thousands of years hence; though we were told in the same breath to look to the fig-tree and all the trees as a sign that it was coming immediately, and that our own generation would not pass away before all had taken place :—would not such a discovery raise in us thoughts and feelings neither wholesome for us nor honourable to the prophet?

I cannot think otherwise. We may be aware of the difficulties which beset this, and any other, interpretation of our Lord's prophecies in Matthew, Mark, and Luke: we may have the deepest respect for those learned and pious divines who from time to time have tried to part the prophecies relating to the fall of Jerusalem from those relating to the end of the world and the day of Judgment. Yet, in the face of such a passage as the text, especially when we cannot agree with those who would make this " generation " mean this " race " or " nation," we may—we have a right to—decline to separate the two sets of passages. We have a right to say,—He who spake as man never spake, and therefore knew the force of words; He who knew what was in man—and therefore what effect His words would produce on His hearers—did deliver a discourse—indeed, many discourses—

which asserted, as far as plain words could be understood by plain men, that the Kingdom of God was at hand; and that the coming of the Son of Man would take place before that generation passed away.

And that all His disciples, and St Paul as much as any, put that meaning upon His words, is a matter of fact and of history, to be seen plainly in Holy Scripture.

But, while the text compels us to believe that the destruction of Jerusalem by the Romans was a coming of the Son of Man—a manifestation of the Kingdom of God—a day of Judgment, in the strictest and most awful sense; yet we are not compelled to limit the meaning of the text to the destruction of Jerusalem.

No prophecy of Scripture is of private interpretation. Prophets, apostles—how much more our Lord Himself—do not merely indulge in presages; they lay down laws —laws moral, spiritual, eternal—which have been fulfilling themselves from the beginning; which are fulfilling themselves now; which will go on fulfilling themselves to the end of time.

So said our Lord Jesus of His own prophecies concerning the destruction of Jerusalem. It was but one example—a most awful one—of the laws of His kingdom. Not in Judæa only, but wherever the carcase was, there would the eagles be gathered together. In the moral, as in the physical word, there were beasts of prey—the scavengers of God—ready to devour out of His kingdom nations, institutions, opinions, which had become dead, and decayed, and ready to infect the air. Many a time since the Roman eagles flocked to Jerusalem has that

prophecy been fulfilled ; and many a time will it be fulfilled once more, and yet once more.

And what else, if we look at them carefully and reverently, is the meaning of the words in this my text,
" Heaven and earth shall pass away, but My words shall
not pass away"?

Shall we translate this,—Heaven and earth shall not
come true: but My words shall come true ? By so doing
we may put some little meaning into the latter half of
the verse; but none into the former. Surely there is a
deeper meaning in the words than that of merely coming
true. Surely they mean that His words are eternal, perpetual; for ever present, possible, imminent; for ever
coming true. So, indeed, they would not pass away. So
they would be like the heavens and the earth, and the
laws thereof; like heat, gravitation, electricity, what not
—always here, always working, always asserting themselves—with this difference, that when the physical laws
of the heavens and the earth, which began in time, in
time have perished, the spiritual laws of God's kingdom,
of Christ's moral government of moral beings, shall
endure for ever and for ever, eternal as that God whose
essence they reflect.

Therefore I mean nothing less than that the great
and final day of Judgment is past; or that we are not to
look for that second coming of our Lord Jesus Christ
which, as our forefathers taught us to hope, shall set right
all the wrong of this diseased world.

God forbid ! For most miserable were the world,
most miserable were mankind, if all that our Lord pro-

phesied had happened, once and for all, at the destruction of Jerusalem by the Roman armies. But most miserable, also, would this world be, and most miserable would be mankind, if these words were not to be fulfilled till some future Last Day, and day of Judgment, for which the Church has now been waiting for more than eighteen centuries—and, as far as we can judge, may wait for as many centuries more. Most miserable, if the Son of Man has never come since He ascended into heaven from Olivet. Most miserable, if the kingdom of God has never been at hand, since He gave that one short gleam of hope to men in Judæa long ago. Most miserable, if there be no kingdom of God among us even now: in one word, if God and Christ be not our King; but the devil, as some fancy; or Man himself, as others fancy, be the only king of this world and of its destinies; if there be no order in this mad world, save what man invents; no justice, save what he executes; no law, save what he finds convenient to lay upon himself for the protection of his person and property. Most miserable, if the human race have no guide, save its own instincts and tendencies; no history, save that of its own greed, ignorance and crime, varied only by fruitless struggles after a happiness to which it never attains. Most miserable world, and miserable man, if that be true after all which to the old Hebrew prophet seemed incredible and horrible—if God does look on while men deal treacherously, and does hold His peace when the wicked devours the man who is more righteous than he; and has made men as the fishes of the sea, as the creeping things that have no ruler over them.

I said—Most miserable, in that case, was the world and man. I did not say that they would consider themselves miserable. I did not say that they would think it a Gospel, and good news, that Christ was their King, and that His Kingdom was always at hand. They never thought that good news. When the prophets told them of it, they stoned them. When the Lord Himself told them, they crucified Him. Worldly men dislike the message now, probably, as much as they ever did. But they escape from it, either by treating it as a self-evident commonplace which no Christian denies, and therefore no Christian need think of; or by smiling at it as an exploded superstition, at least as a "Semitic" form of thought, with which we have nothing to do. They confound it, often I fear purposely, with those fancied miraculous interpositions, those paltry special providences, which fanatics in all ages have believed to be worked for their own special behoof. Altogether they dislike, and express very openly their dislike, of the least allusion to a Divine Providence "interfering," as they strangely term it, with them and their affairs.

And they are wise, doubtless, in their generation. The news that Christ is the King of men and of the world must be unpleasant, even offensive, to too many, both of those who fancy that they are managing this world, and of those who fancy that they could manage the world still better, if they only had their rights. It must be unpleasant to be told that they are not managing the world, and cannot manage it: that it is being managed and ruled by an unseen King, whose ways are far above their ways, and His thoughts above their thoughts.

For then: Prudence might demand of them, that they should find out what are that King's ways, thoughts and laws, and obey them—an enquiry so troublesome, that many very highly educated persons consider it, now-a-days, quite impossible; and tell us that, for practical purposes, God's laws can neither be discovered, nor obeyed.

Moreover, their scheme of this world is one which would work—so they fancy—just as well if there was no God. Unpleasant therefore it must be for them to hear, not merely that there is a God, but that He has His own scheme of the world; and that it is working, whether they like or not; that God, and not they, is making history; God, and not they, appointing the bounds and the times of nations; God, and not they, or any man or men, distributing good and evil among mankind.

They do not object, of course, to the existence of a God. They only object to His being what the Hebrew prophets called Him—a living God; a God who executes justice and judgment by His Son Jesus Christ, to whom He has committed all power both in heaven and earth. They are ready sometimes to allow even that, provided they may relegate it into the past, or into the future. They are ready to allow that God and Christ exerted power over men at the first Advent 1800 years ago, and that they will exert power over men at the second Advent—none knows how long hence. But that God and Christ are exerting power now—in an ever-present and perpetual Advent—in this nineteenth century just as much as in any century before or since—that they had rather not believe. Their creed is, that though heaven and earth have not passed away; though the laws of nature are working for ever as at the beginning: yet Christ's words have passed away, and fallen into abeyance for many centuries past, to remain in abeyance for many centuries to come.

In one word—while they believe more or less in a past God, and a future God, yet as to the existence of a present God, in any practical and real sense—they believe—how little, I dare not say.

Whether this generation will awaken out of that sleep of practical Atheism, which is creeping on them more and more, who can tell? That they are uneasy in the sleep, there are many signs. For in their sleep dreams come of another world, of which their five senses tell them nought. Then do some fly to mediæval superstitions, which give them at least elaborate and agreeable substitutes for a living God. Some fly to impostors, who pretend by juggling tricks to put them in communication with that unseen world which they have so long denied. Some, again, play with unfulfilled prophecy; and fancy that it is for them, though it was not for the apostles, to know the times and seasons which the Father has put in His own power, and the day and hour of which no man knoweth, no not the angels in heaven, nor the Son, but the Father only.

Better that, than that they should believe that there is nothing, and never will 'be anything, in the world, beyond what their five senses can apprehend.

But whether they awake or not out of their sleep, their blindness does not alter the eternal fact, whether men believe it or not. That is true what the Psalmist said of old: "The Lord is King, be the people never so impatient. He sitteth upon His throne, though the earth be never so unquiet."

The utterances of the old Psalmists and prophets concerning the ever-present kingdom of God are facts, not dreams. Whether men believe it or not, it is true that the power, glory, and righteousness of His kingdom may be known unto men; that His kingdom is an everlasting kingdom, and His dominion endureth throughout all ages; that The Lord upholds all such as fall, and lifts up those that are down; that the eyes of all wait on Him, that He may give them their meat in due season; that He opens His hand, and filleth all things living with plenteousness; that the Lord is righteous in all His ways, and holy in all His works; that He is nigh to them that call upon Him, yea to all who call upon Him faithfully. He that planted the ear, shall He not hear? He that made the eye, shall He not see? He that chastiseth the nations; it is He that teacheth man knowledge: shall He not punish?

Whether men believe it or not, that is true which the Psalmist said—Whither shall I flee from His Spirit, or whither shall I go from His presence? If I climb up to heaven, He is there; if I go down to hell, He is there also. If I take the wings of the morning, and dwell in the uttermost part of the sea, even there shall His hand lead me, His right hand hold me still.

Whether men believe it or not, that is true which Christ spake on earth—That the Father hath committed all judgment to Him, because He is the Son of man; that to Him is given all power in heaven and earth; and that He is with us, even to the end of the world.

Whether men believe it or not, that is true which S. Paul spake on Mars' hill, saying that the Lord is not far from any one of us, for in Him we live and move and have our being; and that He hath appointed a day in which He will judge the world in righteousness, by that Man whom He hath ordained, and raised from the dead.

Whether men believe it or not, that is true which Christ spake—Heaven and earth shall pass away; but My words shall not pass away; at least till He has put down all rule and all authority and power, and delivered up the kingdom to God, even the Father, that God may be all in all.

"That one far-off divine event, toward which the whole creation moves," will be, not the resumption, but the triumph, of Christ's rule; of a rule which began before the world, which has endured through all the ages; which endures now, punishing or rewarding each and every one of us, and of our children's children, as long as there shall be a man upon the earth. For by Christ's will alone the world of man consists; in Christ's laws alone is true life, health, wealth, possible for any man, family or nation; out of His kingdom He casts, sooner or later, all things which offend, and whosoever loveth and maketh a lie. He said of Himself—Whosoever falleth on this rock shall be broken; but on whomsoever it shall fall, it shall grind him to powder.

SERMON X.

THE LAW OF THE LORD.

PSALM I. 1, 2.

Blessed is the man who hath not walked in the counsel of the ungodly, nor stood in the path of sinners, nor sat in the seat of the scornful. But his delight is in the law of the Lord; and in his law will he exercise himself day and night.

THE first and second Psalms, taken together, are the key to all the Psalms; I may almost say to the whole Bible. I will say a few words on them this morning, especially to those who are coming to the Holy Communion, to shew their allegiance to that Lord, in whose law alone is life, and who sits on the throne of the universe, King of kings, and Lord of lords: but I say it to the whole congregation likewise; nay, if there were an infidel or a heathen in the Church, I should say it to them. For in this case what is true of one man is true of every man, whether he knows it or not.

We all should like to be blessed. We all should like to be, as the Psalm says, like trees planted by the waterside, whose leaves never wither, and who bring forth their fruit in due season. We should all wish to have it said of us—Whatsoever he doeth it shall prosper.

Then here is the way to inherit that blessing—"*Blessed is the man whose delight is in the law of the Lord, and who exercises himself in His law day and night.*" The Psalmist is not speaking of Moses' Law, nor of any other law of forms and ceremonies. He says expressly "The law of the Lord"—that is, the law according to which the Lord has made him and all the world; and according to which the Lord rules him and all the world. The Psalms—you must remember—say very little about Moses' law; and when they do, speak of it almost slightingly, as if to draw men's minds away from it to a deeper, nobler, more eternal law. In one Psalm God asks, "Thinkest thou that I will eat bulls' flesh, and drink the blood of goats?" And in another Psalm some one answers, "Sacrifice and burnt-offering thou wouldest not. Then said I, Lo I come, to do thy will, O God. Thy law is within my heart." This is that true and eternal law of which Solomon speaks in his proverbs, as the Wisdom by which God made the heavens, and laid the foundation of the earth; and tells us that that Wisdom is a tree of life to all who can lay hold of her; that in her right hand is length of days, and in her left hand riches and honour; that her ways are ways of pleasantness; and all her paths are peace.

This is that law, of which the Prophet says—that God will put it into men's hearts, and write it in their minds; and they shall be His people, and He will be their God. This is that law, which the inspired Philosopher—for a philosopher he was indeed—who wrote the 119th Psalm, continually prayed and strove to learn, intreating the Lord to teach him His law, and make him remember His everlasting judgments. This is that law, which our Lord Jesus Christ perfectly fulfilled, because the law was His Father's law, and therefore His own law, and therefore he perfectly comprehended the law, and perfectly loved the law; and said with His whole heart—I delight to do Thy will, O God.

The will of God. For in one word, this Law, which we have to learn, and by keeping which we shall be blessed, is nothing else than God's Will. God's Will about us. What God has willed and chosen we should be. What God has willed and chosen we should do. The greatest philosopher of the 18th century said that every rational being had to answer four questions— Where am I? What can I know? What must I do? Whither am I going? And he knew well that—as the Bible tells us throughout—the only way to get any answer to those four tremendous questions is—To delight in the law of the Lord; to struggle, think, pray, till we get some understanding of God's will; of God's will about ourselves and about the world; and so be blessed indeed.

But to do that, it is plain that we must heed the warning which the first verse of the Psalm gives us—" Blessed is the man that hath not walked in the counsel of the ungodly." For it is plain that a man will never learn God's will if he takes counsel from ungodly men who care nothing for God's will, and do not believe that God's will governs the world. Neither must he, as the Psalm says, 'stand in the way of sinners'—of profligate and dishonest men who break God's law.　For if he follows their ways, and breaks God's law himself, it is plain that he will learn little or nothing about God's law, save in the way of bitter punishment.　For let him but break God's law a little too long, and then—as the 2nd Psalm says—'God will rule him with a rod of iron, and break him in pieces like a potter's vessel.'　But there is even more hope for him— for he may repent and amend—than if he sits in the seat of the scorners.　The scorners; the sneering, the frivolous, the unearnest, the unbelieving, the envious, who laugh down what they call enthusiasm and romance; who delight in finding fault, and in blackening those who seem purer or nobler than themselves.　These are the men who cannot by any possibility learn anything of the law of God; for they will not even look for it.　They have cast away the likeness of rational men, and have taken upon themselves the likeness of the sneering accusing Satan, who asks in the book of Job—" Doth Job serve God for nought ?"　When the greatest poet of our days tried to picture his idea of a fiend tempting a man to his ruin, he gave his fiend just such a character as this; a very clever, courteous, agreeable man of the world, and yet a being who could not love any one, could not believe in any one; who mocked not only at man but at God and tempted and ruined man, not out of hatred to him, hardly out of envy; but in mere sport, as a cruel child may torment an insect;—in one word, a scorner.　And so true was his conception felt to be, that men of that character are now often called by the very name which he gave to his Satan —Mephistopheles.　Beware therefore of the scornful spirit, as well as of the openly sinful or of the ungodly. If you wish to learn the law of the Lord, keep your souls pious, pure, reverent, and earnest; for it is only the pure in heart who shall see God; and only those who do God's will as far as they know it, who will know concerning any doctrine whether it be true or false; in one word, whether it be of God.

And now bear in mind secondly, that this law is the law of the Lord. You cannot have a law without a law-giver who makes the law, and also without a judge who enforces the law; and the lawgiver and the judge of the law of the Lord is the Lord Himself, our Lord Jesus Christ.

Remembering Him, and that He is King, we can understand the fervour of indignation and pity, with which the writer of the 2nd Psalm bursts out—"Why do the heathen rage, and why do the people imagine a vain thing? The kings of the earth stand up, and the rulers take counsel together, against the Lord, and against His Anointed—

"Let us break their bonds asunder and cast away their cords from us."

For the great majority of mankind, in every age and country, will not believe that there is a Law of the Lord, to which they must conform themselves. Kings, and governments, and peoples, are too often all alike in that. They must needs have their own way. Their will is to be law. Their voice is to be the voice of God. They are they who ought to speak; who is Lord over them? And because the Lord is patient and long-suffering, and does not punish their presumption on the spot by lightning or earthquake, they fancy that He takes no notice of them, and of their crimes and follies; and say—"Tush, shall God perceive it? Is there knowledge in the most High?"

But sooner or later, either by sudden and terrible catastrophes, or by slow decay, brought on sometimes by their own blind presumption, sometimes by their own luxury, they find out their mistake when it is too late. And then—

"He that dwelleth in heaven shall laugh them to scorn. The Lord shall have them in derision. For He has set His King upon the throne" of all the universe.

Yes, Christ the Lord rules, and knows that He rules; whether we know it or not. Christ's law still hangs over our head, ready to lead us to light and life and peace and wealth, or ready to fall on us and grind us to powder, whether we choose to look up and see it or not. The Lord liveth; though we may be too dead to feel Him. The Lord sees us; though we may be too blind to see Him. Man can abolish many things; and does both.—wisely and unwisely—in these restless days of change. But let him try as long as he will—for he has often tried, and will try again—he cannot abolish Christ the Lord.

For Christ is set upon the throne of the universe. The Father of all—if we may dare to hint even in Scriptural words at mysteries which are in themselves unspeakable—is eternally saying to Him—Thou art my Son, this day have I begotten Thee. And Christ answers eternally—I come to do Thy will, O God. The nations are Christ's inheritance ; and the utmost parts of the earth are His possession, now, already ; whether we or they think so or not.

And there are times—there are times, my friends—when the awful words which follow come true likewise—"Thou shalt bruise them with a rod of iron, and break them in pieces like a potter's vessel."

For as to this world in which we live, so to the God who created that world, there is a terrible aspect. There is calm : but there is storm also. There is fertilizing sunshine : but there is also the destroying thunderbolt. There is the solid and fruitful earth, where man can till and build ; but there is the earthquake and the flood likewise, which destroy in a moment the works of man. So there is in God boundless love, and boundless mercy : but there is, too, a wrath of God, and a fire of God which burns eternally against all evil and falsehood. And woe to those who fall under that wrath ; who are even scorched for a moment by that fire.

"It is a fearful thing to fall into the hands of the Living God."

We are all ready enough to forget this ; ready enough to think only of God's goodness, and never of His severity. Ready enough to talk of Christ as gentle and suffering ; because we flatter ourselves that if He is gentle, He may be also indulgent ; if He be suffering, He may be also weak. We like to forget that He is, and was, and ever will be—Lord of heaven and earth ; and to think of Him only in His humiliation in Judæa 1800 years ago, forgetting that during that very humiliation, while He was shewing love, and mercy, and miracles of healing, and sympathy and compassion for every form of human sorrow and weakness, He did not shrink from shewing to men the awful side of His character; did not shrink from saying, "Woe unto you, Scribes and Pharisees, hypocrites. Ye serpents, ye generation of vipers, how can ye escape the damnation of hell?"—did not shrink from declaring that He was coming again, even before that very generation had passed away, to destroy, unless it repented, the wicked city of Jerusalem, with an utter and horrible destruction.

Think of these things, my friends: for true they are, and true they will remain, whether you think of them or not. And take the warning of the second Psalm, which is needed now as much as it was ever needed— "Be wise now therefore, O ye kings, be learned, ye that are judges of the earth. Serve the Lord with fear, and rejoice unto Him with reverence. Worship the Son, lest He be angry, and so ye perish from the right way. If His wrath be kindled, yea, but a little, blessed are all they that put their trust in Him."

But you are no kings, you are no judges. Is it so? And yet you boast yourselves to be free men, in a free country. Not so. Every man who is a free man is a king or a judge, whether he knows it or not. Every one who has a duty, is a king over his duty. Every one who has a work to do, is a judge whether he does his work well or not. He who farms, is a king and a judge over his land. He who keeps a shop, a king and a judge over his business. He who has a family, a king and a judge over his household. Let each be wise, and serve the Lord in fear; knowing that according as he obeys the law of the Lord, he will receive for the deeds done in the body, whether good or evil.

Not kings? not judges? Is not each and every human being who is not a madman, a king over his own actions, a judge over his own heart and conscience? Let him govern himself, govern his own thoughts and words, his own life and actions, according to the law of the Lord who created him; and he will be able to say with the poet,

> My mind to me a kingdom is;
> Such perfect joy therein I find
> As far exceeds all earthly bliss.

But if he governs himself according to his own fancy, which is no law, but lawlessness: then he will find himself rebelling against himself, weakened by passions, torn by vain desires, and miserable by reason of the lusts which war in his members; and so will taste, here in this life, of that anger of the Lord of which it is written ; "If His wrath be kindled, yea, but a little, ye shall perish from the right way."

Therefore let each and all of us, high and low, take the warning of the last verse, and worship the Son of God. Bow low before Him—for that is the true meaning of the words—as subjects before an absolute monarch, who can dispose of us, body and soul, according to His will: but who can be trusted to dispose of us well: because His will is a good will, and the only reason why He is angry when we break His laws, is, that His laws are the Eternal Laws of God, wherein alone is life for all rational beings ; and to break them is to injure our fellow-creatures, and to ruin ourselves, and perish from that right way, to bring us back to which He condescended, of His boundless love, to die on the Cross for all mankind.

SERMON XI.

GOD THE TEACHER.

Psalm CXIX. 33, 34.

Teach me, O Lord, the way of Thy statutes, and I shall keep it unto the end. Give me understanding, and I shall keep Thy Law; yea, I shall observe it with my whole heart.

THIS 119th Psalm has been valued for many centuries, by the wisest and most devout Christians, as one of the most instructive in the Bible; as the experimental psalm. And it is that, and more. It is specially a psalm about education. That is on the face of the text. Teach me, O Lord, Thy statutes, and I shall keep them to the end. These are the words of a man who wishes to be taught, and therefore to learn; and to learn not mere book-learning and instruction, but to acquire a practical education, which he can keep to the end, and carry out in his whole life.

But it is more. It is, to my mind, as much a theological psalm as it is an experimental psalm; and it is just as valuable for what it tells us concerning the changeless and serene essence of God, as for what it tells us concerning the changing and struggling soul of man.

Let us think a little this morning—and, please God, hereafter also—of the Psalm, and what it says. For it is just as true now as ever it was, and just as precious to those who long to educate themselves with the true education, which makes a man perfect, even as his Father in heaven is perfect.

The Psalm is a prayer, or collection of short prayers, written by some one who had two thoughts in his mind, and who was so full of those two thoughts that he repeated them over and over again, in many different forms, like one who, having an air of music in his head, repeats it in different keys, with variation after variation ; yet keeps true always to the original air, and returns to it always at the last.

Now what two thoughts were in the Psalmist's mind?

First: that there was something in the world which he must learn, and would learn ; for everything in this life and the next depended on his learning it. And this thing which he wants to learn he calls God's statutes, God's law, God's testimonies, God's commandments, God's everlasting judgments. That is what he feels he must learn, or else come to utter grief, both body and soul.

Secondly: that if he is to learn them, God Himself must teach them to him. I beg you not to overlook this side of the Psalm. That is what makes it not only a psalm, but a prayer also. The man wants to know something. But beside that, he prays God to teach it to him.

He was not like too many now-a-days, who look on

prayer, and on inspiration, as old-fashioned superstitions; who believe that a man can find out all he needs to know by his own unassisted intellect, and then do it by his own unassisted will. Where they get their proofs of that theory, I know not; certainly not from the history of mankind, and certainly not from their own experience, unless it be very different from mine. Be that as it may, this old Psalmist would not have agreed with them; for he held an utterly opposite belief. He held that a man could see nothing, unless God shewed it to him. He held that a man could learn nothing unless God taught him; and taught him, moreover, in two ways. First taught him what he ought to do, and then taught him how to do it.

Surely this man was, at least, a reasonable and prudent man, and shewed his common-sense. I say—common-sense.

For suppose that you were set adrift in a ship at sea, to shift for yourself, would it not be mere common-sense to try and learn how to manage that ship, that you might keep her afloat and get her safe to land? You would try to learn the statutes, laws, and commandments, and testimonies, and judgments concerning the ship, lest by your own ignorance you should sink her, and be drowned. You would try to learn the laws about the ship; namely the laws of floatation, by fulfilling which vessels swim, and by breaking which vessels sink.

You would try to learn the commandments about her. They would be any books which you could find of rules of navigation, and instruction in seamanship.

You would try to learn the testimonies about the ship. And what would they be? The witness, of course, which the ship bore to herself. The experience which you or others got, from seeing how she behaved—as they say— at sea.

And from whom would you try to learn all this? from yourself? Out of your own brain and fancy? Would you invent theories of navigation and shipbuilding for yourself, without practice or experience? I trust not. You would go to the shipbuilder and the shipmaster for your information. Just as—if you be a reasonable man—you will go for your information about this world to the builder and maker of the world—God himself.

And lastly; you would try to learn the judgments about the ship : and what would they be? The results of good or bad seamanship ; what happens to ships, when they are well-managed or ill-managed.

It would be too hard to have to learn that by experience ; for the price which you would have to pay would be, probably, that you would be wrecked and drowned. But if you saw other ships wrecked near you, you would form judgments from their fate of what you ought to do. If you could find accounts of shipwrecks, you would study them with the most intense interest ; lest you too should be wrecked, and so judgment overtake you for your bad seamanship.

For God's judgment of any matter is not, as superstitious people fancy, that God grows suddenly angry, and goes out of His way to punish those who do wrong, as by a miracle. God judges all things in heaven and earth without anger—ay, with boundless pity : but with no indulgence. The soul that sinneth, it shall die. The ship that cannot swim, it must sink. That is the law of the judgments of God. But He is merciful in this; that He rewardeth every man according to his work. His judgment may be favourable, as well as unfavourable. He may acquit, or He may condemn. But whether He acquits or condemns, we can only know by the event; by the result. If a ship sinks, for want of good sailing or other defect, that is a judgment of God about the ship. He has condemned her. She is not seaworthy. But if the ship arrives safe in port, that too is God's judgment. He has tried her and acquitted her. She is seaworthy ; and she has her reward.

How simple this is. And yet men will not believe it, will not understand it, and therefore they wreck so often each man his own ship—his own life and immortal soul, and sink and perish, for lack of knowledge.

For each one of us is at sea, each in his own ship ; and each must sail her and steer her, as best he can, or sink and drown for ever.

For the sea which each of us is sailing over is this world, and the ship in which each of us sails, is our own nature and character ; what St Paul, like a truly scientific man, calls our flesh ; and what modern scientific men, and rightly, call our organisation. And the land to which we are sailing is eternal Life. Shall we make a prosperous voyage ? Shall we fail, or shall we succeed ? Shall we founder and drown at sea, and sink to eternal death ? Or shall we, as the clergyman prayed for us when we were baptized, so pass through the waves of this troublesome world, that finally we may come to the land of everlasting life? Which shall it be, my friends? Shall we sink, or shall we swim? Certain is one thing—that we shall sink, and not swim, if we do not learn and keep the law, and commandments, and testimonies, and judgments of God, concerning this our mortal life. If we do not, then we shall go through life, without knowing how to go through life, ignorantly and blindly; and the end of that will be failure, and ruin, and death to our souls. If we do not know and keep the Laws of God, the Laws of God will keep themselves, in spite of us, and grind us to powder. Do not fancy that you may do wrong without being punished; and break God's Law, because you are not under the law, but under grace. You are only under grace, as long as you keep clear of God's Law. The moment you do wrong you put yourself under the Law, and the Law will punish you. Suppose that you went into a mill; and that the owner of that mill was your best friend, even your father. Would that prevent your being crushed by the machinery, if you got entangled in it through ignorance or heedlessness? I think not. Even so, though God be your best of friends, ay, your Father in heaven, that will not prevent your being injured, it may be ruined, not only by wilful sins, but by mere folly and ignorance. Therefore your only chance for safety in this life and for ever, is to learn God's laws and statutes about your life, that you may pass through it justly, honourably, virtuously, successfully. And the man who wrote the 119th Psalm knew that, and said, " Oh that my ways were made so direct, that I might keep thy statutes."

But moreover, you must learn God's commandments. He has laid down certain commands, certain positive rules which must be kept if you do not intend to die the eternal death. So says our Lord. "If thou wilt enter into life, keep the commandments." "Thou shalt love the Lord thy God with all thy heart and soul, and thy neighbour as thyself." There the ten commandments are, and kept they must be; and if you break one of them, it will punish you, and you cannot escape. And the man who wrote the 119th Psalm knew that, and said, "With my whole heart have I sought thee: oh let me not go wrong out of Thy commandments."

Moreover, you must learn God's testimonies: what He has witnessed and declared about Himself, and His own character, His power and His goodness, His severity and His love.   And where will you learn that, as in the Bible? The Bible is full of testimonies of God in Christ about Himself; who He is, what He does, what He requires; and of testimonies of holy men of old, concerning God and concerning duty; concerning God's dealings with their souls, and with other men, and with all the nations of the old world, and with all nations likewise to the end of time. And if people will not read and study their Bibles, they cannot expect to know the way to eternal life. That too the man who wrote the 119th Psalm knew, and said, "I have had as great delight in Thy testimonies, as in all manner of riches."

Moreover, you must learn God's judgments; the way

in which He rewards and punishes men. And those too you will learn in the Bible, which is full of accounts of the just and merciful judgments of God. And you may learn them too from your own experience in life; from seeing what actually happens to those whom you know, when they do right things; and what happens again, when they do wrong things. If any man will open his eyes to what is going on around him in a single city, or in the mere private circle of his own kinsfolk and acquaintance; if he will but use his common sense, and look how righteousness is rewarded, and sin is punished, all day long, then he might learn enough and to spare about God's judgments: but men will not. A man will see his neighbour do wrong, and suffer for it: and then go and do exactly the same thing himself; as if there were no living God; no judgments of God; as if all was accident and chance; as if he was to escape scot-free, while his neighbour next door has brought shame and misery on himself by doing the same thing. For it was well written of old, " The fool hath said in his heart— though he is afraid to say it with his lips—There is no God." And the man who wrote the 119th Psalm knew that, and said, " I remembered Thine everlasting judgments, O Lord, and received comfort; for I was horribly afraid for the ungodly who forsake Thy law."

I say again: that the only way to attain eternal life is to know, and keep, and profit by God's laws, God's commandments, God's testimonies, God's judgments; and therefore it is that the Psalmists say so often, that these laws and commandments are Life. Not merely the way to eternal life; but the Life itself, as it is written in the Prayer-Book, "O God, whom truly to know is everlasting life."

But some will say, How shall I learn? I am very stupid, and I confess that freely. And when I have learnt, how shall I act up to my lesson? For I am very weak; and that I confess freely likewise.

How indeed, my friends? Stupid we are, the cleverest of us; and weak we are, the strongest of us. And if God left us to find out for ourselves, and to take care of ourselves, we should not sail far on the voyage of life without being wrecked; and going down body and soul to hell.

But, blessed be God, He has not left us to ourselves. He has not only commanded us to learn: He has promised to teach. And—as I said in the beginning of my Sermon—he who wrote the 119th Psalm knew that well. He knew that God would teach him and strengthen him; enlightening his dull understanding, and quickening his dull will; and therefore his Psalm, as I said, is a prayer, a prayer for teaching, and a prayer for light; and he cries to God—My soul cleaveth to the dust. I am low-minded, stupid, and earthly at the best. Oh quicken Thou me; that is—Oh give me life—more life—according to Thy word.

Thy Word. The Word of God, of whom the Psalmist says—O Lord, Thy Word endureth for ever in heaven. Even the Word of God, Jesus Christ our Lord, the Son of Man who is in heaven; and who, because He is in heaven, both God and man, can and will give us light and life, now and for ever.

And now take home with you this one thought. There is one education which we must all get; one thing which we must all learn, and learn to obey, or come to utter shame and ruin, either in this world or the world to come; and that is the laws, and commandments, and testimonies of God,—God the Father, God the Son, and God the Holy Spirit; for only by keeping them can we enter into eternal life. And if we wish to know them, God himself will teach us them. And if we wish to keep them, God himself will give us strength to keep them. Amen.

SERMON XII.

PSALM CXIX. 33, 94.

*O Lord, teach me Thy statutes, and I shall keep them to the end.
I am Thine, O save me; for I have kept Thy commandments.*

SOME who heard me last Sunday, both morning and afternoon, may have remarked an apparent contradiction between my two sermons. I hope they have done so. For then I shall hope that they are facing one of the most difficult, and yet most necessary, of all problems; namely the difference between the Law and the Gospel. In my morning sermon I spoke of the eternal law of God—how it was unchangeable even as God its author, rigid, awful, inevitable by every soul of man, and certain, if he kept it, to lead him into all good, for body, soul, and spirit : but certain, too, if he broke it, to grind him to powder.

And in the afternoon, I spoke of the Gospel and Free Grace of God—how that too was unchangeable, even as God its author; full of compassion and tender mercy, and forgiveness of sins; willing not the death of a sinner; but rather that he should be converted, and live.

But how are these two statements, both scriptural; both—as I hold from practical experience, true to the uttermost, and not to be compromised or explained away—how are they to be reconciled, I say? By these two texts. By taking them both together, and never one without the other; and by taking them, also, in the order in which you find them, and never—as too many do—the second before the first. At least this was the opinion of the Psalmist. He first seeks God's commandments and statutes, and prays—Give me understanding and I shall keep Thy law, yea, I shall keep it with my whole heart. Make me to go in the path of Thy commandments; for therein is my desire. And then, only then, finding himself in trouble, anxiety, even in danger of death, he feels he has a sort of right to cry to God to help him out of his trouble, and prays—I am Thine, oh save me!

And why? What reason can he give why God should save him? Because, he says, I have sought Thy commandments.

Now let all rational persons lay this to heart; and consider it well. There are very few, heathens and savages, as well as Christians, who will not cry, when they find themselves in trouble—Oh save me. The instinct of every man is, to cry to some unseen persons or powers to help him. If he does not cry to the true and good God, he will cry to some false or bad God; or to some idol, material or intellectual, of his own invention. But that is no reason why his prayers should be heard. We read of old heathens at Rome, who prayed to Mercury, the god of money-making—" Da mihi fallere,"—Help me to cheat my neighbours : while the philosophers, heathen though they were, laughed, with just contempt, at such men and their prayers, and asked—Do you suppose that any God, if he be worth calling a God, will answer such a request as that? Nay, in our own times, have not the brigands of Naples been in the habit of carrying a leaden image of St Januarius in their hats, and praying to it to protect them in their trade of robbery and murder? I leave you to guess what answer good St Januarius, and much more He who made St Januarius, and all heaven and earth, was likely to give to such a prayer as that.

So it is not all prayers for help that are heard, or deserve to be heard. And indeed—I do not wish to be hard, but the truth must be spoken—there are too many people in the world who pray to God to help them, when they are in difficulties or in danger, or in fear of death and of hell, but never pray at any other time, or for any other thing. They pray to be helped out of what is disagreeable. But they never pray to be made good. They are not good, and they do not care to become good. All they care for, is to escape death, or pain, or poverty, or shame, when they see it staring them in the face : and God knows I do not blame them. We are all children, and, like children, we cry out when we are hurt; and that is no sin to us. But that is no part of godliness, not even of mere religion.

But worse—it is still more sad to have to say it, but it is true—most people's notions of the next world, and of salvation, as they call it, are just as childish, material, selfish as their notions of this world.

They all wish and pray to be "saved." What do they mean? To be saved from bodily pain in the next life, and to have bodily pleasure instead. Pain and pleasure are the only gods which they really worship. They call the former—hell. They call the latter—heaven. But they know as little of one as of the other; and their notions of both are equally worthy of—Shall I say it? Must I say it?—equally worthy of the savage in the forest. They believe that they must either go to heaven or to hell. They have, of course, no wish to go to the latter place; for whatever else there is likely to be there—some of which might not be quite unpleasant or new to them, such as evil-speaking, lying, and slandering, envy, hatred, malice and all uncharitableness, bigotry included—there will be certainly there—they have reason to believe—bodily pain; the thing which they, being mostly comfortable people, dread most, and avoid most: contrary, you will remember, to the opinion of the blessed martyrs, who dreaded bodily pain least, and avoided it least, of all the ills which could befal them. Wherefore they are, in the sight of God, and of all true men unto this day—the blessed martyrs.

But these people—and there are too many of them by hundreds of thousands—do not want to be blessed. They only want to be comfortable in this world, and in the next. As for blessedness, they do not even know what it means; and our Lord's seven beatitudes, which begin—"Blessed are the poor in spirit"—are not at all to their mind; even, alas! alas! to the mind of many who call themselves religious and orthodox; at least till they are so explained away, that they shall mean anything, or nothing, save—I trust I am poor in spirit: and nevertheless I am right, and everyone who differs from me is wrong.

The plain truth is—when all fine words, whether said in prayers or sung in hymns, are stript off—that they do not wish to go to hell and pain; and therefore prefer, very naturally, though not very spiritually, to go to heaven and pleasure; and so sing of "crossing over Jordan to Canaan's shore," or of "Jerusalem the golden, with milk and honey blest," and so forth, without any clear notion of what they mean thereby, save selfish comfort without end; they really know not what; they really care not where. And that they may arrive there or at a far better place; and have their wish, and more than their wish: I for one heartily desire. But whether they arrive there, or not; and indeed, whether they arrive at some place infinitely better or infinitely worse, depends on whether they will give up selfish calculations of loss and gain, selfish choosing between mere pain and pleasure: and choose this; choose, whatever it may cost them, between being good and being bad, or even being only half good; as little good as they can afford to be without the pains of hell into the bargain.

My friends—What if Christ should answer such people—I do not say that He does always answer them so, for He is very pitiful, and of tender mercy;—but what if He were to answer them, Save you? Help you? O presumptuous mortal, what have you done that Christ should save or help you? You are afraid of being ruined. Why should you not be ruined? What good will it be to your fellow-men if you keep your money, instead of losing it? You are making nothing but a bad use of your money. Why should Christ help you to keep it, and misuse it still more?

You are afraid of death. You do not wish to die. But why should you not die? Why should Christ save you from death? Of what use is your life to Christ, or to any human being? If you are living a bad life, your life is a bad thing, and does harm not only to yourself, but to your neighbours. Why should Christ keep you alive to hurt and corrupt your neighbours, and to set a bad example to your children? If you are not doing your duty where Christ has put you, you are of no use, a cumberer of the ground. What reason can you shew why He should not take you away, and put some one in your place who *will* do his duty? You are afraid of being lost—why should you *not* be lost? You are offensive, and an injury to the universe. You are an actual nuisance on Christ's earth and in Christ's Kingdom. Why should He not—as He has sworn—cast out of His Kingdom all things which offend, and you among the rest? Why should He not get rid of you, as you get rid of vermin, as you get rid of weeds; and cast you into the fire, to be burned up with all evil things? Answer that: before you ask Christ to save you, and deliver

you from danger, and from death, and from the hell
which you so much—and perhaps so justly—fear.

And how that question is to be answered, I cannot
see.

Certainly the selfish man cannot answer it. The
idle man cannot answer it. The profligate man cannot
answer it. They are doing nothing for Christ; or for
their neighbours, or for the human race; and they cannot
expect Christ to do anything for them.

The only men who can answer it; the only men, it
seems to me, who can have any hope of their prayers
being heard, are those who, like the Psalmist, are trying
to do something for Christ, and their neighbours, and
the human race; who are, in a word, trying to be good.
Those, I mean, who have already prayed, earnestly and
often, the first prayer, "Teach me, O Lord, Thy statutes, and
I shall keep them to the end." They have—not a right:
no one has a right against Christ, no, not the angels and
archangels in heaven—not a right, but a hope, through
Christ's most precious and undeserved promises, that
their prayers will be heard; and that Christ will save
them from destruction, because they are, at least, likely
to become worth saving; because they are likely to be of
use in Christ's world, and to do some little work in
Christ's kingdom.

They are God's: they are soldiers in Christ's army.
They are labourers in Christ's garden. They are on
God's side in the battle of life, which is the battle of
Christ and of all good men, against evil, against sin and
ignorance, and the numberless miseries which sin and

ignorance produce. They are not the profligate; they are not the selfish, the idle; they are not the frivolous, the insolent; they are not the wilfully ignorant who do not care to learn, and do not even—so brutish are they—think that there is anything worth learning in the world, save how to turn sixpence into a shilling, and then spend it on themselves. Not such are those who may hope to have their prayers heard, because they are worth hearing, and worth helping. But they are the people who say to themselves, not once in their lives, not once a week on Sundays, but every day and all day long—I must be good; I will be good. I must be of use; I must be doing some work for God; and therefore I must learn. I must learn God's laws, and statutes, and commandments, about my station, and calling, and business in life. Else how can I do it aright? I dare no more be ignorant, than I dare be idle. I must learn. But how shall I learn? Stupid I am, and ignorant, and the more I try to learn, the more I discover how stupid I am. The more I do actually learn, the more I discover how ignorant I am. There is so much to be learned; and how to learn it passes my understanding. Who will teach me? How shall I get understanding? How shall I get knowledge? And if I get them, how shall I be sure that they are true understanding, and true knowledge? Mad people have understanding enough; and so have some who are not mad, but merely fools. Wit enough they have, active and rapid brains: but their understanding is of no use, for it is only misunderstanding; and therefore the more clever they are, the more foolish they are, and the more dangerous to themselves and their fellow-creatures. Knowledge, too—how shall I be sure that my knowledge, if I get it, is true knowledge, and not false knowledge, knowledge which is not really according to facts? I see too many who have knowledge for which I care little enough. Some know a thousand things which are of no use to them, or to any human being. Others know a thousand things: but know them in a shallow, inaccurate fashion; and so cannot make use of them for any practical purpose. Others know a thousand things: but know them all in a prejudiced and one-sided fashion; till they see things not as things are, but as they are not, and as they never will be; and therefore their knowledge, instead of leading them, misleads them, and they misjudge facts, misjudge men, and earth, and heaven, just as much as the man who should misjudge the sunlight of heaven and fancy it to be green or blue, because he looked at it through a green or blue glass. How then shall I get true knowledge? Knowledge which will be really useful, really worth knowing? Knowledge which I shall know accurately, and practically too, so that I can use it in daily life, for myself and my fellow-men? Knowledge, too, which shall be clear knowledge, not warped or coloured by my own fancies, passions, prejudices, but pure, and calm, and sound; Siccum Lumen, "Dry Light," as the greatest of English Philosophers called it of old?

To all such, who long for light, that by the light they may see to live the life, God answers, through His only-begotten Son, The Word who endureth for ever in heaven :—

"Ask, and ye shall receive; seek, and ye shall find; knock, and it shall be opened to you. For if ye, being evil, know how to give good gifts to your children, much more will your heavenly Father give His Holy Spirit to those who ask Him."

Yes, ask for that Holy Spirit of God, that He may lead you into all truth; into all truth, that is, which is necessary for you to know, in order to see your way through the world, and through your duty in the world. Ask for that Holy Spirit; that He may give you eyes to see things as they are, and courage to feel things as they are, and to do your work in them, and by them, whether they be pleasant or unpleasant, prosperous or adverse. Ask Him; and He will give you true knowledge to know what a serious position you are in, what a serious thing life is, death is, judgment is, eternity is; that you may be no trifler nor idler, nor mere scraper together of gain which you must leave behind you when you die : but a truly serious man, seriously intent on your duty; seriously intent on working God's work in the place and station to which He has called you, before the night comes in which no man can work.

If a man is doing that; if he is earnestly trying to learn what is true, in order that he may do what is right; then he has—I do not say a right—but at least a reason, or a shadow of reason, when he cries to God in his trouble—

"I am Thine, oh save me, for I have sought thy commandments."

"I am Thine." Not merely God's creature: the very birds, and bees, and flowers are that; and do their duty far better than I—God forgive me—do mine.

"I am Thine." Not merely God's child: the sinners and the thoughtless are that, though—God help them—they care not for Him, nor for His laws, nor for themselves and their glorious inheritance as children of God.

And I too am God's child: but I trust that I am more. I am God's school-child. O Lord Jesus Christ, I claim Thy help as my schoolmaster, as well as my Lord and Saviour. I am the least of Thy school-children; and it may be the most ignorant and most stupid. I do not pretend to be a scholar, a divine, a philosopher, a saint. I am a very weak, foolish, insufficient personage; sitting on the lowest form in Thy great school-house, which is the whole world; and trying to spell out the mere letters of Thy alphabet, in hope that hereafter I may be able to make out whole words, and whole sentences, of Thy commandments, and having learnt them, do them. For if Thou wilt but teach me Thy statutes, O Lord, then I will try to keep them to the end. For I long to be on Thy side, and about Thy work. I long to help—if it be ever so little—in making myself better, and my neighbours better. I long to be useful, and not useless; a benefit, and not a nuisance; a fruit-bearing tree, and not a noxious weed, in Thy garden; and therefore I hope that Thou wilt not cut me down, nor root me up, nor let foul creatures trample me under foot.   Have mercy on me, O Lord, in my trouble, for the sake of the truth which I long to learn, and for the good which I long to do.   Poor little weak plant though I may be, I am still a plant of Thy planting, which is doing its best to grow, and flower, and bear fruit to eternal life; and Thou wilt not despise the work of Thine own hands, O Lord, who died that I might live? Thou wilt not let me perish?   I have stuck unto Thy testimonies: O Lord, confound me not.

Therefore remember this.   If you wish to have reasonable hope when you have to pray—"Lord, save me:" pray first, and pray continually—"Teach me, O Lord, Thy statutes, and I will keep them to the end."

SERMON XIII.

THE ONE ESCAPE.

PSALM CXIX. 67.

Before I was troubled, I went wrong: but now have I kept
Thy Word.

LET me speak this afternoon once more about the 119th
Psalm, and the man who wrote it.

And first: he was certainly of a different opinion
from nine persons out of ten, I fear from ninety-nine
out of a hundred, of every country, every age, and every
religion.

For, he says—Before I was troubled, I went wrong:
but now have I kept Thy Word. Whereas nine people
out of ten would say to God, if they dared—Before I was
troubled, I kept Thy Word. But now that I am troubled;
of course I cannot help going wrong.

He makes his troubles a reason for doing right. They
make their troubles an excuse for doing wrong.

Is it not so? Do we not hear people saying, whenever they are blamed for doing what they know to be
wrong—I could not help it? I was forced into it. What
would you have a man do? One must live; and so forth.

One finds himself in danger, and tries to lie himself out of it.   Another finds himself in difficulties, and begins playing ugly tricks in money matters.   Another finds himself in want, and steals.   The general opinion of the world is, that right-doing, justice, truth, and honesty, are very graceful luxuries for those who can afford them; very good things when a man is easy, prosperous, and well off, and without much serious business on hand: but not for the real hard work of life; not for times of ambition and struggle, any more than of distress and anxiety, or of danger and difficulty.   In such times, if a man may not lie a little, cheat a little, do a questionable stroke of business now and then; how is he to live? So it is in the world, so it always was; and so it always will be.   From statesmen ruling nations, and men of business "conducting great financial operations," as the saying is now, down to the beggar-woman who comes to ask charity, the rule of the world is, that honesty is *not* the best policy; that falsehood and cunning are not only profitable, but necessary; that in proportion as a man is in trouble, in that proportion he has a right to go wrong.

A right to go wrong.   A right to make bad worse.   A right to break God's laws, because we are too stupid or too hasty to find out what God's laws are.   A right, as the wise man puts it, to draw bills on nature which she will *not* honour; but return them on a man's hands with "No effects" written across them, leaving the man to pay after all, in misery and shame.   Truly said Solomon of old—The foolishness of fools is folly.

But the Psalmist, because he was inspired by the

Spirit of God, was of quite the opposite opinion. So far from thinking that his trouble gave him a right to go wrong, he thought that his trouble laid on him a duty to go right, more right than he had ever gone before; and that going right was the only possible way of getting out of his troubles.

"Take from me," he cries, "the way of lying, and cause Thou me to make much of Thy law.

I have chosen the way of truth, and Thy judgments have I laid before me.

Incline mine heart unto Thy testimonies, and not unto covetousness.

Oh turn away mine eyes, lest they behold vanity, and quicken Thou me in Thy way.

Thy word is my comfort in my trouble; for Thy word hath quickened me.

The proud have had me exceedingly in derision, yet have I not shrunk from Thy law.

For I remembered Thine everlasting judgments, O God, and received comfort.

Thy statutes have been my songs, in the house of my pilgrimage.

I have thought upon Thy name, O Lord, in the night-season, and have kept Thy law."

This was the Psalmist's plan for delivering himself out of trouble. A very singular plan, which very few persons try, either now, or in any age. And therefore it is, that so many persons are not delivered out of their troubles, but sink deeper and deeper into them, heaping new troubles on old ones, till they are crushed beneath the weight of their own sins.

What the special trouble was, in which the Psalmist found himself, we are not told. But it is plain from his words, that it was just that very sort of trouble, in which the world is most ready to excuse a man for lying, cringing, plotting, and acting on the old devil's maxim that "Cunning is the natural weapon of the weak." For the Psalmist was weak, oppressed and persecuted by the great and powerful. But his method of defending himself against them was certainly not the way of the world.

Princes, he says, sat and spoke against him. But; instead of fawning on them, excusing himself, entreating their mercy: he was occupied in God's statutes.

The proud had him exceedingly in derision—as I am afraid too many worldly men, poor as well as rich, working men as well as idlers, would do now—seeing him occupied in God's statutes, when he might have been occupied in winning money, and place, and renown for himself.

But he did not shrink from God's law. If it was true, he could afford to be laughed at for obeying it.

The congregation of the ungodly robbed him. But he did not forget God's law. If they did wrong, that was no reason why he should do wrong likewise.

The proud imagined a lie against him. But he would keep God's commandments with his whole heart, instead of breaking God's commandments, and justifying their slander, and making their lie true.

Still, it went very hard with him. His honour and

his faith were sorely tried. He was dried up like a bottle in the smoke. It seems to have been with him at times a question of life and death; till he had hardly any hope left. He had to ask, almost in despair—How many are the days of Thy servant? When wilt Thou be avenged of them that persecute me? The proud dug pits for him, contrary to the law of God; contrary to honour and justice; and almost made an end of him upon earth. The ungodly laid wait to destroy him.

But against them all he had but one weapon, and one defence. However much afraid he might be of his enemies, he was still more afraid of doing wrong. His flesh, he said, trembled for fear of God; and he was afraid of God's judgments. Therefore his only safety was, in pleasing God, and not men. I deal, he says, with the thing that is lawful and right. Oh give me not over to my oppressors. Make Thy servant to delight in what is good, that the proud do me no wrong. If he could but keep right, he would be safe at last.

I will consider Thy testimonies, O Lord. I see that all things come to an end. Bad times, and bad chances, and still more bad men, and bad ways for escaping out of trouble—they all come to an end. But Thy commandment is exceeding broad. Exceeding broad. There are depths below depths of meaning in that true saying; depths which you will find true, if you will but read your Bibles, and obey your Bibles. For in them, I tell you openly, you will find rules to guide you in every chance and change of this mortal life. Truly said the good man that there were in the Bible "shallows where a lamb may drink, and deeps wherein an elephant may swim."

There are no possible circumstances, good or bad, pleasant or unpleasant, in which you can find yourselves, be you rich or poor, young or old, without finding in the Bible sound advice, and a clear rule, as to how God would have you behave under those circumstances. For God's commandments are exceeding broad, and take in all cases of conscience, all details of duty; saying to each and every one of us, at every turn—" This is the way, walk ye in it."

At least this is the teaching, this is the testimony, this is the life-experience, of a true hero, namely, the man who wrote the 119th Psalm; a hero according to God, but not according to the world, and the pomp and glory of the world.

No great statesman was he, nor conqueror, nor merchant, nor financier passing millions of money through his hands yearly; and all fancying that they, and not God, govern the nations upon earth, and decide the fate of empires.

He was a man who made no noise in the world: though the world, it seems, made a little noise at him in his time, as it does often bark and yell at those who will not go its way; as it barked at poor Christian, when he went through Vanity Fair, and would not buy its wares, or join in its frivolities. Such a man was this Psalmist; for whom the world had nothing but scorn first, and then forgetfulness. We do not know his name, or where he lived. We do not even know, within a few hundred years, when he lived. I picture him to myself always as a poor, shrivelled, stooping, mean-looking old man; his visage marred more than any man, and his figure more than the sons of men; no form nor comeliness in him, nor beauty that men should desire him; despised and rejected of men: a man of sorrows, and acquainted with grief, even as his Master was after him.

And all that he has left behind him—as far as we can tell—is this one psalm which he wrote, as may be guessed from its arrangement, slowly, and with exceeding care, as the very pith and marrow of an experience spread over many painful years of struggle and of humiliation.

I say of humiliation. For there is not a taint of self-conceit, not even of self-satisfaction, in him. He only sees his own weakness, and want of life, of spirit, of manfulness, of power. His soul cleaveth to the dust. He is tempted, of course, again and again, to give way; to become low-minded, cowardly, time-serving, covetous, worldly. But he dares not. He feels that his only chance is to keep his honour unspotted; and he cries—Whatever happens,—I must do right. I must learn to do right. Teach me to do right. Teach me, O Lord, teach me; and strengthen me, O Lord, strengthen me, and then all must come right at last. That was his cry. And, be you sure, he did not cry in vain.

For this man had one precious possession; which he determined not to lose, not though he died in trying to hold it fast; namely, the Eternal Spirit of God; the

Spirit of Righteousness, and Truth, and Justice, which leads men into all truth. By that Spirit he saw into the Eternal Laws of God. By that Spirit he saw who made and who administers those Eternal Laws, even the Eternal Word of God, who endureth for ever in heaven. By that Spirit he saw that his only hope was to keep those eternal laws. By that Spirit he vowed to keep them. By that Spirit he had strength to keep them. By that Spirit, when he failed he tried again; when he fell he rose and fought on once more, to keep the commandments of the Lord.

And where is he now? Where is he now? Where those will never come—let false preachers and false priests flatter them as they may—who fancy that they can get to heaven without being good and doing good. Where those will never come, likewise, who, when they find themselves in trouble, try to help themselves out of it by false and mean methods; and so begin worshipping the devil, just when they have most need to worship God. He is where the fearful and unbelievers and all liars can never come. He is with the Word of the Lord, who endureth for ever in heaven.

With the Word of the Lord, who endured awhile on earth, even as he the Psalmist endured. Who before Pontius Pilate witnessed a good confession, and endured the cross, despising the shame, because He cared neither for riches, nor for pleasure, for power, nor for glory; but simply for His Father's will, and His Father's law, that He might do to the uttermost the will of His Father who sent Him, and keep to the uttermost that Law of which

His Father says to Him for ever—"Thou art my Son, to-day have I begotten Thee."

Into His presence may we all come at last! But we shall never come thither, unless we keep our honour bright, our courage unbroken, and ourselves unspotted from the world. For so only will be fulfilled in us the sixth Beatitude—Blessed are the pure in heart, for they shall see God. Unto which may God of His free mercy bring us all. Amen.

SERMON XIV.

THE WORD OF GOD.

PSALM CXIX. 89—96.

O Lord, Thy word endureth for ever in heaven. Thy truth also remaineth from one generation to another: Thou hast laid the foundation of the earth, and it abideth. They continue this day according to Thine ordinance: for all things serve Thee. If my delight had not been in Thy law, I should have perished in my trouble. I will never forget Thy commandments: for with them Thou hast quickened me. I am Thine, oh save me: for 1 have sought Thy commandments. The ungodly laid wait for me to destroy me: but I will consider Thy testimonies. I see that all things come to an end: but Thy commandment is exceeding broad.

THIS text is of infinite importance, to you, and me, and all mankind. For if the text is not true; if there is not a Word of God, who endures and is settled for ever in heaven : then this world is a miserable and a mad place; and the best thing, it seems to me, that we poor ignorant human beings can do, is to eat and drink, for to morrow we die.

But that is not the best thing we can do; but the very worst thing. The best thing that we can do, and the only thing worth doing is, to be good, and do good, at all risks and all costs, trusting to the Word of God, who endures for ever in heaven.

But who is this Word of God? I say who, not what. We often call the Bible the Word of God : and so it is in one sense, because it tells us, from beginning to end, about this other Word of God. It is, so to speak, God's word or message about this Word. But it is plain that the Psalmist is not speaking here of the Bible; for he says—

"Thy Word endureth for ever in Heaven :" and the Bible is not in heaven, but on earth.

But in the Bible, usually, this Word of the Lord means not only the message which God sends, but Him by whom God sends it. The Word of God, Word of the Lord, is spoken of again and again, not as a thing, but as a person, a living rational being, who comes to men, and speaks to them, and teaches them; sometimes, seemingly, by actual word of mouth ; sometimes again, by putting thoughts into their minds, and words into their mouths.

Recollect Samuel: how when he was young the Word of the Lord was precious—that is, uncommon, and almost unknown in those days; and how the Lord came and called Samuel, Samuel; and put a word into his mouth against Eli. And so the Lord appeared again in Shiloh; for the Lord revealed Himself to Samuel in Shiloh by The Word of the Lord. In Samuel's case, there was, it seems, an actual voice, which fell on Samuel's ears. In the case of the later prophets, we do not read that they usually heard any actual voice, or saw any actual appearance. It seems that the Word of the Lord who came to them inspired their minds with true thoughts, and inspired their lips to speak those thoughts in noble words, often in regular poetry. But He was The Word of the Lord, nevertheless. Again and again, we read in those grand old prophets, "The Word of the Lord came unto me, saying,"—or again, "The Word which came to Jeremiah from the Lord, saying." It is not the Bible which is meant by such words as these—I am sorry to have to remind a nineteenth century congregation of this fact—but a living being, putting thoughts into the prophets' minds, and words into their mouths, and a divine passion too, into their hearts, which they could not resist; like poor Jeremiah of old, when he was reproached and derided about The Word of the Lord, and said, "I will not make mention of Him, nor speak any more in His name. But He was in my heart as a burning fire shut up in my bones, and I was weary with forbearing, and I could not hold my peace."

But now, what words are these which we read of this same Word of the Lord, in the first chapter of St John's Gospel? "In the beginning was The Word: and The Word was with God, and The Word was God. By Him all things were made, and without Him was not anything made that was made. And in Him was life, and the life was the light of men."

Thus—as always--the Old Testament and the New, the Psalmist and St John, agree together.

This is the gospel and good news, which the Psalmist saw in part, but which St John saw fully and perfectly.

But because the Psalmist saw it even in part, he saw that The Word of the Lord endured for ever in heaven; and that therefore his only hope of safety was to listen eagerly and reverently for what that Word might choose to say to him.

But why does the Psalmist seemingly go out of his way, as it were, to say, "Thou hast laid the foundation of the earth, and it abideth. They continue this day according to Thine ordinance, for all things serve Thee"?

For the very same reason that St John goes, seemingly, out of his way to say, "All things were made by The Word, and without Him was not anything made that was made."

Why is this?

Look at it thus: What an important question it is, whether This Word of God is a being of order; a regular being; a law-abiding being; a being on whose actions men can count; who can be trusted, and depended on, not to alter His own ways, not to deceive us poor mortal men.

The Psalmist wants to know his way through this world, and his duty in this mortal life. Therefore he must learn the laws and rules of this world. And he has the sense to see, that no one can teach him the rules of the world, but the Ruler of the world, and the Maker of the world.

Then comes the terrible question—too many, alas! have not got it answered rightly yet—

But are there any rules at all in the world? Does

The Lord manage the world by rules and laws? Or does He let things go by chance and accident, and take no care about them? Is there such a thing as God's Providence: or is there not? To that the Psalmist answers firmly, because he is inspired by the Spirit of God—

O Lord, Thy Word endureth—is settled—for ever in heaven. In Thee is no carelessness, neglect, slothfulness, nor caprice. Thou hast no variableness, neither shadow of turning. Thou hast laid the foundation of the earth, and it abideth. They continue this day according to Thine ordinance; for all things serve Thee. The world is full of settled and enduring rules and laws; and God keeps to them. The Psalmist looks at the sun, moon and stars over his head, each keeping its settled course, and its settled season: and he sees them all obeying law. He looks at summer and winter, seed-time and harvest: and he sees them obeying law. He looks at birth and growth, at decay and death; and sees them too, obeying law. He looks at the very flowers beneath his feet, and the buds in the woodland, and all the crowd of living things about him, animal, vegetable and mineral: and they too obey law; each after their kind. The world, he says, is full of law. It is a settled world, an orderly world, made and governed by a Lord of order, who makes laws and enforces laws; a Lord whose Word endures for ever in heaven. Therefore—he feels—I can trust that Lord. If He has laws for the beasts and birds, He must have, much more, laws for men. If He has laws for men's bodies, much more has

He laws for their souls. What I have to do, is to ask Him to teach me those laws, that I may live.

But then comes another, and even a more awful question—If I ask Him, will He teach me? Alas! alas! too many have not found the answer yet; too many of those who know most about the Laws of Nature, and reverence those laws most: and all honour to them for so doing; for, even though they know it not, they are preparing the way of the Lord, and making His paths straight. But they have not found the right answer to that question yet. Still there the question is; and you and I, and every soul of man, must get some reasonable answer or other to it, if we wish to be men indeed, men in spirit and in truth; and it is this—

If I ask this Word of God to teach me His Laws— Will He teach me? Will He hear me? Can He hear: or is He Himself a mere brute force, a law of nature and necessity? And even if not, will He hear? Or is He, too, like those Epicurean gods, of whom our great poet sings—a sad and hopeless song :—

They lie beside their nectar, and the bolts are hurled
Far below them in the valleys, and the clouds are lightly curled
Round their golden houses, girdled with the gleaming world,
Where they smile in secret, looking over wasted lands,
Blight and famine, plague and earthquake, roaring deeps and fiery sands,
Clanging fights, and flaming towns, and sinking ships, *and praying hands.*

And praying hands. Oh, my friends, is not the question of all questions for such poor mortal souls as you and me, beset by ignorance and weakness, and passions which are our own worst enemies, and chances and catastrophes which we cannot avert—Is not the question of all questions for such as us—Will this same Word of God—will any unseen being out of the infinite void which surrounds our little speck of a planet, take any notice of our praying hands? Will He hear us, teach us, when we cry? Or is God, and The Word of God, like those old heathen gods? Is He a God who hides Himself, and leaves us to despair and chance: or is He a God who hears, and gives us even a single ray of hope? Is He a gracious God, who will hear every man's tale, however clumsily told, and judge it according to its merits: or even—for that is better than dead silence and carelessness—according to its demerits? Is He a just God? Or has He likes and dislikes, favourites and victims; as human rulers and statesmen, and human parties too, and mobs, are wont to have? May He not, even, like those Epicurean gods, despise men? find a proud satisfaction in deceiving them; or at least letting them deceive themselves?—in playing with their ignorance, and leaving them to reap the fruits of their own childishness ?

To that the Psalmist answers—and I know not how he learnt to answer so, save by the inspiration of the Spirit of God; for I know well that neither flesh and blood, the experience of his own brain, thoughts, and emotions, nor the world around him, either of nature or of man, would ever have revealed that to him—to that he answers confidently, in spite of all appearances—

Thy truth, O Lord, abideth from one generation to another. Thou art a truthful God, a faithful God, whose word can be taken. A God in whom is no variableness, neither shadow of turning; who keepeth His promise for ever; true, as man can be true; and truer than the truest man. And I know it, says he, by experience. God has actually taught me His law: for if my delight had not been in it, I should have perished in my trouble. I will never forget His commandments; for by them He has given me life; has taught me what to do, and en-abled me to do it, to prevent the death and ruin of my body, and soul, and spirit.

Now for the very same reason it is, that St John is so careful, first to tell us that The Word of God made all things; and then to tell us that He is full of grace and truth.

He tells us that The Word made all things, that we may be sure that He is a God of order, because all things which He has made are full of order; a God who acts by rules and laws which we may trust. He tells us that The Word made all things, that we may be sure that all things, being His handy-work, will bear witness of Him and teach us about Him, and shew forth His glory.

But he tells us moreover—Oh gospel, and good news for blind and weak humanity!—that The Word's glory is full of grace; gracious; ready to condescend; ready to teach us, and give us light to see our way through this world which He has made.

He tells us that The Word's glory is full of truth; that He is truthful, accurate, and to be depended on;

and will tell us nothing but what is true. That He is a true Word of God, and when He speaks to us of His Father and of our Father, He tells the truth.

And so do St John and the Psalmist agree in the same gospel, and good news, of the mystery of Christ The Word.

There is an eternal Being in heaven, who is called The Word of God; because He speaks of, and reveals—that is, unveils and shews—to men, and angels, and archangels, and all created beings, that God whom no man hath seen, or can see; a Word who dwells for ever in the bosom of The Father, in the light which no man can approach unto : but who for ever comes forth from thence to proclaim to all created beings—There is a God, and The Word is His likeness; the brightness of His glory, and the express image of His person. None hath seen the Father at any time: but the only-begotten Son, who is in the bosom of the Father, He hath declared Him. None cometh to the Father, but through Him. But he who hath seen Him, hath seen the Father; and He is none other than Jesus Christ our Lord.

He is The Word of God, who speaks to men God's words, because He speaks not His own words but His Father's, and does not His own will but His Father's who sends Him.

He speaks to us and to all men, in many ways; and to each according to his needs. To all men, Christ speaks through their consciences, shewing them what is good, and warning them of what is evil; for He is the Light that lighteth every man that cometh into the

world. To Christians Christ speaks in many ways—
to which, alas, too few give heed—through the Bible,
through the sacraments, through sermons, through the
thoughts and words of all wise and holy men. To
the good He speaks with gracious encouragement; to
the wicked with awful severity. To the hypocrites He
says at times, "Ye serpents, ye generation of vipers,
how can ye escape the damnation of hell?" To the
self-satisfied and bigoted He says, "If ye had been
blind, ye had had no sin: but now ye say, We see;
therefore your sin remaineth." To the careless and
worldly He says, "I know thy works, that thou art
neither cold nor hot. Thou sayest, I am rich and increased with goods, I have need of nothing: and knowest
not that thou art wretched, and miserable, and poor, and
blind, and naked."

To those who are ruining themselves by their own
folly He says, "Why will ye die? I have no pleasure in
the death of him that dieth, saith the Lord: but rather
that he should be converted, and live." To those who
are tormented by their own passions He says, "Take My
yoke upon you and learn of Me, for I am meek and
lowly of heart, and ye shall find rest unto your souls."
To those who are wearied with the burden of their own
sins He says, "Come unto Me, all ye that are weary,
and heavy laden, and I will give you rest."

To those who are struggling, however weakly, to do
what is right He says, "I know thy works. Behold, I
have set before thee an open door, and none can shut it;
for thou hast a little strength, and hast kept My word,

and hast not denied My name. Because thou hast kept the word of My patience, I also will keep thee from the hour of temptation."

And to those who mourn for those whom they have loved and lost He says, "Fear not, I am the first and the last, I am He that liveth, and was dead; and behold, I am alive for evermore, Amen; and have the keys of hell and of death. He that believeth in Me, though he die, yet shall he live; and he that liveth and believeth in Me shall never die."

For every one of us, according to his character and his needs, Christ speaks a fitting word from God, because He is The Word of God; and every word which He speaks to us is true, and sure, and eternal, according to the laws of God His Father. For He is The Word who endures for ever in heaven; and though heaven and earth may pass away, His words cannot pass away.

Yes; Christ The Word speaks to all: but most of all to children: to the children, of whom He said—"Suffer the little children to come to me, and forbid them not;"—of whom He said to grown-up people, not—Except these children be converted and become as you—He left that message for the Pharisees of His own time, and of every age and creed: but—Except you grown people be converted and become as little children, you, and not they, shall in no wise enter into the kingdom of heaven.

Let us tell children that—that Christ Himself is speaking to them. That The Word of God is educating them. That the Light who lightens every man who comes into the world is labouring to enlighten them, their intellect and memory, their emotions and their con-sciences.   Let that be the ground of all our education of children.   Then it will matter little to us who teaches them what is miscalled secular knowledge.   For we shall tell our children—In it, too, Christ is teaching you. The understanding by which you understand the world about you is Christ's gift.   The world which you are to understand is Christ's world; for He laid the foundation of the earth, and it abideth.   The physical laws of the universe are Christ's laws ; for all things serve Him, and continue this day according to His ordinance.   Every natural object is a result of Christ's will, and its organiza-tion a product of Christ's mind ; for without Him was not anything made that was made.   The whole course of events, great and small, is Christ's providence ; for to Him all power is given in heaven and earth.   So far, therefore, from being afraid to teach our children Natural Science, we shall hold it a sacred duty to teach it ; for it is the will and mind of Christ, The Word of God.

And as for morality—we shall be ready to teach that, as far as the prudential and paying virtues are concerned, as boldly and on the very same grounds as the merest Utilitarian.   For we shall teach honesty, courtesy, de-cency, self-restraint, patience, foresight, on the warrant of the Bible ; which is, that Christ has made the world so well, that sooner or later every wise and just act rewards itself, every foolish and unjust act punishes itself, by the very constitution of nature and society, which again are laid down by Christ.   But what of the nobler, the non-prudential, and non-paying virtues?—call them rather graces.—Them we shall teach our children—as I believe we can only teach them rationally and logically, either to children or to grown-up people—by pointing them to Christ upon His cross, and saying to them, " Behold your God !"

For so we shall be able to train them in the orthodox doctrine of morals, which is—

That there is nothing good in man which is not first in God.

We shall be able to make them comprehend what we mean when we tell them that they are members of Christ, and must live the Life of Christ; that they are children of God, and as such must imitate their Father, and become perfect, even as their Father in heaven is perfect.

For we shall say—The pure and perfect graces, the disinterested virtues, the unselfish virtues—obedience, mercy, chivalry, beneficence, magnanimity, heroism,—in one word, self-sacrifice—beautiful these are: but are they necessary? are they mere ornaments? or are they sacred duties? The duty which dares and suffers for the thing it ought to do; the love which dares and suffers for the thing it loves; the unselfish spirit which looks for no reward :—why should these dwell in man? To that we shall answer—Because they dwell for ever in God. If we are asked—Why are they beautiful in man? we shall answer—Because they are the very beauty and glory of God; the glory which the Incarnate Word of God manifested to men, when He hung on the cross of Calvary; and was more utterly then, if possible, than ever, The Word of God : because He then declared most utterly to men the character and essence of God. Love which is not content—as what true love is?—to be a passive sentiment, a self-contained possibility, but which must go out of itself, pitying, yearning, agonizing, to seek, to struggle, to suffer, and, if need be, to die for the creature which it loves, even if that creature love it not again.

We need not say this to children. We need only point them to Christ upon His cross, and trust Christ to say it to them, in their heart of hearts, through instincts too deep for words. All we need say to our children is —"Behold your God! He it is, who inspires you with every dutiful, generous, and unselfish impulse you have ever felt; for they are the fruits of His Spirit. By that Spirit He was once unselfish even to the death. By that Spirit He will enable you to carry out in action, as He did, the unselfish instincts which He has given you; and to live the noble life, the heroic life, the life of self-sacrifice; the life of God; the life of the Father, and of the Son, and of the Holy Spirit; and therefore the only life fit for those who are baptized into that Holy Name."

This is the ground and method on which we should educate our children; for it is the ground and method on which The Word of God is educating us.

SERMON XV.

I.

PSALM CXIX. 94.

I am Thine, oh save me.

LET us think seriously this afternoon of one word; the word which is the key-note of this psalm. A very short word; for in our language there is but one letter in it. A very common word; for we are using it all day long when we are awake, and even at night in our dreams; and yet a very wonderful word, for though we know well whom it means, yet what it means we do not know, and cannot understand, no, nor can the wisest philosopher who ever lived; and a most important word too; for we cannot get rid of it, we cannot help thinking of it, cannot help saying it all our life long from childhood to the grave. After death, too, we shall probably be saying that word to ourselves, each of us, for ever and ever. If the whole universe, sun, moon, and stars, and all that we ever thought of, or can think of, were destroyed and became nothing, that word would probably be left; and we should be left alone with it; and on what we meant by that little word would depend our everlasting happi-

13—2

ness or misery. And what is this wonderful little word? What but the word I? Each one of us says I—I think, I know, I feel, I ought, I ought not, I did that, and cannot undo it: and why? Because we are not things, nor mere animals, but persons, living souls, though our bodies are like the bodies of animals, only more perfect, that they may be fit dwelling-places for more perfect souls. The animals, as far as we know, do not think of themselves each as I. Little children do not at first. They call themselves by names by which they hear others call them: not in the first but in the third person. After a while there grows up in them the wonderful thought that they are persons, different from any other person round them, and they begin to say—I want this, I like that. I trust that I shall not seem to you as one who dreams when I say that I believe that is a revelation from God to each child, and just what makes the difference between him and an animal; that God teaches each child to say I; to know that it is not a mere thing, but a person, a living soul, with a will of its own, and a duty of its own; responsible for itself; which ought to do some things, and ought not to do other things. And what a solemn and awful revelation that is, we shall see more clearly, the more we think of it.

It may be a very dreadful and tormenting thought. It does not torment the mere savage, who has no sense of right and wrong; who follows his own appetites and passions, and has never learnt to say, "I ought," and "I ought not." But it does torment the heathen when they begin to be civilized, and to think; it has tormented them in all ages. It tormented the old Greeks and Romans; it torments some Eastern peoples still—that terrible thought—I am I myself, and cannot be any one else. I am answerable for all that I ever did, or shall do; and no one can be answerable for me. All the bad deeds I ever did, the bad thoughts I ever thought, are mine, parts of me, and will be for ever. I can no more escape from them than I can spring off my own shadow. But men have been always trying to escape; to escape from the burden of their own self, and the dread of an evil conscience; and have invented religion after religion, often fantastic enough, often pathetic enough likewise, in hopes of hiding from themselves the secret thought—I am I, and must be myself for ever. But I am not what I ought to be, and therefore I may be wrong, and miserable for ever. And how many people, in this Christian land, are saying at this very moment to themselves, "Oh that I could get rid of this I myself in me, which is so discontented and unhappy! Oh that I had no conscience! Oh that I could forget myself!" And they try to forget themselves by dissipation, by gaming, by drinking, by taking narcotic drugs, even sometimes by suicide, as a last desperate attempt to escape from themselves, they know not and care not whither. It is all in vain. There is no escape from self. As the pious poet whose bust stands beneath yonder tower has said:

> Each in his separate sphere of joy and woe
> Our hermit spirits dwell, and range apart.

I must be I, thou must be thou, he must be he, she must be she, and no one else, throughout our mortal lives, and, for aught we can tell, for ever; alone, each of us, with our own souls, our own thoughts, our own actions, our own hopes, our own fears, our own deservings. Stay alone:—with all these? Yes, and alone with one more. Each of us is alone with God. Face to face with God, seen by Him through and through, and directly answerable to Him at every moment of our lives, for every deed, and word, and thought. And is that not a more terrible thought than any? Ah! my friends, it may be. But it may be also the most comforting of all thoughts, the only really comforting thought, if we will but look at the question as the Psalmist looks at it, and cry with him to God, " I am Thine, oh save the me whom Thou hast made."

There are those, and those who deserve a respectful hearing, who will differ from all that I have been saying, and indeed from the beliefs of 999 out of 1000 of the human race in every age. They will say—This fancy that you are an I, a self, individual and indivisible, is but a fancy; one of the many idols which man creates for himself, by bestowing reality and personality on mere abstractions like this I and self. Each man is not one indivisible, much less indestructible, thing or being. He is really many things. He is the net result of all the organic cells of his body, and of all the forces which act through them within, and of all the circumstances which influence them from without, ay, and of all the forces and circumstances which have influenced his ancestors ever since man appeared on the earth. But because he remembers many states of consciousness, many moments in which he was aware of sensations within him, and of circumstances without him, therefore he strings all these together, and talks of them as one thing which he calls I; and speaks of them as his remembrances of himself, when really the many things are but links of a chain which is perpetually growing at one end and dropping off at the other. To say, therefore, that he is the same person as he was when a child, or as he would be when an old man,—is, when we know that every atom of his physical frame has changed again and again during the course of years, a popular delusion, or at least a misnomer used for convenience' sake; as when we say that the sun rises and sets, when we know that the earth moves, and not the sun. A man, therefore, according to this school, is really no more a person, one and indivisible, than is the coral with its million polypes, the tree with its million buds, or even the thunderstorm with its million vesicles of attracting and repelling vapour.

Now that a truth underlies such a theory as this, I am the last to deny. How much of the character of each man is inherited, how much of it depends on his actual bodily organization; how much of it, alas! on the circumstances of his youth; how much of it changes with the mere physical change from youth to old age—who does not know all this, who has ever needed to fight for himself the battle of life? Only, I say, this is but half the truth; and these philosophers cannot state their half-truth, without employing the very words which they repudiate; without using the very personal pronouns, the I and me, the thou and thee, the he and him, to which they deny any real existence. Beside, I ask—Is the experience and the conclusion of the vast majority of all mankind to go for nothing? For if there be one point on which human beings have been, and are still, agreed, it is this—that each of them is, to his joy or his sorrow, an I; a separate person. And, I should have said, this conviction becomes stro ger and stronger in each of them, the more human they become, civilized, and worthy of the respect and affection of their fellow-men.

For what rises in them, or seems to rise, more and more painfully and fiercely? What but that protest, that battle, between the everlasting I within them, and their own passions, and motives, and circumstances; which St Paul of old called the battle between the spirit on one side, and the flesh and the world on the other. The nobler, surely, and healthier, even for a moment, the manhood of any man is, the more intense is that inward struggle, which man alone of all the animals endures. Is it in moments of brave endeavour, whether to improve our own character, or to benefit our fellow-men: or is it in moments of depression, disappointment, bodily sickness, that we are tempted to say?—I will fight no more. I cannot mend myself, or the world. I am what nature has made me; and what I am, I must remain. I, and all I know, and all I love, are things, not persons; parts of nature, even as the birds upon the bough, only more miserable, because tormented by a hope which never will be fulfilled; an empty pageant of mere phenomena, blown onward toward decay, like dying autumn leaves, before the "everlasting storm which no one guides." Is this the inward voice of health and strength? or rather, for evil or for good, that voice which bids the man, the woman, in the mysterious might of the free I within, trample on their own passions, defy their own circumstances, even to the death; fall back, in utter need, on the absolute instinct of self; and even though all seem lost, say with Medea in the tragedy—

Che resta? Io !

Medea ?—Some one will ask, and have a right to ask— Is that the model which you set before us ? The imperious sorceress, who from the first has known no law but self, her own passions, her own intellect ; who, at last, maddened by a grievous wrong, asserts that self by the murder of her own babes ? You might as well set before us as a model Milton's Satan.

Just so. Remember first, nevertheless, the old maxim, that the best, when corrupted, is the worst; that the higher the nature, when used aright in its right place, the baser it becomes when used wrongly, in its wrong place. When Satan fell from his right place, said the old Jews, he became, remember, not a mere brute: but worse, a fiend. There is a deep and true philosophy in that. As long as he was what he was meant to be— the servant of God—he was an archangel and more ; the fairest of all the sons of the morning. When he rebelled; when in pride and self-will he tore himself—his person— away from that God in whom he lived and moved and had his being: the personality remained; he could still, like Medea, fall back, even when he knew that he had rebelled against his Creator, on his indomitable self, and reign a self-sufficing king, even in the depths of hell.

But the very strength and richness of that personality made him, like Medea, only the more capable of evil. He stood, that is, his moral health endured, only by loyalty to God. When he lost that, he fell; to moral disease: disease the vaster, the vaster were his own capacities.

And so it is with you, and me, and every soul of man. Only by loyalty to God can this undying I, this self, this person, which each of us has—or rather which each of us is—be anything but a torment and a curse; the more terrible to us, and those around us, the stronger and the richer are the nature and faculties through which it works.

Wouldest thou not be a curse unto thy self? Then cry with him who wrote the 119th Psalm—I am Thine. Oh save the me, whom Thou, O God, hast made.

For he who wrote that psalm had an intense conviction of his own personality. I, and me, are words for ever in his mouth: but not in self-satisfied conceit; nor in self-tormenting superstition, crying perpetually, Shall I be saved? shall I be lost? No. Faith in God delivers him from either of these follies. He is forced to think of self. Sad, persecuted, seemingly friendless, he is alone with self: yet not alone. For at every moment he is referring himself to his true place in the universe; to God; God's law, God's help. The burden of self—of mingled responsibility and weakness—is to him past bearing. It would be utterly past bearing, if he could not cast it down, at least at moments, at the foot of the throne of God, and cry, I am Thine. Oh save me.

And if any should ask—as has been asked ere now—
But is there not in this tone of mind something undignified, something even abject? thus to cry for help,
instead of helping oneself? thus to depend on another
being, instead of bearing stoically with manly indepen-
dence? I answer—The Psalmist does bear stoically,
just because he cries for help. For the old Stoics cried
for help; the earlier and truer-hearted of them, at least.
Some here, surely, have read Epictetus, the heathen
whose thought most exactly coincides with that of the
Psalmist. If so, do they not see what enabled him, the
slave of Nero's minion, to assert himself, and his own
unconquerable personality; to defy circumstance; and to
preserve his own calm, his own honour, his own purity,
amid a degradation which might well have driven a good
man to suicide? And was it not this—The intensity of
his faith in God? In God the helper, God the guide?

If any man here have learnt, to his own loss, to
undervalue the experience of prophets, psalmists, apostles:
then let him turn to Epictetus the heathen; and learn
from that heroic slave, that the true dignity of man lies
in true faith in God.

Nay more. It is a serious question, whether ungodliness—by which I mean, as the Psalmist means, the
assertion of self, independent of God—whether ungodliness, I say, is ever dignified; whether, as has been often
said, Milton's still dignified Satan is not an impossible
character; whether Goethe's utterly undignified Mephistopheles is not the true ideal of an utterly evil spirit.
Ungodliness, as we see it manifested in human beings,

may be repulsive, as in the mere ruffian, whose mouth is filled with cursing, and his feet swift to shed blood It may, again, be pitiable, as in those human butterflies, who live only to enjoy, or to minister to, what they call luxury and fashion. And it may be again—when it calmly and deliberately asserts itself to be a philosophy, and an explanation of man and of the universe, and gives itself magisterial airs, however courteously and kindly—it may be then, I dare to think, a little ludicrous.

But as for its dignity, I leave to you to say which of the two beings is the more dignified, which the more abject—a little organism of flesh and blood, at most not more than six feet high, liable to be destroyed by a tile off the roof, or a blast of foul gas, or a hundred other accidents; standing self-poised and self-complacent in the centre of such an universe as this, and asserting that it acknowledges no superior, and needs no guide—or the same being, awakened to the mystery of his own actual weakness, his possible strength; his own actual ignorance, his possible wisdom; his own actual sinfulness, his possible holiness: and then; by a humility which is the highest daring; by a self-distrust which is the truest self-assertion, vindicating the divine element within, by taking personal and voluntary service under no less a personage than Him who made him; and crying directly to the Creator of sun and stars and all the universe—I am Thine. Oh save the me which Thou hast made?

Make up your own minds, make up your minds, which of the two figures is the more abject, which the more dignified. For me, I have had too good cause, long since, to make up mine.

And if you wish to judge further for yourselves, whether the teaching of the Psalmist is more likely to produce an abject or a dignified character, I advise you to ponder carefully a certain singular—I had almost said unique—educational document, written by men who had thoroughly imbibed the teaching of this psalm; a document which, the oftener I peruse it, arouses in me more and more admiration; not only for its theology, but for its knowledge of human nature; and not only for what it does, but for what it does not, say. I mean the Catechism of the Church of England.

You will remark at first sight, that it does not affect to teach the child; with one remarkable exception to be hereafter noticed. It does not tell the child—You should do this, you should not do that.

It is strictly an Educational Catechism. It tries to educe—that is, draw out—what is in the child already; its own native instincts and native conscience. Therefore it makes the child speak for itself. It makes each child feel that he or she is an I; a person, a responsible soul. It begins—What is your name? It makes the child confess that it has a name, as a sign that it is a person, a self, a soul, different from all other persons in earth or heaven; and that its name was given it at baptism, for a sign that God made it a person, and wishes it to know that it is a person, and will teach it how to be a true person, and a good person. It teaches the child to say—I, and me, not in fear and dread, like those heathen of whom I spoke just now, but with manly confidence, and self-respect, and gratitude to God who has made it a person, and an immortal soul.

To say—I am a person; and in order that I might be a right kind of person, and not a wrong kind, I was made a member of Christ, a child of God, and an inheritor of the kingdom of heaven.

To say—I am a person; and that I may be a right kind of person, I must know and believe certain things concerning God Himself, Father, Son, and Holy Ghost. I am a person; and that I may be a right kind of person, I must keep certain commandments and do certain duties toward God, and my parents, and my Queen, and my country, and my neighbour, and all toward whom I am responsible for right behaviour.

And then, and only then, after it has made the child say all this for itself and about itself, the Catechism does begin to teach; and in a few very short words, tell the child about that which is not itself—

" My good child, know this, that thou art not able to do these things of thyself, nor to walk in the Commandments of God, and to serve Him, without His special grace ; which thou must learn at all times to call for by diligent prayer."

Now consider these words. There is comfort and strength in them; comfort for the child; comfort for you, and me, and every human being who has awakened to the sense of his own personal responsibility, and finds it too often a burden heavier than he—and, alas, often, she—can bear.

The Catechism tells the child that it must not merely know doctrines about God, or do duties to God; but more : that it is alone with God Himself, face to face with God Himself day and night.   But that therefore it is to dread God, and look up to God as a taskmaster and tyrant, and try to hide from God's awful eye, and forget God, and forget itself—if it can ?—God forbid ; God forbid.   The Catechism leaves such teaching for those Pharisees who tell little children that unless they are converted, and become as them, they shall in no wise enter into the kingdom of heaven.   The Catechism says, My good child—not, My bad child—know this.   Know that thou art weak : but know that God is strong ; and look up to Him as the Father of all fathers, the Teacher of all teachers, the Helper of all helpers, the Friend of all friends, who has called thee unto His kingdom of grace, that He might shew thee graciousness ; and make thee gracious and graceful in all thy thoughts, and works, and ways : and, therefore, far from trying to hide from Him, call on Him with diligent prayer.   For the Father of all fathers is the Father of thy soul, the Son of all sons died for thee upon the Cross, the Holy Spirit of all holy spirits will make thee a holy spirit and person, even as He is a Holy Spirit and Person Himself.

Believing those words, no one will dare to forget to say his prayers.   For when he prays, he is indeed a person.   He is himself; and not ashamed, however sinful, to be himself; and to tell God about himself. Oh, think of that.   You, each of you, have a right, as God's children, to speak to the God who made the universe. Therefore be sure, that when you dislike to say your prayers, it is because you do not like to be what you are, a person; and prefer—ah foolish soul—to be a thing, and an animal.

Believing those words, no man need long to forget himself, to escape from himself. He can lift up himself to God who made him, with reverence, and fear, and yet with gratitude and trust, and say—

I, Lord, am I; and what I am—a very poor, pitiful, sinful person. But Thou, Lord, art Thou; and what Thou art—happily for me, and for the whole universe—Perfect. Thou art what Thou oughtest to be—Goodness itself. And therefore Thou canst, and Thou wilt, make me what I ought to be at last, a good person. To thee, O Lord, I can bring the burden of this undying I, which I carry with me, too often in shame and sadness, and ask Thee to help me to bear it; saying—"Thou knowest, Lord, the secrets of our hearts. Shut not Thy merciful ears to our prayers: but spare us, O Lord most Holy, O God most Mighty, Thou worthy Judge Eternal, and suffer us not, for any temptation of the world, the flesh or the devil, to fall from Thee." Guide me, teach me, strengthen me, till I become such a person as Thou wouldst have me be; pure and gentle, truthful and high-minded, brave and able, courteous and generous, dutiful and useful, like Thy Son Jesus Christ when He increased not only in stature, but in favour with God and man.

To which may God in His mercy bring us all! Amen.

SERMON XVI.

THE CEDARS OF LEBANON.

PSALM CIV. 16.

The trees of the Lord are full of sap; the cedars of Lebanon,
which He hath planted.

LET me say a few words this afternoon about the noble 104th Psalm, which was read this afternoon, as it is now in many churches, and most wisely and rightly, as the Harvest Psalm. It is a fit psalm for a service in which we thank God for such harvest as He has thought best to send us, whether it be above or below the average. But it is also a fit psalm to be thought earnestly over just now, considering the turn which men's minds are taking more and more in these times in which it has pleased God that we should live. For we have lost, all of us, unlearned as well as learned, the old superstitious notions about this world around us which our forefathers held for many hundred years. No rational person now believes that witches can blight crops or cattle, or that evil spirits cause storms. No one now believes that nymphs and fairies live in fountains or in trees; or that the spirits of the planets rule the fates of men. That

K. S.14

old belief is gone, for good and for evil, and it was good that it should go; for it was false: and falsehoods can do no good, but only harm, to any man, in body and in soul alike. It has died out quickly and strangely. Some say that modern science has destroyed it. I can hardly agree to that: for it has died out—and that almost since my own recollection and under my own eyes—in the minds of country people, who know nothing of science. I had rather say—as I presume the man who wrote the 104th Psalm would have said—The Lord has taken the belief out of men's hearts and minds. And I cannot but hope that He has taken it away, and allows us to believe no more in demons and fairies ruling the world around us, in order that we may believe in Him, and nothing but Him, the true Ruler of the world; in Him of whom it is written, "Him shalt thou worship, and Him only shalt thou serve;" even God the Father, of whom are all things, and God the Son, by whom are all things, and God the Holy Spirit, who is the Lord and Giver of life, alike to sun and stars over our heads, and to the meanest weed and insect under our feet; the Lord and Giver of life alike to matter and spirit, soul and body, worm and man, and angel and archangel before the throne of God. I hope it is so. I trust it is so. For we never had more need than now to believe with all our hearts in the living God; to take into all our hearts the teaching of the 104th Psalm. For now that we have given up believing in superstitions, we are in danger of going to the other extreme, and believing in nothing at all which we cannot see with our eyes, and handle with our hands. Now that we have given up believing in the fabled supernatural; in ghosts, fairies, demons, witches, and such-like : we are in danger of giving up believing in the true and eternal supernatural, which is the Holy Spirit of God, by whom the whole creation is kept alive and sound. We are in danger of falling into a low, stupid, brutish view of this wonderful world of God in which we live; in danger of thinking of nature—that is, of the things which we can see and handle—only as something of which we can make use— till we fall as low as that poor ruffian, of whom the poet says :

> A primrose on the river's brim
> A yellow primrose was to him,
> And it was nothing more.

Lower, that is, than even our own children, whom God has at least taught to admire and love the primroses for their beauty—as something precious and divine, quite independent of their own emotions about them. Men in these days are but too likely to fall into the humour of those poor savages, of whom one who knows them well said to me once—bitterly but truly—that when a savage sees anything new, however wonderful or beautiful, he has but two thoughts about it; first—Will it hurt me? and next—Can I eat it? And from that truly brutish view of God's world, we shall be delivered, I believe, only by taking in with our whole hearts the teaching of the 104th Psalm; which is indeed the teaching of all Holy Scripture throughout.

The Psalmist, in the passage which I have chosen, is

talking of the circulation of water on the earth; how wisely and well it is ordered; how the vapours rise off the sea, till the waters stand above the mountain-tops, to be brought down in thunder-storms—for in his country, as in many hot ones, thunder was generally needed, at the end of the dry season, to bring down the rain; how it forms springs in the highland, and flows down from thence in brooks and rivers, making the whole lowland green and fertile. Well—all very true, you may say. But that is simply a matter of science, or indeed of common observation and common sense. It is not a subject for a psalm or for a sermon.

True: in the words in which I have purposely put it. But not in the words in which the Psalmist puts it; and which I purposely left out, to shew you just the difference between even the soundest science, and faith. He brings in another element, which is the true cause of the circulation of water; and that is, none other but Almighty God.

This is the way in which the inspired Psalmist puts it; and this is the truth of it all; this is the very kernel and marrow and life and soul of it all: while the facts which I told you just now are the mere shell and dead skeleton of it—"*Thou* sendest the springs into the rivers."

Thou art the Lord of the lightning and of the clouds, the Lord of the highlands and of the lowlands, and the Lord of the rainfall and of the drought, the Lord of good seasons and of bad, of rich harvests and of scanty. They, like all things, obey Thine everlasting laws; and of them, whatever may befal, poor purblind man can say in faith and hope—"It is the Lord, let Him do what seemeth Him good."

Yes. He was not of course a man of science, in the modern sense of the word, this old Psalmist. But this I know, that he was a man of science in the soundest and deepest sense; an inspired philosopher, as well as an inspired poet; and had the highest of all sciences, which is the science and knowledge of the living God. For he saw God in everything and everything in God.

But—he says—the trees of the Lord are full of sap; even the cedars of Lebanon which He hath planted. Why should he say that specially of the cedars? Did not God make all trees? Does He not plant all wild trees, and every flower and seed? My dear friends, happy are you if you believe that in spirit and in truth. But let me tell you that I think you would not have believed that, unless the Psalmist, and others who wrote the Holy Scriptures, had told you about trees of God, and rivers of God, and winds of God, and had taught you that the earth is the Lord's and the fulness thereof. You do not know—none of us can know—how much we owe to the Bible for just and rational, as well as orthodox and Christian, notions of the world around us. We, and—thank God—our forefathers for hundreds of years, have drunk in Bible thoughts, as it were, with our mother's milk; till much that we have really learnt from the Bible we take as a matter of course, as self-evident truths which we have found out for ourselves by common sense.

And yet, so far from that being the case, if it had not been for the Bible, we might be believing at this moment, that one god made one tree, and another another; that one tree was sacred to one god, and another flower to another goddess, as the old Greeks believed; and that the wheat and barley were the gift, and therefore the property, of some special deity; and be crying now in fear and trembling to the sun-god, or the rain-god, or some other deified power of nature, because we fancied that they were angry with us, and had therefore sent us too much rain and a short harvest.

It is difficult, now-a-days, to make even cultivated people understand the follies of those who, like the heathen round the Jews, worshipped many gods: and all the more because our modern folly runs in a different channel; because we are tempted, not to believe in many gods, but in no God at all; to believe not that one god made one thing and another another, but that all things have made themselves.

When Hiram, king of Tyre, sent down timber cut from the cedars of Lebanon, to build the temple of God for Solomon; his heathen workmen, probably, were angry and terrified at what they were doing. They said among themselves—"These cedars belong to Baal, or to Melkart, the gods of Tyre. Our king has no right to send them to build the temple of Jehovah, the God of the Jews. It is a robbery, and a sacrilege; and Baal will be angry with us; and curse us with drought and blight."

But now-a-days men say—"The cedars of Lebanon are not God's trees, nor are any other trees. They belong to nature." Now I believe in nature no more than I do in Baal. Nature is merely things—a great many things it is true, but only things—and when I add them all up together, and call them nature, as if they were one thing, I make an abstraction of them. There is no harm in that: but if I treat that abstraction as if it really existed, and did anything, then I make of it an idol, the which I have no mind to do. I believe, I say, in nature no more than I do in Baal. Both words were at first symbols; and both have become in due course of time mere idols. But those who worship nature and not God, say now—God did not make trees; they were made by the laws of nature and nothing else. Well: I believe that the so-called philosophers who say that, will be proved at last to be no more right, and no more rational, than those heathen workmen of Tyre. But meanwhile, what the Psalmist says, and what the Bible says, is—Those trees belong to God. He made them, He made all things; the sap—the mysterious life in them, by which each grows and seeds according to its kind—is His gift. Their growth is ordered by Him; and so are all things in earth and heaven.

Then why speak of them especially as trees of God? Because, my friends, we can only find out that something is true of many things, by finding out that it is true of one thing; and that we usually find out by some striking instance; some case about which there can be no mistake. And these cedars of Lebanon were, and are still, such a striking instance, which there was no mistaking. Upon the slopes of the great snow-mountain of Lebanon stood those gigantic cedar-trees—whole forests of them then —now only one or two small groups, but awful, travellers tell us, even in their decay. Whence did they come? There are no trees like them for hundreds, I had almost said for thousands, of miles. There are but two other patches of them left now on the whole earth, one in the Atlas, one in the Himalaya. The Jews certainly knew of no trees like them; and no trees either of their size. There were trees among them then, probably, two and three hundred feet in height; trees whose tops were as those minster towers; whose shafts were like yonder pillars; and their branches like yonder vaults. No king, however mighty, could have planted them up there upon the lofty mountain-slopes. The Jew, when he entered beneath the awful darkness of these cedars; the cedars with a shadowy shroud—as the Scripture says—the cedars high and lifted up, whose tops were among the thick boughs, and their height exalted above all the trees of the field; fair in their greatness; their boughs multiplied, and their branches long—for it is in such words of awe and admiration that the Bible talks always of the cedars —then the Jew said, "God has planted these, and God alone." And when he thought, not merely of their grandeur and their beauty, but of their use; of their fragrant and incorruptible timber, fit to build the palaces of kings, and the temples of gods; he said—and what could he say better?—"These are trees of God;" wonderful and glorious works of a wonderful and a glorious Creator. If he had not, he would have had less reason in him, and less knowledge of God, than the Hindoos of old; who when they saw the other variety of the cedar growing, in like grandeur, on the slopes of the Himalaya, called them the Deodara—which means, in the old Sanscrit tongue, neither more nor less than "the timber of God," "the lance of God"—and what better could they have said?

My friends, I speak on this matter from the fulness of my heart. It has happened to me—through the bounty of God, for which I shall be ever grateful—to have spent days in primeval forests, as grand, and far stranger and far richer than that of Lebanon and its cedars; amid trees beside which the hugest tree in Britain would be but as a sapling; gorgeous too with flowers, rich with fruits, timbers, precious gums, and all the yet unknown wealth of a tropic wilderness. And as I looked up, awe-struck and bewildered, at those minsters not made by hands, I found the words of Scripture rising again and again unawares to my lips, and said—Yes: the Bible words are the best words, the only words for such a sight as this. These too are trees of God which are full of sap. These, too, are trees, which God, not man, has planted. Mind, I do not say that I should have said so, if I had not learnt to say so from the Bible. Without the Bible I should have been, I presume, either an idolater or an atheist. And mind, also, that I do not say that the Psalmist learnt to call the cedars trees of God by his own unassisted reason. I believe the very opposite. I believe that no man can see the truth of a thing unless God shews it him; that no man can find out God, in earth or heaven, unless God condescends to reveal Himself to that man. But I believe that God did reveal Himself to the Psalmist; did enlighten his reason by the inspiration of His Holy Spirit; did teach him, as we teach a child, what to call those cedars; and, as it were, whispered to him, though with no audible voice: "Thou wishest to know what name is most worthy whereby to call those mighty trees: then call them trees of God. Know that there is but one God, of whom are all things; and that they are His trees; and that He planted them, to shew forth His wisdom, His power, and His good will to man."

And do you fancy that because the Jew called the great cedars trees of God, that therefore he thought that the lentiscs and oleanders, by the brook outside, were not God's shrubs; or the lilies and anemones upon the down below were not God's flowers? Some folk have fancied so.—It seems to me most unreasonably. I should have thought that here the rule stood true; that that which is greater contains the less; that if the Psalmist knew God to be mighty enough to make and plant the cedars, he would think Him also mighty enough to make and plant the smallest flower at his feet. I think so. For I know it was so with me. My feeling that those enormous trees over my head were God's trees, did not take away in the least from my feeling of God's wisdom and power in the tiniest herb at their feet. Nay rather, it increased my feeling that God was filling all things with life and beauty; till the whole forest,—if I may so speak in all humility, but in all honesty—from the highest to the lowest, from the hugest to the smallest, and every leaf and bud therein, seemed full of the glory of God. And if I could feel that,—

being the thing I am—how much more must the inspired Psalmist have felt it? You see by this very psalm that he did feel it. The grass for the use of cattle, and the green herb for men, and the corn and the wine and the oil, he says, are just as much God's making, and God's gift. The earth is "filled," he says, "with the fruit of God's works." Filled : not dotted over here and there with a few grand and wonderful things which God cares for, while He cares for nothing else : but filled. Let us take the words of Scripture honestly in their whole strength ; and believe that if the Psalmist saw God's work in the great cedars, he saw it everywhere else likewise.

Nay, more : I will say this. That I believe it was such teaching as that of this very 104th Psalm—teaching which runs, my friends, throughout the Old Testament, especially through the Psalmists and the Prophets—which enabled the Jews to understand our Lord's homely parables about the flowers of the field and the birds of the air. Those of them at least who were Israelites indeed ; those who did understand, and had treasured up in their hearts, the old revelation of Moses, and the Psalmists, and the Prophets ; those who did still believe that the cedars were the trees of God, and that God brought forth grass for the cattle, and green herb for the service of men ; and who could see God's hand, God's laws, God's love, working in them—those men and women, be sure, were the very ones who understood our Lord, when He said, "Consider the lilies of the field, how they grow. They toil not, neither do they spin. And yet I say unto you, that Solomon in all his glory was not compared unto one of these."

And why should it not be so with you, townsfolk though you are? Every Londoner has now, in the public parks and gardens, the privilege of looking on plants and flowers, more rich, more curious, more varied than meet the eye of any average countryman. Then when you next avail yourselves of that real boon of our modern civilization, let me beg you not to forget the lesson which I have been trying to teach you.

You may feel—you ought to feel—that those strange and stately semitropic forms are indeed plants of God; the work of a creative Spirit who delights to employ His Almighty power in producing ever fresh shapes of beauty —seemingly unnecessary, seemingly superfluous, seemingly created for the sake of their beauty alone—in order that the Lord may delight Himself in His works. Let that sight make you admire and reverence more, not less, the meanest weed beneath your feet. Remember that the very weeds in your own garden are actually more highly organized; have cost—if I may so say, with all reverence, but I can only speak of the infinite in clumsy terms of the finite—the Creator more thought, more pains, than the giant cedars of Lebanon, and the giant cypresses of California. Remember that the smallest moss or lichen which clings upon the wall, is full of wonders and beauties, as inexplicable as unexpected; and that of every flower on your own window-sill the words of Christ stand literally true—that Solomon in all his glory was not arrayed as one of these: and how your hearts and souls before the magnificent prodigality, the exquisite perfection of His work, who can be, as often as He will, greatest in that which is least, because to His infinity nothing is great, and nothing small; who hath created all things, and for His pleasure they are, and were created; who rejoices for ever in His own works, because He beholds for ever all that He makes, and it is very good.

And then refresh your hearts as well as your brains— tired it may be, too often, with the drudgery of some mechanical, or merely calculating, occupation—refresh your hearts, I say, by lifting them up unto the Lord, in truly spiritual, truly heavenly thoughts; which bring nobleness, and trust, and peace, to the humblest and the most hardworked man.

For you can say in your hearts—All the things which I see, are God's things. They are thoughts of God. God gives them law, and life, and use. My heavenly Father made them. My Saviour redeemed them with His most precious blood, and rules and orders them for ever. The Holy Spirit of God, which was given me at my baptism, gives them life and power to grow and breed after their kinds. The divine, miraculous, and supernatural power of God Himself is working on them, and for them, perpetually: and how much more on me, and for me, and all my children, and fellow-creatures for whom Christ died. Without my Father in heaven not a sparrow falls to the ground: and am I not of more value than many sparrows? God feeds the birds: and will He not feed me? God clothes the lilies of the field: and will He not clothe me? Ah, me of little faith, who forget daily that in God I live, and move, and have my being, and am, in spite of all my sins, the child of God. Him I can trust in prosperous times, and in disastrous times; in good harvests and in bad harvests; in life and in death, in time and in eternity. For He has given all things a law which cannot be broken. And they continue this day as at the beginning, serving Him. And if I serve Him likewise, then shall I be in harmony with God, and with God's laws, and with God's creatures, great and small. The whole powers of nature as well as of spirit will be arrayed on my side in the struggle for existence; and all things will work together for good to those who love God.

SERMON XVII.

LIFE.

PSALM CIV. 24, 28—30.

O Lord, how manifold are Thy works! in wisdom hast Thou made
them all: the earth is full of Thy riches.

That Thou givest them they gather. Thou openest Thine hand,
they are filled with good. Thou hidest Thy face, they are troubled. Thou takest away their breath, they die, and return to
their dust. Thou sendest forth Thy Spirit, they are created:
and Thou renewest the face of the earth.

WHAT is the most important thing to you, and me,
and every man?

I suppose that most, if they answered honestly,
would say—Life. I will give anything I have for my
life.

And if some among you answered—as I doubt not
some would—No: not life: but honour and duty.
There is many a thing which I would rather die than
do—then you would answer like valiant and righteous
folk; and may God give you grace to keep in the same
mind, and to hold your good resolution to the last. But
you, too, will agree that, except doing your duty, life
is the most important thing you have. The mother,

when she sacrifices her life to save her child, shews thereby how valuable she holds the child's life to be; so valuable that she will give up even her own to save it.

But did you never consider, again—and a very solemn and awful thought it is—that this so important thing called life is the thing, above all other earthly things, of which we know least—ay, of which we know nothing?

We do not know what death is. We send a shot through a bird, and it falls dead—that is, lies still, and after a while decays again into the dust of the earth, and the gases of the air. But what has happened to it? How does it die? How does it decay? What is this life which is gone out of it? No man knows. Men of science, by dissecting and making experiments, which they do with a skill and patience which deserve not only our belief, but our admiration, will describe to us the phenomena, or outward appearances, which accompany death, and follow death. But death itself—for want of what the animal has died—what has gone out of it—they cannot tell. No man can tell; for that is invisible, and not to be discovered by the senses. They are therefore forced to explain death by theories, which may be true, or false: but which are after all not death itself, but their own thoughts about death put into their own words. Death no man can see: but only the phenomena and effects of death; and still more, life no man can see: but only the phenomena and effects of life.

For if we cannot tell what death is, still more we cannot tell what life is. How life begins; how it organizes each living thing according to its kind; and makes it grow; how it gives it the power of feeding on other things, and keeping up its own body thereby: of this all experiments tell us as yet nothing. Experiment gives us, here again, the phenomena—the visible effects. But the causes it sees not, and cannot see.

This is not a matter to be discussed here. But this I say, that scientific men, in the last generation or two, have learnt, to their great honour, and to the great good of mankind—everything, or almost everything, about it—except the thing itself; and that, below all facts, below all experiments, below all that the eye or brain of man can discover, lies always a something nameless, invisible, imponderable, yet seemingly omnipresent and omnipotent; retreating before the man of science deeper and deeper, the deeper he delves: namely, the life, which shapes and makes all phenomena, and all facts. Scientific men are becoming more and more aware of this unknown force, I had almost said, ready to worship it. More and more the noblest-minded of them are becoming engrossed with that truly miraculous element in nature which is always escaping them, though they cannot escape it. How should they escape it? Was it not written of old—Whither shall I go from Thy presence? and whither shall I flee from Thy Spirit?

What then can we know of this same life, which is so precious in most men's eyes?

My friends, it was once said—That man's instinct

was in all unknown matters to take refuge in God. The words were meant as a sneer. I, as a Christian, glory in them; and ask, Where else should man take refuge, save in God? When man sees anything—as he must see hundreds of things—which he cannot account for; things mysterious, and seemingly beyond the power of his mind to explain: what safer, what wiser word can he say than—This is the Lord's doing, and it is marvellous in our eyes? God understands it: though I do not. Be it what it may, it is a work of God. From God it comes: by God it is ruled and ordered. That at least I know: and let that be enough for me. And so we may say of life. When we are awed, and all but terrified, by the unfathomable mystery of life, we can at least take refuge in God. And if we be wise, we shall take refuge in God. Whatever we can or cannot know about it, this we know; that it is the gift of God. So thought the old Jewish Prophets and Psalmists; and spoke of a breath of God, a vapour, a Spirit of God, which breathed life into all things. It was but a figure of speech, of course: but if a better one has yet been found, let the words in which it has been written or spoken be shewn to me. For to me, at least, they are yet unknown. I have read, as yet, no wiser words about the matter than those of the old Jewish sages, who told how, at the making of the world, the Spirit, or breath, of God moved on the face of the waters, quickening all things to life; or how God breathed into man's nostrils the breath or spirit of life, and man became a living soul.

And in the same temper does that true philosopher and truly inspired Psalmist, who wrote the 139th Psalm, speak of the Spirit or breath of God. He considers his own body: how fearfully and wonderfully it is made; how God did see his substance, yet being imperfect; and in God's book were all his members written, which day by day were fashioned, while as yet there was none of them. "Thou," he says, "O God, hast fashioned me behind and before, and laid Thine hand upon me. Such knowledge is too wonderful and excellent for me; I cannot attain to it." "But," he says to himself, "there is One Who has attained to it; Who does know; for He has done it all, and is doing it still: and that is God and the Spirit of God. Whither"—he asks—"shall I go then from God's Spirit? Whither shall I flee from God's presence?" And so he sees by faith—and by the highest reason likewise—The Spirit of God, as a living, thinking, acting being, who quickens and shapes, and orders, not his mortal body merely, but all things; giving life, law, and form to all created things, from the heights of heaven to the depths of hell; and ready to lead him and hold him, if he took the wings of the morning and fled into the uttermost parts of the sea.

And so speaks again he who wrote the 104th Psalm, and the text which I have chosen. To him, too, the mystery of death, and still more the mystery of life, could be explained only by faith in God, and in the Spirit of God. If things died, it was because God took away their breath, and therefore they returned to their dust. And if things lived, it was because the Spirit of

God, breathed forth, and proceeding, from God, gave them life. He pictured to himself, I dare to fancy, what we may picture to ourselves—for such places have often been, and are now, in this world—some new and barren land, even as the very gravel on which we stand was once, just risen from the icy sea, all waste and lifeless, without a growing weed, an insect, even a moss. Then, gradually, seeds float thither across the sea, or are wafted by the winds, and grow; and after them come insects; then birds; then trees grow up; and larger animals arrive to feed beneath their shade; till the once barren land has become fertile and rich with life, and the face of the earth is renewed. But by what? "God," says the Psalmist, "has renewed the face of the earth." True, the seeds, the animals came by natural causes: but who was the Cause of those causes? Who sent the things thither, save God? And who gave them life? Who kept the life in floating seeds, in flying spores? Who made that life, when they reached the barren shore, grow and thrive in each after their kind? Who, but the Spirit of God, the Lord and Giver of life? God let His Spirit proceed and go forth from Himself upon them; and they were made; and so He renewed the face of the earth.

That, my good friends, is not only according to Scripture, but according to true philosophy. Men are slow to believe it now: and no wonder. They have been always slow to believe in the living God; and have made themselves instead dead gods—if not of wood and stone, still out of their own thoughts and imaginations; and talk of laws of nature, and long abstractions ending in ation and ality, like that "Evolution" with which so many are in love just now; and worship them as gods; mere words, the work of their own brains, though not of their own hands—even though they be—as many of them are—Evolution, I hold, among the rest—true and fair approximations to actual laws of God. But before them, and behind them, and above them and below them, lives the Author of Evolution, and of everything else. For God lives, and reigns, and works for ever. The Spirit of God proceedeth from the Father and the Son, giving, evolving, and ruling the life of all created things; and what we call nature, and this world, and the whole universe, is an unfathomable mystery, and a perpetual miracle, The one Author and Ruler of which is the ever-blessed Trinity, of whom it is written—"The glorious majesty of the Lord shall endure for ever: the Lord shall rejoice in His works."

I believe, therefore, that the Psalmist in the text is speaking, not merely sound doctrine but sound philosophy. I believe that the simplest and the most rational account of the mystery of life is that which is given by the Christian faith; and that the Nicene Creed speaks truth and fact, when it bids us call the Holy Spirit of God the Lord and Giver of life.

That this is according to the orthodox Catholic Faith there is no doubt. Many mistakes were made on this matter, in the early times of the Church, even by most learned and holy divines; as was to be expected, considering the mysteriousness of the subject. They were inclined, often, to what is called Pantheism—that is, to fancy that all living things are parts of God; that God's Spirit is in them, as our soul is in our body, or as heat is in a heated matter; and to speak of God's Spirit as the soul and life of the world.

But this is exactly what the Nicene Creed does not do. It does not say that the Holy Spirit is life: but that He is the Lord and Giver of life—a seemingly small difference in words: but a most vast and important difference in meaning and in truth.

The true doctrine, it seems to me, is laid down most clearly by the famous bishop, Cyril of Alexandria; who, whatever personal faults he had—and they were many—had doubtless dialectic intellect enough for this, and even deeper questions. And he says—" The Holy Spirit moves all things that are moved; and holds together, and animates, and makes alive, the whole universe. Nor is He another Nature different from the Father and the Son: but as He is in us; of the same nature and the same essence as they." And so says another divine, Eneas of Gaza—" The Father, with the Son, sends forth the Holy Spirit; and inspiring with this Spirit all things, beyond sense and of sense—invisible and visible—fills them with power, and holds them together, and draws them to Himself." And he prays thus to the Holy Spirit a prayer which is to my mind as noble as it is true—" O Holy Spirit, by whom God inspires, and holds together, and preserves all things, and leads them to perfection." I quote such words to shew you that I am not giving you new fancies of my own: but simply what I believe to be the ancient, orthodox and honest meaning of that same Nicene Creed, which you just now heard; where it says that the Holy Spirit is the Lord and Giver of life; and the meaning of the 104th Psalm also, where it says—"Thou lettest Thy breath—Thy Spirit—go forth, and they shall be made, and Thou shalt renew the face of the earth."

And now—if anyone shall say—This may be all very true. But what is it to me? You are talking about nature; about animals and plants, and lands and seas. What I come to church to hear of, is about my own soul—

I should answer such a man—My good friend, you come to church to hear about God as well as about what you call your soul. And any sound knowledge which you can learn about God, must be—believe me—of use to your immortal soul. For if you have wrong notions concerning God: how can you avoid having wrong notions concerning your soul, which lives and moves and has its being in God?

But look at it thus. At least I have been speaking of the works of God. And are not you, too, a work of God? The Lord shall rejoice in His works, even to the tiniest gnat that dances in the sun. Is the Lord rejoicing in you? I have said—Whither shall a man go from God's presence? Are you forgetting or remembering God's presence? And—Whither shall a man flee from God's Spirit? Are you, O man, fleeing from God's Spirit, and forgetting His gracious inspirations; all pure and holy, and noble, and just and lovely and truly human, thoughts, in the whirl of pleasure, or covetousness, or ambition, or actual sin? If so, look at the tiniest gnat which dances in the air, the meanest flower beneath your feet; and be ashamed, and fear, and tremble before the Living God, and before His Spirit. For the gnat and the flower are doing their duty, and pleasing the Holy Spirit of God; and you are not doing your duty, and are grieving the Holy Spirit of God. For simply: because that Spirit is the Spirit of God, He is a Holy Spirit, who tries to make you—O man and not animal—holy; a moral, and spiritual, and good being. Because you are a moral and spiritual being, God's Spirit exercises over you a moral power which He does not exercise over the plants and animals. He works not merely on your body and your brain: but on your heart and immortal soul. But if you choose to be immoral, when He is trying to keep you moral; if you choose to be carnal like the brutes, while He is trying to make you spiritual, like Jesus Christ, from whom He proceeds: then, oh then, tremble, and beware, and be ashamed before the very flowers which grow in your own garden-bed; for they fulfil the law which God has given them. They are what they ought to be, each after its kind. But you are not what you ought to be, after your kind; which is a good man, or a good woman, or a good child.

Oh beware lest the Lord should fulfil in you the awful words of this Psalm; lest He should hide His face from you, and you be troubled; and lest when He takes away your breath you should die, and turn again to your dust; and find, too late, that the wages of sin are death—death not merely of the body, but of the soul. Rather repent, and amend, and remember that most blessed, and yet most awful fact—that God's Spirit is with you from your baptism until now, putting into your heart good desires, and ready to enable you—if you will—to bring those good desires to good effect: instead of leaving them only as good intentions, with which, says the too true proverb, hell is paved.

So will be fulfilled in you the blessed words of the next verse—When Thou lettest Thy Spirit go forth, they shall be made; and Thou shalt renew the face of the earth—words which St Augustine of old applied to the work of God's Spirit on the souls of men.

For well it is with us—as St Augustine says—when God takes away from us our own spirit, the spirit of pride and self-will and self-righteousness; and we see that we are but dust and ashes; worse than the animals, in that we have sinned, and they have not. Confess— he says—thy weakness and thy dust: and then listen to what follows:—Thou shalt take away from them their own spirit; but Thou shalt send forth Thy Spirit on them, and they shall be made and created anew. As the Apostle says, "We are God's own workmanship, created in Christ Jesus unto good works." And so— he says—God will indeed renew the face of the earth with converted and renewed men, who confess that they are not righteous in themselves, but made righteous by the grace of the Spirit of God; and so the Lord shall rejoice in His works; you will be indeed His work, and He will rejoice in you.

Yes. God will indeed rejoice in us, if we obey the

godly inspirations of His Spirit. But again, we shall
rejoice in God; if we be but led by His Spirit into all
truth, and thence into all righteousness. Then we shall
be in harmony with God, and with the whole universe of
God. We shall have our share in that perpetual worship
which is celebrated throughout the universe by all creatures, rational and irrational, who are obeying the laws
of their being; the laws of the Spirit of God, the Lord
and Giver of life. We shall take our part in that perpetual Hymn which calls on all the works of the Lord,
from angels and powers, sun and stars, winds and seasons,
seas and floods, trees and flowers, beasts and cattle, to
the children of men, and the servants of the Lord, and
the spirits and souls of the righteous, and the holy and
humble men of heart—"O all ye works of the Lord, bless
ye the Lord, praise Him and magnify Him for ever."

SERMON XVIII.

DEATH.

PSALM CIV. 20, 21.

Thou makest darkness, and it is night: wherein all the beasts of the
forest do creep forth. The lions roar after their prey, and seek
their meat from God.

LET me say a few words on this text. It is one which
has been a comfort to me again and again. It is one
which, if rightly understood, ought to give comfort to
pitiful and tender-hearted persons.

Have you never been touched by, never been even
shocked by, the mystery of pain and death? I do not
speak now of pain and death among human beings: but
only of that pain and death among the dumb and irrational creatures, which from one point of view is more
pitiful than pain and death among human beings.

For pain, suffering, and death, we know, may be of
use to human beings. It may make them happier and
better in this life, or in the life to come; if they are the
Christians which they ought to be. But of what use can
suffering and death be to dumb animals? How can it
make them better in this life, and happier in the life to

come? It seems, in the case of animals, to be only so much superfluous misery thrown away. Would to God that people would remember that, when they unnecessarily torment dumb creatures, and then excuse themselves by saying—Oh, they are not human beings; they are not Christians; and therefore it does not matter so much. I should have thought that therefore it mattered all the more: and that just because dumb animals have, as far as we know, only this mortal life, therefore we should allow them the fuller enjoyment of their brief mortality.

And yet, how much suffering, how much violent death, there is among animals. How much? The world is full of it, and has been full of it for ages. I dare to say, that of the millions on millions of living creatures in the earth, the air, the sea, full one-half live by eating each other. In the sea, indeed, almost every kind of creature feeds on some other creature: and what an amount of pain, of terror, of violent death that means, or seems to mean!

We here, in a cultivated country, are slow to take in this thought. We have not here, as in India, Africa, America, lion and tiger, bear and wolf, jaguar and puma, perpetually prowling round the farms, and taking their tithe of our sheep and cattle. We have never heard, as the Psalmist had, the roar of the lion round the village at night, or seen all the animals, down to the very dogs, crowding together in terror, knowing but too well what that roar meant. If we had; and had been like the Psalmist, thoughtful men: then it would have been a very solemn question to us—From whom the lion was asking for his nightly meal; whether from God, or from some devil as cruel as himself?

But even here the same slaughter of animals by animals goes on. The hawk feeds on the small birds, the small birds on the insects, the insects, many of them, on each other. Even our most delicate and seemingly harmless songsters, like the nightingale, feed entirely on living creatures—each one of which, however small, has cost God as much pains—if I may so speak in all reverence—to make as the nightingale itself; and thus, from the top to the bottom of creation, is one chain of destruction, and pain, and death.

What is the meaning of it all? Ought it to be so, or ought it not? Is it God's will and law, or is it not? That is a solemn question; and one which has tried many a thoughtful, and tender, and virtuous soul ere now, both Christian and heathen; and has driven them to find strange answers to it, which have been, often enough, not according to Scripture, or to the Catholic Faith.

Some used to say, in old times; and they may say again—This world, so full of pain and death, is a very ill-made world. We will not believe that it was made by the good God. It must have been made by some evil being, or at least by some stupid and clumsy being—the Demiurgus, they called him—or the world-maker—some inferior God, whom the good God would conquer and depose, and so do away with pain, and misery, and death. A pardonable mistake: but, as we are bound to believe, a mistake nevertheless.

Others, again, good Christians and good men like

wise, have invented another answer to the mystery—like that which Milton gives in his 'Paradise Lost.' They have said—Before Adam fell there was no pain or death in the world. It was only after Adam's fall that the animals began to destroy and devour each other. Ever since then there has been a curse on the earth, and this is one of the fruits thereof.

Now I say distinctly, as I have said elsewhere, that we are not bound to believe this or anything like it. The book of Genesis does not say that the animals began to devour each other at Adam's fall. It does not even say that the ground is cursed for man's sake now, much less the animals. For we read in Genesis ix. 21—"And the Lord said, I will not any more curse the ground for man's sake." Neither do the Psalmists and Prophets give the least hint of any such doctrine. Surely, if we found it anywhere, we should find it in this very 104th Psalm, and somewhere near the very verse which I have taken for my text. But this Psalm gives no hint of it. So far from saying that God has cursed His own works, or looks on them as cursed: it says—"The Lord shall rejoice in His works."

Others will tell us that St Paul has said so, where he says that "by one man sin entered into the world, and death by sin." But I must very humbly, but very firmly, demur to that. St Paul shews that when he speaks of the world he means the world of men; for he goes on to say, "And so death passed upon all men, in that all have sinned." By mentioning men, he excludes the animals; he excludes all who have not sinned: according to a sound rule of logic which lawyers know well. What St Paul meant, I believe, is most probably this: that Adam, by sinning, lost his heavenly birthright; and put on the carnal and fleshly likeness of the animals, instead of the likeness of God in which he was created; and therefore, sowing to the flesh, of the flesh reaped corruption; and became subject to death even as the dumb beasts are.

Be that as it may, we know—as certainly as we can know anything from the use of our own eyes and common sense—that long ages before Adam, long ages before men existed on this earth, the animals destroyed and ate each other, even as they are doing now. We know that ages ago, in old worlds, long before this present world in which we live, the seas swarmed with sharks and other monsters, who not only died as animals do now, but who did devour—for there is actual proof of it—other living creatures; and that the same process went on on the land likewise. The rocks and soils, for miles beneath our feet, are one vast graveyard, full of the skeletons of creatures, almost all unlike any living now, who, long before the days of Adam, and still more before the days of Noah, lived and died, generation after generation; and sought their meat—from whom—if not from God?

Yes, that last is the answer—the only answer which can give a thoughtful and tender-hearted soul comfort, at the sight of so much pain and death on earth—In every unknown question, to take refuge in God. And that is the answer which the inspired Psalmist gives, in the 104th Psalm—"The lions roaring after their prey do seek their meat from God." And if they seek it from

God, all must be right: we know not how; but He who made them knows.

Consider, with respect and admiration, the manful, cheerful view of pain and death, and indeed of the whole creation, which the Psalmist has, because he has faith. There is in him no sentimentalism, no complaining of God, no impious, or at least weak and peevish, cry of " Why hast Thou made things thus?" He sees the mystery of pain and death. He does not attempt to explain it: but he faces it; faces it cheerfully and manfully, in the strength of his faith, saying—This too, mysterious, painful, terrible as it may seem, is as it should be; for it is of the law and will of God, from whom come all good things; of The God in whom is light, and in Him is no darkness at all. Therefore to the Psalmist the earth is a noble sight; filled, to his eyes, with the fruit of God's works. And so is the great and wide sea likewise. He looks upon it; "full of things creeping innumerable, both small and great beasts," for ever dying, for ever devouring each other. And yet it does not seem to him a dreadful and a shocking place. What impresses his mind is just what would impress the mind of a modern poet, a modern man of science; namely, the wonderful variety, richness, and strangeness of its living things. Their natures and their names he knows not. It was not given to his race to know. It is enough for him that known unto God are all His works from the foundation of the world. But one thing more important than their natures and their names he does know; for he perceives it with the instinct of a true poet and a true philosopher—

"These all wait upon thee, O God, that Thou mayest give them meat in due season."

But more.—"There go the ships;" things specially wonderful and significant to him, the landsman of the Judæan hills, as they were afterward to Muhammed, the landsman of the Arabian deserts. And he has talked with sailors from those ships; from Tarshish and the far Atlantic, or from Ezion-geber and the Indian seas. And he has heard from them of mightier monsters than his own Mediterranean breeds; of the Leviathan, the whale, larger than the largest ship which he has ever seen, rolling and spouting among the ocean billows, far out of sight of land, and swallowing, at every gape of its huge jaws, hundreds of living creatures for its food. But he does not talk of it as a cruel and devouring monster, formed by a cruel and destroying deity, such as the old Canaanites imagined, when—so the legend ran—they offered up Andromeda to the sea-monster, upon that very rock at Joppa, which the Psalmist, doubtless, knew full well. No. This psalm is an inspired philosopher's rebuke to that very superstition; it is the justification of the noble old Greek tale, which delivers Andromeda by the help of a hero, taught by the Gods who love to teach mankind.

For what strikes the Psalmist is, again, exactly what would strike a modern poet, or a modern man of science: the strength and ease of the vast beast; its enjoyment of its own life and power. It is to him the Leviathan, whom "God has made to play in the sea;" "to take his pastime therein."

Truly this was a healthy-minded man; as all will be, and only they, who have full faith in the one good God, of whom are all things, both in earth and heaven.

Then he goes further still. He has looked into the face of life innumerable. Now he looks into the face of innumerable death; and sees there too the Spirit and the work of God.

> Thou givest to them; they gather:
> Thou openest thy hand; they are filled with good:
> Thou hidest thy face; they are troubled:
> Thou takest away their breath; they die, and are
>   turned again to their dust.

Poetry? Yes: but, like all highest poetry, highest philosophy; and soundest truth likewise. Nay, he goes further still—further, it may be, than most of us would dare to go, had he not gone before us in the courage of his faith. He dares to say, of such a world as this—"The glory of the Lord shall endure for ever. The Lord shall rejoice in His works."

The glory of the Lord, then, is shewn forth, and endures for ever, in these animals of whom the Psalmist has been speaking, though they devour each other day and night. The Lord rejoices in His works, even though His works live by each other's death. The Lord shall rejoice in His works—says this great poet and philosopher.

But what Lord, and what God? Ah, my friends, all depends on the answer to that question. "There be," says St Paul, "lords many, and gods many:" and since his time, men have made fresh lords and gods for themselves, and believed in them, and worshipped them, while they fancied that they were believing in the one true God, in the same God in whom the man believed who wrote the 104th Psalm.

Do we truly believe in that one true God, Father, Son and Holy Spirit?

Let me beg you to consider that question earnestly. The Psalmist, when he talked of the Lord, did not mean merely what some people call the Deity, or the Supreme Being, or the Creator. You will remark that I said— What. I do not care to say, Whom, of such a notion ; that is, of a God who made the world, and set it going once for all, but has never meddled with it; never, so to speak, looked at it since: so that the world would go on just the same, and just as well, if God thenceforth had ceased to be. No : that is a dead God; an absentee God—as one said bitterly once. But the Psalmist believed in the living God, and a present God, in whom we live and move and have our being; in a God who does not leave the world alone for a moment, nor in the smallest matter, but is always interested in it, attending to it, enforcing His own laws, working—if I may so speak in all reverence—and using the most pitifully in-sufficient analogy—working—I say—His own machinery; making all things work together for good, at least to those who love God; a God without whom not a sparrow falls to the ground, and in whose sight all the hairs of our heads are numbered.

In one word, he believed in a living God. If anyone had said to the Psalmist, as I have heard men say now-a-days—Of course we believe, with you, in a general Providence of God over the whole universe. But you do not surely believe in special Providences? That would be superstition. God governs the world by law, and not by special Providences. Then I believe that the Psalmist would have answered—Laws? I believe in them as much as you, and perhaps more than you. But as for special Providences, I believe in them so much, that I believe that the whole universe, and all that has ever happened in it from the beginning, has happened by special Providences; that not an organic being has assumed its present form, after long ages and generations, save by a continuous series of special Providences; that not a weed grows in a particular spot, without a special Providence of God that it should grow there, and nowhere else; then, and nowhen else. I believe that every step I take, every person I meet, every thought which comes into my mind—which is not sinful—comes and happens by the perpetual special Providence of God, watching for ever with Fatherly care over me, and each separate thing that He has made.

And if a modern philosopher—or one so called—had said to him,—'This is unthinkable and inconceivable, and therefore cannot be. I cannot "think of"—I cannot conceive a mind—or as I call it—"a series of states of consciousness," as antecedent to the infinity of processes simultaneously going on in all the plants that cover the globe, from scattered polar lichens to crowded tropical palms, and in all the millions of animals which roam among them, and the millions of millions of insects which buzz among them:'—Then the Psalmist would have answered him, I believe,—'If you cannot, my friend, I can. And you must not make your power of thought and conception the measure of the universe, or even of other men's intellects; or say—" Because I cannot conceive a thing, therefore no man can conceive it, and therefore it does not exist." But pray, O philosopher, if you cannot think and conceive of the omnipresence and omnipotence of God, what can you think and conceive?'

Then if that philosopher had answered him—as some would now-a-days—'I can conceive that the properties of very different elements,—and therefore the infinite variety and richness of nature which I cannot conceive as caused by a God—that the properties—I say—of different elements result from differences of arrangement arising by the compounding and recompounding of ultimate homogeneous units'—Then, I think, the Psalmist would have replied, as soon as he had—like Socrates of old in a like case—recovered from the 'dizziness' caused by an eloquence so unlike his own—' Why, this proposition is far more "unthinkable" to me, and will be to 999 of 1000 of the human race, than mine about a God and a Providence. Alas! for the vagaries of the mind of man. When it wants to prove a pet theory of its own, it will strain at any gnat, and swallow any camel.'

But again—if a philosopher of more reasonable mood had said to him—as he very likely would say—'This is a grand conception of God: but what proof have you of it? How do you know that God does interfere, by spe-

cial Providences, in the world around us; not only, as
you say, perpetually: but even now and then, and
at all ?'

Then the Psalmist, like all true Jews, would have
gone back to a certain old story which is to me the most
precious story, save one, that ever was written on earth;
and have taken his stand on that. He would have gone
back—as the Scripture always goes back—to the story of
Moses and the Israelites in Egypt, and have said—
'Whatever I know or do not know about the Laws of
nature, this I know—That God can use them as He
chooses, to punish the wicked, and to help the miserable. For He did so by my forefathers. When we Jews
were a poor, small, despised tribe of slaves in Egypt,
The God who made heaven and earth shewed Himself
at once the God of nature, and the God of grace. For
He took the powers of nature; and fought with them
against proud Pharaoh and all his hosts; and shewed
that they belonged to Him; and that He could handle
them all to do His work. He shewed that He was
Lord, not only of the powers of nature which give life
and health, but of those which give death and disease.
Nothing was too grand, nor too mean, for Him to use.
He took the lightning and the hail, and the pestilence,
and the darkness, and the East wind, and the spring-
tides of the Red sea; and He took also the locust-
swarms, and the frogs, and the lice, and the loathsome
skin-diseases of Egypt, and the microscopic atomies
which turn whole rivers into blood, and kill the fish;
and with them He fought against Pharaoh the man-God,

the tyrant ruling at his own will in the name of his father the sun-God and of the powers of nature; till Egypt was destroyed, and Pharaoh's host drowned in the sea; And He brought out my forefathers with a mighty hand and an outstretched arm, because He had heard their cry in Egypt, and saw their oppression under cruel taskmasters, and pitied them, and had mercy on them in their slavery and degradation.' That is my God—the old Psalmist would have said. Not merely a strong God, or a wise God; but a good God, and a gracious God, and a just God likewise; a God who not only made heaven and earth, the sea, and all that therein is, but who keepeth His promise for ever; who helpeth them to right who suffer wrong, and feedeth the hungry.

Yes, my friends, it is this magnificent conception of God's living and actual goodness and justice, which the Psalmist had, which made him trust God about all the strange and painful things which he saw in the world— about, for instance, the suffering and death of animals; and say—'If the lion roaring after his prey seeks his meat, he seeks his meat from God: and therefore he ought to seek it, and he will find it. It is all well: I know not why: but well it is, for it is the law and will of the good and righteous and gracious God, who brought His people out of the land of Egypt. And that is enough for me.'

Enough for him? and should it not be enough for us, and more than enough?—We know what the Psalmist knew not. We know God to be more good, more righteous, more gracious than any Prophet or Psalmist could know. We know that God so loved the world, that He spared not His only-begotten Son, but freely gave Him for us. We know that the only-begotten Son Jesus Christ so loved the world that He stooped to be born and suffer as mortal man, and to die on the cross, even while He was telling men that not a sparrow fell to the ground without the knowledge of their heavenly Father, and bidding them see how God fed the birds and clothed the lilies of the field. Ah, my friends, in this case, as in all cases, rest and comfort for our doubts and fears is to be found in one and the same place—at the foot of the Cross of Christ. If we believe that He who hung upon that Cross is—as He is—the maker and ruler of the universe, the same from day to day and for ever: then we can trust Him in darkness as well as in light; in doubt as well as in certainty; in the face of pain, disease, and death, as well as in the face of joy, health, and life; and say—Lord, we know not, but Thou knowest. Lord, we believe, help Thou our unbelief. Make us sure that Thou, Lord, shalt save both man and beast. For great are Thy mercies, O Lord; and the children of men shall put their trust under the shadow of Thy wings.

Yes, my friends, this is, after all, a strange world, a solemn world, a world full of sad mysteries, past our understanding. As was said once by the holiest of modern Englishmen, now gone home to his rest—whose bust stands worthily in yonder chapel—This is a world in which men must be sometimes sad who love God, and care for their fellow-men.

But it is not over the dumb animals that we must mourn. For they fulfil the laws of their being; and whatever meat they seek, they seek their meat from God.

Rather must we mourn over those human beings who, being made in the likeness of God, and redeemed again into that likeness by our Lord Jesus Christ, and baptized into that likeness by the Holy Spirit, put on again of their own will the likeness of the beasts which perish; and find too often, alas! too late, that the wages of sin are death.

Rather must we mourn for those human beings who do not fulfil the laws of their being: but break those laws by sin; till they are ground by them to powder.

Rather must we mourn for those who seek their meat, not from God, but from the world and the flesh; and neglect the bread which cometh down from heaven, and the meat which endureth to eternal life, whereof the Lord who gives it said—Seek ye first the kingdom of God, and His righteousness, and all other things shall be added unto you.

Rather must we pray for ourselves, and for all we love, that God's Spirit of eternal life would raise us up, more and more day by day, out of the likeness of the old Adam, who was of the earth, earthy; of whom it is written that—like the animals—dust he was, and unto dust he must return; and would mould us into the likeness of the new Adam, who is the Lord from heaven, into the likeness of which it is written, that it is created after God's image, in righteousness and true holiness, the end of which is not death, but everlasting life through Jesus Christ our Lord.

And so will be fulfilled in us the saying of the Psalmist; and the Lord shall rejoice in His works: for we too, not only body and soul, but spirit also, shall be the work of God; and God will rejoice in us, and we in God.

SERMON XIX.

SIGNS AND WONDERS.

JOHN IV. 48—50.

Then said Jesus unto him, Except ye see signs and wonders, ye will not believe. The nobleman saith unto him, Sir, come down ere my child die. Jesus saith unto him, Go thy way; thy son liveth.

THESE words of our Lord are found in the Gospel for this day. They are a rebuke, though a gentle one. He reproved the nobleman, seemingly, for his want of faith : but He worked the miracle, and saved the life of the child.

We do not know enough of the circumstances of this case, to know exactly why our Lord reproved the nobleman; and what want of faith He saw in him. Some think that the man's fault was his mean notion of our Lord's power; his wish that He should come down the hills to Capernaum, and see the boy Himself, in order to cure him; whereas he ought to have known that our Lord could cure him—as He did—at a distance, and by a mere wish, which was no less than a command to nature, and to that universe which He had made.

I cannot tell how this may be: but of one thing I think we may be sure—That this saying of our Lord's is very deep, and very wide; and applies to many people, in many times—perhaps to us in these modern times.

We must recollect one thing—That our Lord did not put forward the mere power of His miracles as the chief sign of His being the Son of God. Not so: He declared His almighty power most chiefly by shewing mercy and pity. Twice He refused to give the Scribes and Pharisees a sign from heaven. "An evil and adulterous generation," He said, "seeketh after a sign: but there shall be no sign given them, but the sign of the prophet Jonas." And what was that,—but a warning to repent, and mend their ways, ere it was too late?

Now the slightest use of our common sense must tell us, that our Lord could have given a sign of His almighty power if He had chosen; and such a sign as no man, even the dullest, could have mistaken. What prodigy could He not have performed, before Scribes and Pharisees, Herod, and Pontius Pilate? "Thinkest thou," He said Himself, "that I cannot now pray to My Father, and He will send Me presently more than twelve legions of angels?" Yet how did our Lord use that miraculous and almighty power of His? Sparingly, and secretly. Sparingly; for He used it almost entirely in curing the diseases of poor people; and secretly; for He used it almost entirely in remote places. Jerusalem itself, recollect, was at best a remote city compared with any of the great cities of the Roman empire. And even there He refused to cast Himself down from a pinnacle of the temple, for a sign and wonder to the Jews.   If He, the Lord of the world, had meant to convert the world by prodigious miracles, He would surely have gone to Rome itself, the very heart and centre of the civilized world, and have shewn such signs and wonders therein, as would have made the Cæsar himself come down from his throne, and worship Him, the Lord of all.

But no.   Our Lord wished for the obedience, not of men's lips, but of their hearts.   It was their hearts which He wished to win, that they might love Him—and be loyal to Him—for the sake of His goodness; and not fear and tremble before Him for the sake of His power. And therefore He kept, so to speak, His power in the background, and put His goodness foremost; only shewing His power in miracles of healing and mercy; that so poor neglected, oppressed, hardworked souls might understand that whoever did not care for them, Christ their Lord did; and that their disease and misery were not His will; nor the will of His Father and their Father in heaven.

But because, also, Christ was Lord of heaven and earth; therefore—if I may make so bold as to guess at the reason for anything which He did—He seems to have interfered as little as possible with those regular rules and customs of this world about us, which we now call the Laws of Nature.   He did not offer—as the magicians of His time did offer—and as too many have pretended since to do—to change the courses of the elements, to bring down tempests or thunderbolts, to shew prodigies in the heaven above, and in the earth beneath. Why should He? Heaven and earth, moon and stars, fire and tempest, and all the physical forces in the universe, were fulfilling His will already; doing their work right well according to the law which He had given them from the beginning. He had no need to disturb them, no need to disturb the growth of a single flower at His feet.

Rather He loved to tell men to look at them, and see how they went well, because His Father in heaven cared for them. To tell people to look, not at prodigies, comets, earthquakes, and the seeming exceptions of God's rule: but at the common, regular, simple, peaceful work of God, which is going on around us all day long in every blade of grass, and flower, and singing bird, and sunbeam, and shower. To consider the lilies of the field how they grow: which toil not, neither do they spin: and yet I say unto you, that Solomon in all his glory was not arrayed like one of these.—And the birds of the air: They sow not, neither reap, nor gather into barns; and yet your heavenly Father feedeth them. How much more will He feed you, who can sow, and reap, and gather into barns?—O ye of little faith, who fancy always that besides sowing and reaping honestly, you must covet, and cheat, and lie, and break God's laws instead of obeying them; or else, forsooth, you cannot earn your living? To see that the signs of God's Kingdom are not astonishing convulsions, terrible catastrophes and disorders: but order, and peace, and usefulness, in creatures which are happy, because they live according to the law which God has given them, and do their duty—that duty, of which the great poet of the English Church has sung—

> Stern Lawgiver! Thou yet dost wear
>   The Godhead's most benignant grace
> Nor know we anything so fair
>   As is the smile upon thy face.
> Flowers laugh before thee on their beds,
>   And fragrance in thy footing treads;
> Thou dost preserve the stars from wrong,
> And the most ancient heavens, through thee, are fresh and strong.

But men would not believe that in our Lord's time; neither would they believe it after His time. Will they believe it even now? They craved after signs and wonders; they saw God's hand, not in the common sights of this beautiful world; not in seed-time and harvest, summer and winter; not in the blossoming of flowers, and the song of birds: but only in strange portents, absurd and lying miracles, which they pretended had happened, because they fancied that they ought to have happened: and so built up a whole literature of *un*reason, which remains to this day, a doleful monument of human folly and superstition.

But is not this too true of some at least of us in this very day? Must not people now see signs and wonders before they believe in God?

Do they not consider whatever is strange and inexplicable, as coming immediately from God? While whatever they are accustomed to, or fancy that they can explain, they consider comes in what they call the course of nature, without God's having anything to do with it?

If a man drops down dead, they say he died "by the hand of God," or "by the visitation of God:" as if any created thing or being could die, or live either, save by the will and presence of God: as if a sparrow could fall to the ground without our Father's knowledge. But so it is; because men's hearts are far from God.

If an earthquake swallowed up half London this very day, how many would be ready to cry, "Here is a visitation of God. Here is the immediate hand of God. Perhaps Christ is coming, and the end of the world at hand." And yet they will not see the true visitation, the immediate hand of God, in every drop of rain which comes down from heaven; and returneth not again void, but gives seed to the sower and bread to the eater. But so it always has been. Men used to see God and His power and glory almost exclusively in comets, auroras, earthquakes. It was not so very long ago, that the birth of monstrous or misshapen animals, and all other prodigies, as they were called, were carefully noted down, and talked of far and wide, as signs of God's anger, presages of some coming calamity.—Atheists while they are in safety, superstitious when they are in danger —Requiring signs and wonders to make them believe— Interested only in what is uncommon and seems to break God's laws—Careless about what is common, and far more wonderful, because it fulfils God's laws—Such have most men been for ages, and will be, perhaps, to the end;

shewing themselves, in that respect, carnal and no wiser than dumb animals.

For it is carnal, animal and brutish, and a sign of want of true civilization, as well as of true faith, only to be interested and surprised by what is strange; like dumb beasts, who, if they see anything new, are attracted by it and frightened by it, at the same time: but who, when once they are accustomed to it, and have found out that it will do them no harm, are too stupid to feel any curiosity or interest about it, though it were the most beautiful or the most wonderful object on earth.

But I will tell you of a man after God's own heart, who was not like the dumb animals, nor like the ungodly and superstitious; because he was taught by the Spirit of God, and spoke by the Spirit of God. One who saw no signs and wonders, and yet believed in God—namely, the man who wrote the 139th Psalm. He needed no prodigies to make him believe. The thought of his own body, how fearfully and wonderfully it was made, was enough to make him do that. He looked on the perfect order and law which ruled over the development of his own organization, and said—" I will praise Thee. For I am fearfully and wonderfully made. Marvellous are Thy works, and that my soul knoweth right well. Thine eyes did see my substance, yet being imperfect; and in Thy Book were all my members written, which day by day were fashioned, when as yet there was none of them. How dear are Thy counsels unto me, O God! how great is the sum of them !"

And I will tell you of another man who needed no

signs and wonders to make him believe—the man, namely, who wrote the 19th Psalm. He looked upon the perfect order and law of the heavens over his head, and the mere sight of the sun and moon and stars was enough for him; and he said—" The heavens declare the glory of God, the firmament sheweth His handy-work. One day telleth another, and one night certifieth another. There is neither speech nor language, where their voice is not heard among them."

And I will tell you of yet another man who needed no signs and wonders to make him believe—namely, the man who wrote the 104th Psalm. He looked on the perfect order and law of the world about his feet; and said,—" O Lord, how manifold are Thy works. In wisdom hast Thou made them all: the earth is full of Thy riches. So is the great and wide sea also, wherein are things creeping innumerable, both small and great beasts. These all wait upon Thee, that Thou mayest give them their meat in due season. Thou givest to them; they gather. Thou openest Thy hand; they are filled with good. Thou hidest Thy face; they are troubled. Thou takest away their breath, they die, and return to their dust. Thou sendest forth Thy breath, they are created; and Thou renewest the face of the earth. The glory of the Lord shall endure for ever. The Lord shall rejoice in His works."

My friends, let us all pray to God and to Christ, that They will put into our hearts the Spirit by which those psalms were written: that They will take from us the evil heart of unbelief, which must needs have signs and wonders, and forgets that in God we live and move and have our being. For are we not all—even the very best of us—apt to tempt our Lord in this very matter?

When all things go on in a common-place way with us—that is, in this well-made world, comfortably, easily, prosperously—how apt we all are—God forgive us—to forget God. How we forget that on Him we depend for every breath we draw; that Christ is guarding us daily from a hundred dangers, a hundred sorrows, it may be from a hundred disgraces, of which we, in our own self-satisfied blindness, never dream. How dull our prayers become, and how short. We almost think, at times, that there is no use in praying, for we get all we want without asking for it, in what we choose to call the course of circumstances and nature.—God forgive us, indeed.

But when sorrow comes, anxiety, danger, how changed we are all of a sudden. How gracious we are when pangs come upon us—like the wicked queen-mother in Jerusalem of old, when the invaders drove her out of her cedar palace. How we cry to the Lord then, and get us to our God right humbly. Then, indeed, we feel the need of prayer. Then we try to wrestle with God, and cry to Him—and what else can we do?—like children lost in the dark; entreat Him, if there be mercy in Him—as there is, in spite of all our folly—to grant some special providence, to give us some answer to our bitter entreaties. If He will but do for us this one thing, then we will believe indeed. Then we will trust Him, obey Him, serve Him, as we never did before.

Ah, if there were in Christ any touch of pride or

malice! Ah, if there were in Christ aught but a magnanimity and a generosity altogether boundless! Ah, if He were to deal with us as we have dealt with Him! Ah, if He were to deal with us after our sins, and reward us according to our iniquities!

If He refused to hear us; if He said to us,—You forgot me in your prosperity, why should I not forget you in your adversity?—What could we answer? Would that answer not be just? Would it not be deserved, however terrible? But our hope and trust is, that He will not answer us so; because He is not our God only, but our Saviour; that He will deal with us as one who seeks and saves that which is lost, whether it knows that it is lost or not.

Our hope is, that the Lord is very pitiful and of tender mercy; that because He is man, as well as God, He can be touched with the feeling of our infirmities; that He knoweth our frame, He remembereth of what we are made: else the spirit would fail before Him, and the souls which He has made. So we can have hope, that, though Christ rebuke us, He will yet hear us, if our prayers are reasonable, and therefore according to His will. And surely, surely, surely, if our prayers are for the improvement of any human being; if we are praying that we, or any human being, may be made better men and truer Christians at last, and saved from the temptations of the world, the flesh, and the devil—oh then, then shall we not be heard? The Lord may keep us long waiting, as He kept St Monica of old, when she wept over St Augustine's youthful sins and follies. But

He may answer us, as He answered her by the good bishop—"Be of good cheer. It is impossible that the son of so many prayers should perish." And so, though He may shame us, in our inmost heart, by the rebuke—"Except ye see signs and wonders, ye will not believe"—He will in the same breath grant our prayer, undeserved though His condescension be, and say—" Go in peace, thy son liveth."

SERMON XX.

THE JUDGMENTS OF GOD.

LUKE XIII. 1—5.

There were present at that season some that told him of the Galilæans, whose blood Pilate had mingled with their sacrifices. And Jesus answering said unto them, Suppose ye that these Galilæans were sinners above all the Galilæans, because they suffered such things? I tell you, Nay: but, except ye repent, ye shall all likewise perish. Or those eighteen, upon whom the tower in Siloam fell, and slew them, think ye that they were sinners above all men that dwelt in Jerusalem? I tell you, Nay: but, except ye repent, ye shall all likewise perish.

THIS story is often used, it seems to me, for a purpose exactly opposite to that for which it is told. It is said that because these Galilæans, whom Pilate slew, and these eighteen on whom the tower in Siloam fell, were no worse than the people round them, that therefore similar calamities must not be considered judgments and punishments of God; that it is an offence against Christian charity to say that such sufferers are the objects of God's anger; that it is an offence against good manners to introduce the name of God, or the theory of a Divine Providence, in speaking of historical events. They must be ascribed to certain brute forces of nature; to certain inevitable laws of history; to the passions of men, to chance, to fate, to anything and everything: rather than to the will of God.

No man disagrees more utterly than I do with the latter part of this language. But I cannot be astonished at its popularity. It cannot be denied that the theory of a Divine Providence has been much misstated; that the doctrine of final causes has been much abused; that, in plain English, God's name has been too often taken in vain, about calamities, private and public. Rational men of the world, therefore, may be excused for begging at times not to hear any more of Divine Providence; excused for doubting the existence of final causes; excused for shrinking, whenever they hear a preacher begin to interpret the will of God about this event or that. They dread a repetition of the mistake—to call it by the very gentlest term—which priests, in all ages, have been but too ready to commit. For all priesthoods—whether heathen or Christian, whether calling themselves priests, or merely ministers and preachers—have been in all ages tempted to talk as if Divine Providence was exercised solely on their behalf; in favour of their class, their needs, their health and comfort; as if the thunders of Jove never fell save when the priesthood needed, I had almost said commanded, them. Thus they have too often arrogated to themselves a right to define who was cursed by God, which has too soon, again and again, degenerated into a right to curse men in God's name; while they have too often taught men to believe only in a Providence who interfered now and then on behalf of certain favoured persons, instead of a Providence who rules, always and everywhere, over all mankind. But men have again and again reversed their judgments. They have had to say—The facts are against you. You prophesied destruction to such and such persons; and behold: they have not been destroyed, but live and thrive. You said that such and such persons' calamities were a proof of God's anger for their sins. We find them, on the contrary, to have been innocent and virtuous persons; often martyrs for truth, for humanity, for God. The facts, we say, are against you. If there be a Providence, it is not such as you describe. If there be judgments of God, you have not found out the laws by which He judges: and rather than believe in your theory of Providence, your theory of judgments, we will believe in none.

Thus, in age after age, in land after land, has fanaticism and bigotry brought forth, by a natural revulsion, its usual fruit of unbelief.

But—let men believe or disbelieve as they choose—the warning of the Psalmist still stands true—"Be wise. Take heed, ye unwise among the people. He that nurtureth the heathen; it is He that teacheth man knowledge, shall He not punish?" For as surely as there is a God, so surely does that God judge the earth; and every individual, family, institution, and nation on the face thereof; and judge them all in righteousness by His Son Jesus Christ, whom He hath appointed heir of all things, and given Him all power in heaven and earth;

who reigns and will reign till He hath put all enemies under His feet.

This is the good news of Advent. And therefore it is well that in Advent, if we believe that Christ is ruling us, we should look somewhat into the laws of His king-dom, as far as He has revealed them to us; and among others, into the law which—as I think—He laid down in the text.

Now I beg you to remark that the text, taken fully and fairly, means the very opposite to that popu-lar notion of which I spoke in the beginning of my sermon.

Our Lord does not say—Those Galilæans were not sinners at all. Their sins had nothing to do with their death. Those on whom the tower fell were innocent men. He rather implies the very opposite.

We know nothing of the circumstances of either calamity: but this we know—That our Lord warned the rest of the Jews, that unless they repented—that is, changed their mind, and therefore their conduct, they would all perish in the same way. And we know that that warning was fulfilled, within forty years, so hideously, and so awfully, that the destruction of Jerusalem remains, as one of the most terrible cases of wholesale ruin and horror recorded in history; and—as I believe—a key to many a calamity before and since. Like the taking of Babylon, the fall of Rome, and the French Revolution, it stands out in lurid splendour, as of the nether pit itself, forcing all who believe to say in fear and trembling— Verily there is a God that judgeth the earth—and a warning to every man, class, institution, and nation on earth, to set their houses in order betimes, and bear fruit meet for repentance, lest the day come when they too shall be weighed in the balance of God's eternal justice, and found wanting.

But another lesson we may learn from the text, which I wish to impress earnestly on your minds. These Galilæans, it seems, were no worse than the other Galilæans: yet they were singled out as examples: as warnings to the rest.

Believing—as I do—that our Lord was always teaching the universal through the particular, and in each parable, nay in each comment on passing events, laying down world-wide laws of His own kingdom, enduring through all time—I presume that this also is one of the laws of the kingdom of God. And I think that facts— to which after all is the only safe appeal—prove that it is so; that we see the same law at work around us every day. I think that pestilences, conflagrations, accidents of any kind which destroy life wholesale, even earth- quakes and storms, are instances of this law; warnings from God; judgments of God, in the very strictest sense; by which He tells men, in a voice awful enough to the few, but merciful and beneficent to the many, to be prudent and wise; to learn henceforth either not to interfere with the physical laws of His universe, or to master and to wield them by reason and by science.

I would gladly say more on this point, did time allow: but I had rather now ask you to consider, whether this same law does not reveal itself throughout history; in many great national changes, or even calamities; and in the fall of many an ancient and time-honoured institution. I believe that the law does reveal itself; and in forms which, rightly studied, may at once teach us Christian charity, and give us faith and comfort, as we see that God, however severe, is still just.

I mean this—The more we read, in history, of the fall of great dynasties, or of the ruin of whole classes, or whole nations, the more we feel—however much we may acquiesce with the judgment as a whole—sympathy with the fallen. It is not the worst, but often the best, specimens of a class or of a system, who are swallowed up by the moral earthquake, which has been accumulating its forces, perhaps for centuries. Innocent and estimable on the whole, as persons, they are involved in the ruin which falls on the system to which they belong. So far from being sinners above all around them, they are often better people than those around them. It is as if they were punished, not for being who they were, but for being what they were.

History is full of such instances; instances of which we say and cannot help saying—What have they done above all others, that on them above all others the thunderbolt should fall?

Was Charles the First, for example, the worst, or the best, of the Stuarts; and Louis the Sixteenth, of the Bourbons? Look, again, at the fate of Sir Thomas More, Bishop Fisher, and the hapless monks of the Charterhouse. Were they sinners above all who upheld the Romish system in England? Were they not rather among the righteous men who ought to have saved it, if it could have been saved? And yet on them— the purest and the holiest of their party—and not on hypocrites and profligates, fell the thunderbolt.

What is the meaning of these things?—for a meaning there must be; and we, I dare to believe, must be meant to discover it; for we are the children of God, into whose hearts, because we are human beings and not mere animals, He has implanted the inextinguishable longing to ascertain final causes; to seek not merely the means of things, but the reason of things; to ask not merely How? but Why?

May not the reason be—I speak with all timidity and reverence, as one who shrinks from pretending to thrust himself into the counsels of the Almighty—But may not the reason be that God has wished thereby to condemn not the persons, but the systems? That He has punished them, not for their private, but for their public faults? It is not the men who are judged, it is the state of things which they represent; and for that very reason may not God have made an example, a warning, not of the worst, but of the very best, specimens of a doomed class or system, which has been weighed in His balance, and found wanting?

Therefore we need not suppose that these sufferers themselves were the objects of God's wrath. We may believe that of them, too, stands true the great Law, "Whom the Lord loveth, He chasteneth, and scourgeth every son whom He receiveth." We may believe that of them, too, stands true St Paul's great parable in 1 Cor. xii., which, though a parable, is the expression of a perpetually active law. They have built, it may be, on the true foundation: but they have built on it wood, hay, stubble, instead of gold and precious stone. And the fire of God, which burns for ever against the falsehoods and follies of the world, has tried their work, and it is burned and lost. But they themselves are saved; yet as through fire.

Looking at history in this light, we may justify God for many a heavy blow, and fearful judgment, which seems to the unbeliever a wanton cruelty of chance or fate; while at the same time we may feel deep sympathy with—often deep admiration for—many a noble spirit, who has been defeated, and justly defeated, by those irreversible laws of God's kingdom, of which it is written— "On whomsoever that stone shall fall, it will grind him to powder." We may look with reverence, as well as pity, on many figures in history, such as Sir Thomas More's; on persons who, placed by no fault of their own in some unnatural and unrighteous position; involved in some decaying and unworkable system; conscious more or less of their false position; conscious, too, of coming danger, have done their best, according to their light, to work like men, before the night came in which no man could work; to do what of their duty seemed still plain and possible; and to set right that which would never come right more: forgetting that, alas, the crooked cannot be made straight, and that which is wanting cannot be numbered; till the flood came and swept them away, standing bravely to the last at a post long since untenable, but still—all honour to them—standing at their post.

When we consider such sad figures on the page of history, we may have, I say, all respect for their private virtues. We may accept every excuse for their public mistakes. And yet we may feel a solemn satisfaction at their downfall, when we see it to have been necessary for the progress of mankind, and according to those laws and that will of God and of Christ, by which alone the human race is ruled. We may look back on old orders of things with admiration; even with a touch of pardonable, though sentimental, regret. But we shall not forget that the old order changes, giving place to the new;

> And God fulfils Himself in many ways,
> Lest one good custom should corrupt the world.

And we shall believe, too, if we be wise, that all these things were written for our example, that we may see, and fear, and be turned to the Lord, each asking himself solemnly, What is the system on which I am governing my actions? Is it according to the laws and will of God, as revealed in facts? Let me discover that in time: lest, when it becomes bankrupt in God's books, I be involved—I cannot guess how far—in the common ruin of my compeers.

What is my duty? Let me go and work at it, lest a night come, in which I cannot work. What fruit am I expected to bring forth? Let me train and cultivate my mind, heart, whole humanity to bring it forth, lest the great Husbandman come seeking fruit on me, and find none. And if I see a man who falls in the battle of life, let me not count him a worse sinner than myself; but let me judge myself in fear and trembling; lest God judge me, and I perish in like wise.

SERMON XXI.

THE WAR IN HEAVEN.

REV. XIX. 11—16.

And I saw heaven opened, and behold a white horse; and he that
sat upon him was called Faithful and True, and in righteousness
he doth judge and make war. His eyes were as a flame of fire,
and on his head were many crowns; and he had a name written,
that no man knew, but he himself. And he was clothed with a
vesture dipped in blood: and his name is called The Word of
God. And the armies which were in heaven followed him upon
white horses, clothed in fine linen, white and clean. And out of
his mouth goeth a sharp sword, that with it he should smite the
nations: and he shall rule them with a rod of iron: and he
treadeth the winepress of the fierceness and wrath of Almighty
God. And he hath on his vesture and on his thigh a name
written, KING OF KINGS, AND LORD OF LORDS.

LET me ask you to consider seriously this noble passage.
It was never more worth men's while to consider it than
now, when various selfish and sentimental religions—
call them rather superstitions—have made men altogether forget the awful reality of Christ's kingdom; the
awful fact that Christ reigns, and will reign, till He has
put all enemies under His feet.

Who, then, is He of whom the text speaks? Who is this personage, who appears eternally in heaven as a warrior, with His garments stained with blood, the leader of armies, smiting the nations, and ruling them with a rod of iron?

St John tells us that He had one name which none knew save Himself. But he tells us that He was called Faithful and True; and he tells us, too, that He had another name which St John did know; and that is, "The Word of God."

Now who the Word of God is, all are bound to know who call themselves Christians; even Jesus Christ our Lord, who was born of the Virgin Mary, crucified under Pontius Pilate, rose again the third day, ascended into heaven, and sitteth at the right hand of God.

He it is who makes everlasting war as King of kings and Lord of lords. But against what does He make war? His name tells us that. For it is—Faithful and True; and therefore He makes war against all things and beings who are unfaithful and false. He Himself is full of chivalry, full of fidelity; and therefore all that is unchivalrous and treacherous is hateful in His eyes; and that which He hates, He is both able and willing to destroy.

Moreover, He makes war in righteousness. And therefore all men and things which are unrighteous and unjust are on the opposite side to Him; His enemies, which He will trample under His feet. The only hope for them, and indeed for all mankind, is that He does make war in righteousness, and that He Himself is faithful and true, whoever else is not; that He is always just, always fair, always honourable and courteous; that He always keeps His word; and governs according to fixed and certain laws, which men may observe and calculate upon, and shape their conduct accordingly, sure that Christ's laws will not change for any soul on earth or in heaven. But, within those honourable and courteous conditions, He will, as often as He sees fit, smite the nations, and rule them with a rod of iron; and tread the winepress of the fierceness and wrath of Almighty God.

And if any say—as too many in these luxurious unbelieving days will say—What words are these? Threatening, terrible, cruel? My answer is,—The words are not mine. I did not put them into the Bible. I find them there, and thousands like them, in the New Testament as well as in the Old, in the Gospels and Epistles as well as in the Revelation of St John. If you do not like them, your quarrel must be, not with me, but with the whole Bible, and especially with St John the Apostle, who said—"Little children, love one another;" and who therefore was likely to have as much love and pity in his heart as any philanthropic, or sentimental, or superstitious, or bigoted, personage of modern days.

And if any one say,—But you must mistake the meaning of the text. It must be understood spiritually. The meek and gentle Jesus, who is nothing but love and mercy, cannot be such an awful and destroying being as you would make Him out to be. Then I must answer—That our Lord was meek and gentle when on earth, and therefore is meek and gentle for ever and ever, there can be no doubt. "I am meek and lowly of heart," He said of Himself. But with that meekness and lowliness, and not in contradiction to it, there was, when He was upon earth, and therefore there is now and for ever, a burning indignation against all wrong and falsehood; and especially against that worst form of falsehood—hypocrisy; and that worst form of hypocrisy—covetousness which shelters itself under religion.

When our Lord saw men buying and selling in the temple, He made a scourge of cords, and drove them out, and overthrew the tables of the money-changers, and said,—"It is written, my Father's house is a house of prayer, but ye have made it a den of thieves."

When He faced the Pharisees, who were covetous, He had no meek and gentle words for them : but, "Ye serpents, ye generation of vipers, how can ye escape the damnation of hell?"

And because His character is perfect and eternal : because He is the same yesterday, to-day, and for ever, we are bound by the Christian faith to believe that He has now, and will have for ever, the same Divine in- dignation against wrong, the same determination to put it down : and to cast out of His kingdom, which is simply the whole universe, all that offends, and whoso- ever loveth and maketh a lie.

And if any say, as some say now-a-days—"Ah, but you cannot suppose that our Lord would propagate His Gospel by the sword, or wish Christians to do so."

My friends, this chapter and this sermon has nothing
to do with the propagation of the Gospel, in the popular
sense; nothing to do with converting heathens or others
to Christianity. It has to do with that awful government
of the world, of which the Bible preaches from beginning
to end; that moral and providential kingdom of God,
which rules over the destiny of every kingdom, every
nation, every tribe, every family, nay, over the destiny
of each human being; ay, of each horde of Tartars on
the furthest Siberian steppe, and each group of savages
in the furthest island of the Pacific; rendering to each
man according to his works, rewarding the good, punishing the bad, and exterminating evildoers, even wholesale and seemingly without discrimination, when the
measure of their iniquity is full. Christ's herald in this
noble chapter calls men, not to repentance, but to inevitable doom. His angel—His messenger—stands in
the sun, the source of light and life; above this petty
planet, its fashions, its politics, its sentimentalities, its
notions of how the universe ought to have been made
and managed; and calls to whom?—to all the fowl that
fly in the firmament of heaven—"Come and gather
yourselves together, to the feast of the great God, that
ye may eat the flesh of kings, and of captains, and of
mighty men; and the flesh of horses and of them that
sit on them; and the flesh of all men, both free and
slave, both small and great."

What those awful words may mean I cannot say. But
this I say, that the Apostle would never have used such
words, conveying so plain and so terrible a meaning to

anyone who has ever seen or heard of a battle-field, if he had really meant by them nothing like a battle-field at all.

It may be that these words have fulfilled themselves many times—at the fall of Jerusalem—at the wars which convulsed the Roman empire during the first century after Christ—at the final fall of the Roman empire before the lances of our German ancestors—in many another great war, and national calamity, in many a land since then. It may be, too, that, as learned divines have thought, they will have their complete fulfilment in some war of all wars, some battle of all battles; in which all the powers of evil, and all those who love a lie, shall be arrayed against all the powers of good, and all those who fear God and keep His commandments: to fight it out, if the controversy can be settled by no reason, no persuasion; a battle in which the whole world shall discover that, even in an appeal to brute force, the good are stronger than the bad; because they have moral force also on their side; because God and the laws of His whole universe are fighting for them, against those who transgress law, and outrage reason.

The wisest of living Britons has said,—" Infinite Pity, yet infinite rigour of Law. It is so that the world is made." I should add, It is so the world must be made, because it is made by Jesus Christ our Lord, and its laws are the likeness of His character; pitiful, because Christ is pitiful; and rigorous, because He is rigorous. So pitiful is Christ, that He did not hesitate to be slain for men, that mankind through Him might be saved. But so rigorous is Christ, that He does not hesitate to slay men, if needful, that mankind thereby may be saved. War and bloodshed, pestilence and famine, earthquake and tempest—all of them, as sure as there is a God, are the servants of God, doing His awful but necessary work, for the final benefit of the whole human race.

It may be difficult to believe this : at least to believe it with the same intense faith with which prophets and apostles of old believed it, and cried—" When Thy judgments, O Lord, are abroad in the earth, then shall the inhabitants of the world learn righteousness." But we must believe it : or we shall be driven to believe in no God at all ; and that will be worse for us than all the evil that has happened to us from our youth up until now.

But most people find it very difficult to believe in such a God as the Scripture sets forth—a God of boundless tenderness ; and yet a God of boundless indignation.

The covetous and luxurious find it very difficult to understand such a being. Their usual notion of tenderness is a selfish dislike of seeing any one else uncomfortable, because it makes them uncomfortable likewise. Their usual notion of indignation is a selfish desire of revenge against anyone who interferes with their comfort. And therefore they have no wholesome indignation against wrong and wrong-doers, and a great deal of unwholesome tenderness for them. They are afraid of any one's being punished ; probably from a fellow-feeling ; a suspicion that they deserve to be punished themselves. They hate and dread honest severity, and stern exercise of lawful power. They are indulgent to the bad, severe upon the good; till, as has been bitterly but too truly said,—" Public opinion will allow a man to do anything, except his duty."

Now this is a humour which cannot last. It breeds weakness, anarchy, and at last ruin to society. And then the effeminate and luxurious, terrified for their money and their comfort, fly from an unwholesome tenderness to an unwholesome indignation; break out into a panic of selfish rage; and become, as cowards are apt to do, blindly and wantonly cruel; and those who fancied God too indulgent to punish His enemies, will be the very first to punish their own.

But there are those left, I thank God, in this land, who have a clear understanding of what they ought to be, and an honest desire to be it; who know that a manful indignation against wrong-doing, a hearty hatred of falsehood and meanness, a rigorous determination to do their duty at all risks, and to repress evil with all severity, may dwell in the same heart with gentleness, forgiveness, tenderness to women and children; active pity to the weak, the sick, the homeless; and courtesy to all mankind, even to their enemies.

God grant that that spirit may remain alive among us. For without it we shall not long be a strong nation; not indeed long a nation at all. And it is alive among us. Not that we, any of us, have enough of it—God forgive us for all our shortcomings. And God grant it may remain alive among us; for it is, as far as it goes, the likeness of Christ, the Maker and Ruler of the world.

"Christian," said a great genius and a great divine,

> "If thou wouldst learn to love,
> Thou first must learn to hate."

And if any one answer—"Hate? Even God hateth nothing that He has made." The rejoinder is,—And for that very reason God hates evil; because He has not made it, and it is ruinous to all that He has made.

Go you and do likewise. Hate what is wrong with all your heart, and mind, and soul, and strength. For so, and so only, you will shew that you love God with all your heart, and mind, and soul, and strength, likewise.

Oh pray—and that not once for all merely, but day by day, ay, almost hour by hour—Strengthen me, O Lord, to hate what Thou hatest, and love what Thou lovest; and therefore, whenever I see an opportunity, to put down what Thou hatest, and to help what Thou lovest—That so, at the last dread day, when every man shall be rewarded according to his works, you may have some answer to give to the awful question—On whose side wert thou in the battle of life? On the side of good men and of God, or on the side of bad men and the devil? Lest you find yourselves forced to reply—as too many will be forced—with surprise, and something like shame and confusion of face—I really do not know. I never thought about the matter at all. I never knew that there was any battle of life.

Never knew that there was any battle of life? And yet

you were christened, and signed with the sign of the Cross, in token that you should fight manfully under Christ's banner against sin, the world, and the devil, and continue Christ's faithful soldier and servant to your life's end.   Did it never occur to you that those words might possibly mean something? And you used to sing hymns, too, on earth, about "Soldiers of Christ, arise, And put your armour on."   What prophets, and apostles, and martyrs, and confessors meant by those words, you should know well enough.   Did it never occur to you that they might possibly mean something to you? That as long as the world was no better than it is, there was still a battle of life; and that you too were sworn to fight in it? How many will answer—Yes—Yes—But I thought that these words only meant having my soul saved, and going to heaven when I died.   And how did you expect to do that? By believing certain doctrines which you were told were true; and leading a tolerably respectable life, without which you would not have been received into society? Was that all which was needed to go to heaven? And was that all that was meant by fighting manfully under Christ's banner against sin, the world, and the devil? Why, Cyrus and his old Persians, 2,400 years ago, were nearer to the kingdom of God than that. They had a clearer notion of what the battle of life meant than that, when they said that not only the man who did a merciful or just deed, but the man who drained a swamp, tilled a field, made any little corner of the earth somewhat better than he found it, was fighting against Ahriman the evil spirit of darkness, on the side of Ormuzd the good god of light; and that as he had taken his part in Ormuzd's battle, he should share in Ormuzd's triumph.

Oh be at least able to say in that day,—Lord, I am no hero. I have been careless, cowardly, sometimes all but mutinous. Punishment I have deserved, I deny it not. But a traitor I have never been; a deserter I have never been. I have tried to fight on Thy side in Thy battle against evil. I have tried to do the duty which lay nearest me; and to leave whatever Thou didst commit to my charge a little better than I found it. I have not been good: but I have at least tried to be good. I have not done good, it may be, either: but I have at least tried to do good. Take the will for the deed, good Lord. Accept the partial self-sacrifice which Thou didst inspire, for the sake of the one perfect self-sacrifice which Thou didst fulfil upon the Cross. Pardon my faults, out of Thine own boundless pity for human weakness. Strike not my unworthy name off the roll-call of the noble and victorious army, which is the blessed company of all faithful people; and let me, too, be found written in the Book of Life: even though I stand the lowest and last upon its list. Amen.

SERMON XXII.

HEBREWS XII. 22, 23.

Ye are come to the city of the living God, and to the spirits of just men made perfect.

I HAVE quoted only part of the passage of Scripture in which these words occur. If you want a good employment for All Saints' Day, read the whole passage, the whole chapter; and no less, the 11th chapter, which comes before it: so will you understand better the meaning of All Saints' Day. But sufficient for the day is the good thereof, as well as the evil; and the good which I have to say this morning is—You are come to the spirits of just men made perfect; for this is All Saints' Day.

Into the presence of this noble company we have come: even nobler company, remember, than that which was spoken of in the text. For more than 1800 years have passed since the Epistle to the Hebrews was written: and how many thousands of just men and women, pure, noble, tender, wise, beneficent, have graced the earth since then, and left their mark upon mankind, and helped forward the hallowing of our heavenly Father's name, the coming of His kingdom, the doing of His will on earth as it is done in heaven; and helped therefore to abolish the superstition, the misrule, the vice, and therefore the misery of this struggling, moaning world. How many such has Christ sent on this earth during the last 1800 years. How many before that; before His own coming, for many a century and age. We know not, and we need not know. The records of Holy Scripture and of history strike with light an isolated mountain peak, or group of peaks, here and here through the ages; but between and beyond all is dark to us now. But it may not have been dark always. Scripture and history likewise hint to us of great hills far away, once brilliant in the one true sunshine which comes from God, now shrouded in the mist of ages, or literally turned away beyond our horizon by the revolution of our planet: and of lesser hills, too, once bright and green and fair, giving pasture to lonely flocks, sending down fertilizing streams into now forgotten valleys; themselves all but forgotten now, save by the God who made and blessed them.

Yes: many a holy soul, many a useful soul, many a saint who is now at God's right hand, has lived and worked, and been a blessing, himself blest, of whom the world, and even the Church, has never heard, who will never be seen or known again, till the day in which the Lord counteth up His jewels.

Let us rejoice in that thought on this day, above all days in the year. On this day we give special thanks to God for all His servants departed this life in His faith and fear.   Let us rejoice in the thought that we know not how many they are; only that they are an innumerable company, out of all tongues and nations, whom no man can number.   Let us rejoice that Christ's grace is richer, and not poorer, than our weak imaginations can conceive, or our narrow systems account for.   Let us rejoice that the goodly company in whose presence we stand, can be limited and defined by no mortal man, or school of men: but only by Him from whom, with the Father, proceeds for ever the Holy Spirit, the inspirer of all good; and who said of that Spirit—"The wind bloweth where it listeth, and thou hearest the sound thereof, but canst not tell whence it cometh, and whither it goeth.   So is every one who is born of the Spirit" —and who said again, "John came neither eating nor drinking, and ye said, He hath a devil.   The Son of man came eating and drinking, and ye say, Behold a man gluttonous and a winebibber, a friend of publicans and sinners.   But I say unto you, Verily wisdom is justified of all her children"—and who said again—when John said to Him, "Master, we saw one casting out devils in Thy name, and he followeth not us"—"Forbid him not. For I say to you, that he that doeth a miracle in My name will not lightly speak evil of Me"—and who said, lastly—and most awfully—that the unpardonable sin, either in this life or the life to come, was to attribute beneficent deeds to a bad origin, because they were performed by one who differed from us in opinion; and to say, "He casteth out devils by Beelzebub, prince of the devils."

These are words of our Lord, which we are specially bound to keep in our minds, with reverence and godly fear, on All Saints' Day, lest by arranging our calendar of saints according to our own notions of who ought to be a saint, and who ought not—that is, who agrees with our notions of perfection, and who does not—we exclude ourselves, by fastidiousness, from much unquestionably good company; and possibly mix ourselves up with not a little which is, to say the least, questionable.

Men in all ages, Churchmen or others, have fallen into this mistake. They have been but too ready to limit their calendar of saints; to narrow the thanksgivings which they offer to God on All Saints' Day.

The Romish Church has been especially faulty on this point. It has assumed, as necessary preliminaries for saintship — at least after the Christian era — the practice of, or at least the longing after, celibacy; and after the separation of the Eastern and Western Churches, unconditional submission to the Church of Rome. But how has this injured, if not spoiled, their exclusive calendar of saints. Amid apostles, martyrs, divines, who must be always looked on as among the very heroes and heroines of humanity, we find more than one fanatic persecutor; more than two or three clearly insane personages; and too many who all but justify the terrible sneer—that the Romish Calendar is the "Pantheon of Hysteria."

And Protestants, too—How have they narrowed the number of the spirits of just men made perfect; and confined the Pæan which should go up from the human race on All Saints' Day, till a "saint" has too often meant with them only a person who has gone through certain emotional experiences, and assented to certain subjective formulas, neither of which, according to the opinion of some of the soundest divines, both of the Romish, Greek, and Anglican communions, are to be found in the letter of Scripture as necessary to salvation; and who have, moreover, finished their course—doubtless often a holy, beneficent, and beautiful course—by a rapturous death-bed scene, which is more rare in the actual experience of clergymen, and, indeed, in the conscience and experience of human beings in general, than in the imaginations of the writers of religious romances.

But we of the Church of England, as by law established —and I recognize and obey, and shall hereafter recognize and obey, no other—have no need so to narrow our All Saints' Day; our joy in all that is noble and good which man has said or done in any age or clime. We have no need to define where formularies have not defined; to shut where they have opened; to curse where they either bless, or are humbly, charitably, and therefore divinely, silent. With a magnificent faith in the justice of the Father, and in the grace of Christ, and in the inspiration of the Holy Spirit, our Church bids us—Judge not the dead, lest ye be judged. Condemn not the dead, lest ye be condemned. For she bids us commit to the earth the corpses of all who die not "unbaptized," "excommunicate," or wilful suicides, and who are willing to lie in our consecrated ground; giving thanks to God that our dear brother has been delivered from the miseries of this sinful world, and in sure and certain hope of the resurrection to eternal life.

At least: we of the Abbey of Westminster have a right to hold this; for we, thank God, act on it, and have acted on it for many a year. We have a right to our wide, free, charitable, and truly catholic conception of All Saints' Day. Ay, if we did not use our right, these walls would use it for us; and in us would our Lord's words be fulfilled—If we were silent, the very stones beneath our feet would cry out.

For hither we gather, as far as is permitted us, and hither we gather proudly, the mortal dust of every noble soul who has done good work for the British nation; accepting each and all of them as gifts from the Father of lights, from whom proceedeth every good and perfect gift, as sent to this nation by that Lord Jesus Christ who is the King of all the nations upon earth; and acknowledging—for fear of falling into that Pelagian heresy, which is too near the heart of every living man—that all wise words which they have spoken, all noble deeds which they have done, have come, must have come, from The One eternal source of wisdom, of nobleness, of every form of good; even from the Holy Spirit of God.

We make no severe or minute inquiries here. We leave them, if they must be made, to God the Judge of all things, and Christ who knows the secrets of the hearts; to Him who is merciful in this: that He rewardeth every man according to his works.

All we ask is—and all we dare ask—of divine or statesman, poet or warrior, musician or engineer—of

Dryden or of Handel—of Isaac Watts or of Charles Dickens—but why go on with the splendid diversities of the splendid catalogue?—What was your work? Did we admire you for it? Did we love you for it? And why? Because you made us in some way or other better men. Because you helped us somewhat toward whatsoever things are pure, true, just, honourable, of good report. Because, if there was any virtue—that is, true valour and manhood; if there was any praise—that is, just honour in the sight of men, and therefore surely in the sight of the Son of man, who died for men; you helped us to think on such things. You, in one word, helped to make us better men.

Welcome then, friends unknown—and, alas! friends known, and loved, and lost—welcome into England's Pantheon, not of superstitious and selfish hysteria, but of beneficent and healthy manhood.

Your words and your achievements have gone out into all lands, and your sound unto the ends of the world; and let them go, and prosper in that for which the Lord of man has sent them. Our duty is, to guard your sacred dust. Our duty is, to point out your busts, your monuments around these ancient walls, to all who come, of every race and creed; as proofs that the ancient spirit is not dead; that Christ has not deserted the nation of England, while He sends into it such men as you; that Christ has not deserted the Church of England, while He gives her grace to recognize and honour such men as you, and to pray Christ that He would keep up the sacred succession of virtue, talent, beneficence, patriotism; and make us, most unworthy, at last worthy, one at least here and there, of the noble dead, above whose dust we now serve God.

Yes, so ought we in Westminster to keep our All Saints' Day; in giving thanks to God for the spirits of just men made perfect. Not only for those just men and women innumerable, who—as I said at first—have graced this earth during the long ages of the past: but specially for those who lie around us here; with whom we can enter, and have entered already, often, into spiritual communion closer than that, almost, of child with parent; whose writings we can read, whose deeds we can admire, whose virtues we can copy, and to whom we owe a debt of gratitude, we and our children after us, which never can be repaid.

And if ever the thought comes over us—But these men had their faults, mistakes—Oh, what of that?

> Nothing is left of them
> Now, but pure manly.

Let us think of them: not as they were, compassed round with infirmities—as who is not?—knowing in part, and seeing in part, as St Paul himself, in the zenith of his inspiration, said that he knew; and saw, as through a glass, darkly.

Let us think of them not as they were, the spirits of just men imperfect: but as the spirits of just men made, or to be made hereafter, perfect; when, as St Paul says, "that which is in part is done away, and that which is perfect is come." And let us trust Christ for them, as we would trust Him for ourselves; sure "that the path of the just is as a shining light, which shineth more and more unto the perfect day."

Ah, how many lie in this Abbey, to meet whom in the world to come, would be an honour most undeserved !

How many more worthy, and therefore more likely, than any of us here, to behold that endless All Saints' Day, to which may God in His mercy, in spite of all our shortcomings, bring us all.   Amen.

SERMON XXIII.

DE PROFUNDIS.

Out of the deep have I called unto Thee, O Lord: Lord, hear my
voice. O let Thine ears consider well the voice of my complaint.
If Thou, Lord, wilt be extreme to mark what is done amiss, O
Lord, who may abide it? For there is mercy with Thee, therefore shalt Thou be feared. I look for the Lord; my soul doth
wait for Him: in His word is my trust. My soul fleeth unto
the Lord before the morning watch: I say, before the morning
watch. O Israel, trust in the Lord: for with the Lord there is
mercy, and with Him is plenteous redemption. And He shall
redeem Israel from all his sins.

LET us consider this psalm awhile, for it is a precious
heirloom to mankind. It has been a guide and a comfort to thousands and tens of thousands. Rich and poor,
old and young, Jews and Christians, Romans, Greeks,
and Protestants, have been taught by it the character of
God; and taught to love Him, and trust in Him, in
whom is mercy, therefore He shall be feared.

The Psalmist cries out of the deep; out of the deep
of sorrow, perhaps, and bereavement, and loneliness; or
out of the deep of poverty; or out of the deep of persecution and ill-usage; or out of the deep of sin, and

shame, and weakness which he hates yet cannot conquer; or out of the deep of doubt, and anxiety—and ah! how common is that deep; and how many there are in it that swim hard for their lives : may God help them and bring them safe to land;—or out of the deep of overwork, so common now-a-days, when duty lies sore on aching shoulders, a burden too heavy to be borne.

Out of some one of the many deeps into which poor souls fall at times, and find themselves in deep water where no ground is, and in the mire wherein they are ready to sink, the Psalmist cries. But out of the deep he cries—to God. To God, and to none else.

He goes to the fountain-head, to the fount of deliverance, and of forgiveness. For he feels that he needs, not only deliverance, but forgiveness likewise. His sorrow may not be altogether his own fault. What we call in our folly "accident" and "chance," and "fortune,"—but which is really the wise providence and loving will of God—may have brought him low into the deep. Or the injustice, cruelty, and oppression of men may have brought him low; or many another evil hap. But be that as it may, he dares not justify himself. He cannot lift up altogether clean hands. He cannot say that his sorrow is none of his own fault, and his mishap altogether undeserved. If Thou, Lord, wert extreme to mark what is done amiss, O Lord, who could abide it? "Not I," says the Psalmist. "Not I," says every human being who knows himself; and knows too well that—"If we say we have no sin, we deceive ourselves, and the truth is not in us."

But the Psalmist says likewise, "There is forgiveness with Thee, therefore shalt Thou be feared."

My friends, consider this; the key of the whole psalm; the gospel and good news, for the sake of which the psalm has been preserved in Holy Scripture, and handed down to us.

God is to be feared, because He is merciful. It is worth while to fear Him, because He is merciful, and of great kindness, and hateth nothing that He hath made; and willeth not the death of a sinner, but rather that he should turn from his wickedness and live.

Superstitious people, in all ages, heathens always, and sometimes, I am sorry to say, Christians likewise, have had a very different reason, an opposite reason, for fearing God.

They have said: Not—there is mercy: but there is anger with God: therefore shall He be feared. They have said—We must fear God, because He is wrathful, and terrible, and ready to punish; and is extreme to mark what is done amiss, and willeth the death of a sinner: and therefore they have not believed, when Holy Scripture told them, that God was love, and that God so loved the world, that He gave His only-begotten Son, and sent Him to visit the world in great humility, that the world through Him might be saved.

God has seemed to them only a proud, stern, and formidable being; a condemning judge, and not a merciful Father; and therefore, when they have found themselves in the deep of misery, they have cried out of it to saints, angels, the Virgin Mary; or even to sun, moon, and stars, and all the powers of nature; or even, again—what is more foolish still,—to astrologers, wizards, mediums, and quacks of every shape and hue; to any one and any thing, rather than to God.

But do not you do so, my friends. Fix it in your hearts and minds; and fix it now, before you fall into the deep, as most are apt to do before they die; lest, when the dark day comes, you have no time to learn in adversity the lesson which you should have learnt in prosperity. Fix in your hearts and minds the blessed Gospel and good news—"There is mercy with Thee, O God; therefore shalt Thou be feared." There is mercy with Him, pity, tenderness, sympathy; a heart which can be touched with the feeling of our infirmities; which knoweth what is in man; which despiseth not the work of His own hands; which remembereth our weak frame, and knoweth that we are but dust: else the spirit would fail before Him, and the souls which He has made. Think of God as that which He is—a compassionate God, a long-suffering God, a generous God, a magnanimous God, a truly royal God; in one word, a Perfect God; who causeth His sun to shine on the evil and on the good, and sendeth His rain on the just and on the unjust; a God who cannot despise, cannot neglect, cannot lose His patience with any poor soul of man; who sets Himself against none but the insolent, the proud, the malicious, the mean, the wilfully stupid and ignorant and frivolous. Against those who exalt themselves, whether as terrible tyrants or merely contemptible boasters, He exalts Himself; and will shew them, sooner or later, whether He or they be the stronger; whether He or they be the wiser. But for the poor soul who is abased, who is down, and in the depth; who feels his own weakness, folly, ignorance, sinfulness, and out of that deep cries to God as a lost child crying after its father—even a lost lamb bleating after the ewe—of that poor soul, be his prayers never so confused, stupid and ill-expressed—of him it is written: "The Lord helpeth them that fall, and lifteth up all those that are down. He is nigh to all that call on Him, yea, to all that call upon Him faithfully. He will fulfil the desire of those that fear Him, He also will hear their cry and will help them."

Yes. To all such does God the Father, God who made heaven and earth, hold up, as it were, His only-begotten Son, Christ, hanging on the Cross for us; and say: Behold thy God. Behold the brightness of God's glory, and the express image of God's person. Behold what God gave for thee, even His only-begotten Son. Behold that in which God the Father was well pleased: in His Son; not condemning you, not destroying you, but humbling Himself, dying Himself awhile, that you may live for ever. Look; and by seeing the Son, see the Father also—your Father, and the Father of the spirits of all flesh; and know that His essence and His name is—Love.

Therefore, when you are in the deep of sorrow, whatever that depth may be, cry to God. To God Himself; and to none but God. If you can go to the pure fountain-head, why drink of the stream, which must have gathered something of defilement as it flows? If you can get light from the sun itself, why take lamp or candle in place of his clear rays? If you can go to God Himself, why go to any of God's creatures, however holy, pure, and loving? Go to God, who is light of light, and life of life; the source of all light, the source of all life, all love, all goodness, all mercy. From Him all goodness flows. All goodness which ever has been, shall be, or can be, is His alone, the fruit of His Spirit. Go then to Him Himself. Out of the depth, however deep, cry unto God and God Himself. If David, the Jew of old, could do so, much more can we, who are baptized into Christ; much more can we, who have access by one Spirit to the Father; much more can we, who—if we know who we are and where we are—should come boldly to the throne of grace, to find mercy and grace to help us in the time of need.

Boldness. That is a bold word: but it is St Paul's, not mine. And by shewing that boldness, we shall shew that we indeed fear God. We shall shew that we reverence God. We shall shew that we trust God. For so, and so only, we shall obey God. If a sovereign or a sage should bid you come to him, would you shew reverence by staying away? Would you shew reverence by refusing his condescension? You may shew that you are afraid of him; that you do not trust him: but that is not to shew reverence, but irreverence.

If God calls, you are bound by reverence to come, however unworthy. If He bids you, you must obey, however much afraid. You must trust Him; you must take Him at His word; you must confide in His goodness, in His justice, in His wisdom: and since He bids you, go boldly to His throne, and find Him what He is, a gracious Lord.

My friends, to you, every one of you—however weak, however ignorant, ay, however sinful, if you desire to be delivered from those sins—this grace is given; liberty to cry out of the depth to God Himself, who made sun and stars, all heaven and earth; liberty to stand face to face with the Father of the spirits of all flesh, and cling to the one Being who can never fail nor change; even to the one immortal eternal God, of whom it is written, "Thou, Lord, in the beginning hast laid the foundation of the earth, and the heavens are the work of Thy hands. They shall perish, but Thou shalt endure. They all shall wax old, like a garment, and as a vesture shalt Thou change them, and they shall be changed. But Thou art the same, and Thy years shall not fail."

But it is written again, "My soul waits for the Lord." Yes, if you can trust in the God who cannot change, you can afford to wait; you need not be impatient; as it is written—"Fret not thyself, lest thou be moved to do evil;" and again—"He that believeth shall not make haste." For God, in whom you trust, is not a man that He should lie, nor a son of man that He should repent. Hath He promised, and shall He not do it? His word is like the rain and dew, which fall from heaven, and return not to it again useless, but give seed to the sower and bread to the eater. So is every man that trusteth in Him. His kingdom, says the Lord, is as if a man should put seed into the ground, and sleep and wake, and the seed should grow up, he knoweth not how. So the seed which we sow—the seed of repentance, the seed of humility, the seed of sorrowful prayers for help—it too shall take root, and grow, and bring forth fruit, we know not how, in the good time of God, who cannot change. We may be sad; we may be weary; our eyes may wait and watch for the Lord as the Psalmist says; more than they that watch for the morning: but it must be as those who watch for the morning, for the morning which must and will come, for the sun which will surely rise, and the day which will surely dawn, and the Saviour who will surely deliver, and the God who is merciful in this— that He rewardeth every man according to his work.

"Oh trust in the Lord. For with the Lord there is mercy, and with Him is plenteous redemption; and He shall deliver His people from all their sins."

From their sins. Not merely from the punishment of their sins; not always from the punishment of their sins in this life: but, what is better far, from the sins themselves; from the sins which bring them into fresh and needless troubles; and which make the old troubles, which cannot now be escaped, intolerable.

From all their sins. Not only from the great sins, which, if persisted in, will surely destroy both body and soul in hell: but from the little sins which do so easily beset us; from little bad habits, tempers, lazinesses, weaknesses, ignorances, which hamper and hinder us all every day when we try to do our duty. From all these will the Lord deliver us, by the blood of Christ, and by the inspiration of His Holy Spirit, that we may be able at last to say to children and friends, and all whom we love and leave behind us—

"Oh taste and see that the Lord is gracious. Blessed is the man that trusteth in Him."

Yes. This at least we may do—Trust in our God, and thank God that we may do it; for if men may not do that, then is that true of them which Homer said of old—that man is more miserable than all the beasts of the field. For the animals look neither forward nor back. They live but for the present moment; and pain and grief, being but for the moment, fall lightly upon them. But we—we who have the fearful power of looking back, and looking forward—we who can feel regret and remorse for the past, anxiety and terror for the future—to us at times life would be scarce worth having, if we had not a right to cry with all our hearts—

"O God, in Thee have I trusted, let me never be confounded."

SERMON XXIV.

THE BLESSING AND THE CURSE.

Preached on Whit-Sunday.

DEUT. XXX. 19, 20.

I call heaven and earth to record this day against you, that I have set before you life and death, blessing and cursing: therefore choose life, that both thou and thy seed may live: that thou mayest love the Lord thy God, and that thou mayest obey His voice, and that thou mayest cleave unto Him: for He is thy life, and the length of thy days: that thou mayest dwell in the land which the Lord sware unto thy fathers, to Abraham, to Isaac, and to Jacob, to give them.

THESE words, the book of Deuteronomy says, were spoken by Moses to all the Israelites shortly before his death. He had led them out of Egypt, and through the wilderness. They were in sight of the rich land of Canaan, where they were to settle and to dwell for many hundred years. Moses, the book says, went over again with them all the Law, the admirable and divine Law, which they were to obey, and by which they were to govern and order themselves in the land of Canaan. He had told them that they owed all to God Himself; that God had delivered them out of slavery in Egypt; God had led them to the land of Canaan; God had given them just laws and right statutes, which if they kept, they would live long in their new home, and become a great and mighty nation. Then he calls heaven and earth to witness that he had set before them life and death, blessing and cursing. If they trusted in the one true God, and served Him, and lived as men should, who believed that a just and loving God cared for them, then they would live; then a blessing would come on them, and their children, on their flocks and herds, on their land and all in it. But if they forgot God, and began to worship the sun, and the moon, and the stars, the earth and the weather, like the nations round them, then they would die; they would grow superstitious, cowardly, lazy, and profligate, and therefore weak and miserable, like the wretched Canaanites whom they were going to drive out; and then they would die. Their souls would die in them, and they would become less than men, and at last—as the Canaanites had become—worse than brutes, till their numbers would diminish, and they would be left, Moses says, few in number and at last perish out of the good land which God had given them.

So, he says, you know how to live, and you know how to die. Choose between them this day.

They knew the road to wealth, health, prosperity and order, peace and happiness, and life: and they knew the road to ruin, poverty, weakness, disease, shame and death.

They knew both roads; for God had set them before them.

And you know both roads; for God has set them before you.

Then he says—I call heaven and earth to witness against you this day, that I have set before you life and death, blessing and cursing.

He called heaven and earth to witness. That was no empty figure of speech. If you will recollect the story of the Israelites, you will see plainly enough what Moses meant.

The heaven would witness against them. The same stars which would look down on their freedom and prosperity in Canaan, had looked down on all their slavery and misery in Egypt, hundreds of years before. Those same stars had looked down on their simple forefathers, Abraham, Isaac, and Jacob, wandering with their flocks and herds out of the mountains of the far north. That heaven had seen God's mercies and care of them, for now five hundred years. Everything had changed round them: but those stars, that sun, that moon, were the same still, and would be the same for ever. They were witnesses to them of the unchangeable God, those heavens above. They would seem to say—Just as the heavens above you are the same, wherever you go, and whatever you are like, so is the God who dwells above the heaven; unchangeable, everlasting, faithful, and true, full of light and love; from whom comes down every good and perfect gift, in whom is neither variableness nor shadow of turning. Do you turn to Him continually, and as often as you turn away from Him: and you shall find Him still the same; governing you by unchangeable law, keeping His promise for ever.

And the earth would witness against them. That fair land of Canaan whither they were going, with its streams and wells spreading freshness and health around; its rich corn valleys, its uplands covered with vines, its sweet mountain pastures, a very garden of the Lord, cut off and defended from all the countries round by sandy deserts and dreary wildernesses; that land would be a witness to them, at their daily work, of God's love and mercy to their forefathers. The ruins of the old Canaanite cities would be a witness to them, and say— Because of their sins the Lord drove out these old heathens from before you. Copy their sins, and you will share their ruin. Do as they did, and you will surely die like them. God has given you life, here in this fair land of Canaan; beware how you choose death, as the Canaanites chose it. They died the death which comes by sin; and God has given you life, the life which is by righteousness. Be righteous men, and just, and God-fearing, if you wish to keep this land, you, and your children after you.

And now, my dear friends, if Moses could call heaven and earth to witness against those old Jews, that he had set before them life and death, a blessing and a curse, may we not do the same? Does not the heaven above our heads, and the earth beneath our feet, witness against us here? Do they not say to us—God has given you life and blessing. If you throw that away, and choose instead death and a curse; it is your own fault, not God's?

Look at the heaven above us. Does not that witness against us? Has it not seen, for now fifteen hundred years and more, God's goodness to us, and to our forefathers? All things have changed; language, manners, customs, religion. We have changed our place, as the Israelites did; and dwell in a different land from our forefathers: but that sky abides for ever. That same sun, that moon, those stars shone down upon our heathen forefathers, when the Lord chose them, and brought them out of the German forests into this good land of England, that they might learn to worship no more the sun, and the moon, and the storm, and the thunder-cloud, but to worship Him, the living God who made all heaven and earth. That sky looked down upon our forefathers, when the first missionaries baptized them into the Church of Christ, and England became a Christian land, and made a covenant with God and Christ for ever to walk in His laws which He has set before us. From that heaven, ever since, hath God been sending rain and fruitful seasons, filling our hearts with food and gladness, for a witness of His love and fostering care; prospering us, whensoever we have kept His laws, above all other nations upon earth. Shall not that heaven witness against us? Into that heaven ascended Christ the Lord, that He might fill all things with His power and His rule, and might send from thence on us His Holy Spirit, the Spirit whom we worship this day, the spirit of wisdom and understanding, the spirit of counsel and might, the spirit of knowledge and the fear of the Lord. By that same Spirit, and by none other, have been thought all the noble thoughts which Englishmen ever thought. By that Spirit have been spoken all the noble words which Englishmen ever spoke. By that Spirit have been done all the noble deeds which Englishmen have ever done. To that Spirit we owe all that is truly noble, truly strong, truly stable, in our English life. It is He that has given us power to get wealth, to keep wealth, to use wealth. And if we begin to deny that, as we are inclined to do now-a-days; if we lay our grand success and prosperity to the account of our own cleverness, our own ability; if we say, as Moses warned the Israelites they would say, in the days of their success and prosperity, not—" It is God who has given us power to get wealth," but—"Mine arm, and the might of my hand, has gotten me this wealth;"—in plain words—If we begin to do what we are all too apt to do just now, to worship our own brains instead of God: then the heaven above us will witness against us, this Whitsuntide above all seasons in the year; and say—Into heaven the Lord ascended who died for you on the Cross. From heaven He sent down gifts for you, and your forefathers, even while you were His enemies, that the Lord God might dwell among you. And behold, instead of thanking God, fearing God, and confessing that you are nothing, and God is all, you talk as if you were the arbiters of your own futures, the makers of your own gifts. Instead of giving God the glory, you take the glory to yourselves. Instead of declaring the glory of God, like the heavens, and shewing his handiwork, like the stars, you shew forth your own glory and boast of your own handiwork. Beware, and fear; as your forefathers feared, and lived, because they gave the glory to God.

And shall not the earth witness against us? Look round, when you go out of church, upon this noble English land. Why is it not, as many a land far richer in soil and climate is now, a desolate wilderness; the land lying waste, and few men left in it, and those who are left robbing and murdering each other, every man's hand against his fellow, till the wild beasts of the field increase upon them? In that miserable state now is many a noble land, once the very gardens of the world—Judæa, and almost all the East, which was once the very garden of the Lord, as thick with living men as a hive is with bees, and vast sheets both of North Africa, and of South and of North America. Why is not England thus? Why, but because the Lord set before our forefathers life and death, blessing and cursing; and our forefathers chose life, and lived; and it was well with them in the land which God gave to them, because they chose blessing, and God blessed them accordingly? In spite of many mistakes and shortcomings—for they were sinful mortal men, as we are—they chose life and a blessing; and clave unto the Lord their God, and kept His covenant; and they left behind, for us their children, these churches, these cathedrals, for an everlasting sign that the Lord was with us, as He had been with them, and would be with our children after us.

Ah, my friends, while we look round us over the face of this good land, and see everywhere the churches pointing up to heaven, each amid towns and villages which have never seen war or famine for now long centuries, all thriving and improving year by year, and which never for 800 years have been trodden by the foot of an invading enemy, one ought to feel, if one has a thoughtful and God-fearing heart—Verily God has set before us life and blessing, and prospered us above all nations upon earth; and if we do not cleave to Him, we shall shew ourselves fools above all nations upon earth.

And then when one reads the history of England; when one thinks over the history of any one city, even one country parish; above all, when one looks into the history of one's own foolish heart: one sees how often, though God has given us freely life and blessing, we have been on the point of choosing death and the curse instead; of saying—We will go our own way and not God's way. The land is ours, not God's; the houses are our own, not God's; our souls are our own, not God's. We are masters, and who is master over us? That is the way to choose death, and the curse, shame and poverty and ruin, my friends; and how often we have been on the point of choosing it. What has saved us? What has kept us from it? Certainly not our own righteousness, nor our own wisdom, nor our own faith. After reading the history of England; or after recollecting our own lives—the less we say of them the better.

What has kept us from ruin so long? We are all day long forgetting the noble things which God did for our forefathers. Why does not God in return remember our sins, and the sins of our forefathers? Why is He not angry with us for ever? Why, in spite of all our shortcomings and backslidings, are we prospering here this day?

I know not, my friends, unless it be for this one reason, That into that heaven which witnesses against us, the merciful and loving Christ is ascended; that He is ever making intercession for us, a High-priest who can be touched with the feeling of our infirmities; and that He has received gifts for men, even for His enemies —as we have too often been—that the Lord God might dwell among us. Yes. He ascended on high that He might send down His Holy Spirit; and that Spirit is among us, working patiently and lovingly in many hearts —would that I could say in all—giving men right judgments; putting good desires into their hearts; and enabling them to put them into good practice.

The Holy Spirit is the life of England, and of the Church of England, and of every man, whether he belongs to the Church or not, who loves the good, and desires to do it, and to see it done. And those in whom the Holy Spirit dwells, are the salt of England, which keeps it from decay. They are those who have chosen life and blessing, and found them. Oh may God increase their number more and more; till all know Him from the least unto the greatest; and the land be filled with the knowledge of the Lord, as the waters cover the sea.

And then shall all days be Whit-Sundays; and the Name of the Father be hallowed indeed, and His kingdom come, and His will be done on earth, as it is in heaven.

SERMON XXV.

THE SILENCE OF FAITH.

PSALM CXXXI.

Lord, my heart is not haughty, nor mine eyes lofty: neither do I
exercise myself in great matters, or in things too high for me.
Surely I have behaved and quieted myself, as a child that is
weaned of his mother: my soul is even as a weaned child.   Let
Israel hope in the Lord from henceforth and for ever.

WE know not at what period of David's life this psalm
was written.   We know not what matters they were
which were too high for him to meddle with; matters
about which he had to refrain his soul; to quiet his
feelings; to suspend his judgment; to check his curiosity,
and say about them simply—Trust in the Lord.

We do not know, I say, what these great matters,
these mysteries were.   But that concerns us little.   Human life, human fortune, human history, human agony—
nay, the whole universe, the more we know of it, is full
of such mysteries.   Only the shallow and the conceited
are unaware of their presence.   Only the shallow and
the conceited pretend to explain them, and have a Why
ready for every How.   David was not like them.   His
was too great a mind to be high-minded; too deep a

heart to have proud looks, and to pretend, to himself or to others, that he knew the whole counsel of God.

Solomon his son had the same experience. For him, too, in spite of all his wisdom, the mystery of Providence was too dark. Though a man laboured to seek it, yet should he not find it out. All things seemed, at least, to come alike to all. There was one event to the righteous and to the wicked; to the clean and to the unclean. Vanity of vanity; all was vanity. Of making books there was no end, and much study was a weariness to the flesh. And the conclusion of the whole matter was—Fear God, and keep His commandments. That—and not to pry into the unfathomable will of God—was the whole duty of man.

Job, too: what is the moral of the whole book of Job, save that God's ways are unsearchable, and His paths past finding out? The Lord, be it remembered, in the closing scene of the book, vouchsafes to Job no explanation whatsoever of his affliction. Instead of telling him why he has been so sorely smitten; instead of bidding him even look up and trust, He silences Job by the mere plea of His own power. Where wast thou when I laid the foundation of the earth? Declare, if thou hast understanding. When the morning stars sang together; and all the sons of God shouted for joy. Shall he that contendeth with The Almighty instruct Him? He that reproveth God, let him answer.

But, it may be said, these are Old Testament sayings. The Patriarchs and Prophets had not that full light of knowledge of the mind of God which the Evangelists and

Apostles had. What do the latter, the writers of the New Testament, say, with that fuller knowledge of God, which they gained through Jesus Christ our Lord?

My friends—This is not, I trust, by God's great goodness, the last time that I am to preach in this Abbey. What the Evangelists and Apostles taught, which the Prophets and Psalmists did not teach, I hope to tell you, as far as I know, hereafter.

But this I am bound to tell you beforehand—That there are no truer words in the Articles of the Church of England than those in the VIIth Article—that the Old Testament is not contrary to the New; for both in the Old and New Testament everlasting life is offered to mankind by Christ, the only Mediator between God and man, being both God and man.

Yes. That the Old Testament is not contrary to the New, I believe with my whole heart and soul. And therefore to those who say that the Apostles had solved the whole mystery of human life, its sins, its sorrows, its destinies, I must reply that such is not the case, at least with the most gifted of all the writers of the New Testament. We may think fit to claim omniscience for St Paul: but he certainly does not claim it for himself.

When he is vouchsafed a glimpse of the high counsels of God, he exclaims, as one dazzled—"Oh the depth of the riches both of the wisdom and knowledge of God! How unsearchable are His judgments, and His ways past finding out! For who hath known the mind of the Lord, or who hath been His counsellor?"—While of himself he speaks in a very different tone—"Even though he have been," as he says, "caught up into the third heaven, and heard words unspeakable, which it is not lawful for a man to utter," yet " he knows," he says, " in part ; he prophesies in part ; but when that which is perfect comes, that which is partial shall be done away."   He is as the child to the full-grown man, into which he hopes to develop in the future life.   He " sees as in a glass darkly, but then face to face."   He "knows now in part."   Then—but not till then—will he " know even as he is known."   Nay, more. In the ninth chapter of his Epistle to the Romans, he does not hesitate to push to the utmost that plea of God's absolute sovereignty which we found in the book of Job.

" He has mercy on whom He will have mercy; and whom He will He hardeneth."   And if any say, " Why doth He then find fault ?   For who hath resisted His will ?"   " Who art thou that repliest against God ?   Shall the thing formed say to him that formed it, Why hast thou made me thus ?   Hath not the potter power over the clay, of the same lump to make one vessel to honour, and another to dishonour ?"

What those words may mean, or may not mean, I do not intend to argue now.   I only quote them to shew you that St Paul, just as much as any Old Testament thinker, believed that there were often mysteries, ay, tragedies, in the lives, not only of individuals, nor of families, but of whole races, to which we shortsighted mortals could assign no rational or moral final cause, but must simply do that which Spinoza forbade us to do, namely—" In every unknown case, flee unto God;" and say—" It is the Lord, let Him do what seemeth Him good ;"—certain of this, which the Cross and Passion of our Lord Jesus Christ shewed forth as nothing else in heaven or earth could shew—that the will of God toward man is an utterly good will ; and that therefore what seemeth good to Him, will be good in act and fact.

It is this faith, and I believe this faith alone, which can enable truly feeling spirits to keep anything like equanimity, if they dwell long and earnestly on the miseries of mankind; on sorrow, pain, bereavement ; on the fate of many a widow and orphan ; on sudden, premature, and often agonizing death—but why pain you with a catalogue of ills, which all, save—thank God—the youngest, know too well?

And it is that want of faith in the will and character of a living God, which makes, and will always make, infidelity a sad state of mind—a theory of man and the universe, which contains no gospel or good news for man.

I do not speak now of atheism, dogmatic, selfsatisfied, insolent cynic. I speak especially to-night of a form of unbelief far more attractive, which is spreading, I believe, among people often of high intellect, often of virtuous life, often of great attainments in art, science, or literature. Such repudiate, and justly, the name of theists : but they decline, and justly, the name of atheists. They would—the finest and purest spirits among them—accept only too heartily the whole of the Psalm which I have chosen for my text, save its ascription and the last verse. We too—they would say—do not wish to be high-minded, and dogmatize, and assert, and condemn. We too do not wish to meddle with matters too high for us, or for any human intellect. We too wish to refrain ourselves from asserting what—however pleasant—we cannot prove; and to wean ourselves—however really painful the process—from the milk, the mere child's food, on which Mother Church has brought up the nations of Europe for the last 1500 years. But for that very reason, as for asking us to trust in The Lord, either for this life, or an eternal life to come, do not ask that of us.

We do not say that there is no God; no Providence of God; no life beyond the grave: only we say, that we cannot find them. They may exist: or they may not. But to us; and as we believe to all mankind if they used their reason aright, they are unthinkable, and therefore unknowable. God we see not: but this we see—Man, tortured by a thousand ills; and then, alas, perishing just as the dumb beasts perish. We see death, decay, pain, sorrow, bereavement, weakness; and these produced, not merely by laws of nature, in which, however terrible, we could stoically acquiesce; but worse still, by accident—the sports of seeming chances—and those often so slight and mean. Man in his fullest power, woman in her highest usefulness, the victim not merely of the tempest or the thunderstroke, but of a fallen match, a stumbling horse.

Therefore the sight of so much human woe, without a purpose, and without a cause, is too much for them: as, without faith in God, it ought to be too much for us.

And therefore in their poetry and in their prose—and they are masters, some of them, both of poetry and of prose—there is a weary sadness, a tender despair, which one must not praise: yet which one cannot watch without sympathy and affection. For the mystery of human vanity and vexation of spirit; the mystery which weighed down the soul of David, and of Solomon, and of him who sang the song of Job, and of St Paul, and of St Augustine, and all the great Theologians of old time, is to them nought but utter darkness. For they see not yet, as our great modern poet says,

> Hands
> Athwart the darkness, shaping man.

They see not yet athwart the darkness a face, most human yet divine, of utter sympathy and love; and hear not yet—oh let me say once more not yet of such fine souls—the only words which can bring true comfort to one who feels for his fellow-men, amid the terrible chances and changes of this mortal life—

"Let not your heart be troubled. Believe in God, and believe also in Me."

"All power is given to Me in heaven and in earth."

"Lo I am with you even to the end of the world."

Oh let us, to whom God has given that most undeserved grace, by the confession of a true faith to acknowledge the glory of the eternal Trinity, and in the power of the Divine Majesty to worship the Unity—Let us, I say, beseech God that He would give to them, as well as to us, that comfortable and wholesome faith;

and evermore defend them and us—if it seem good in
His gracious sight—from all adversity.

And surely we need that faith—those of us at least
who know what we have lost—in the face of such a cata-
strophe as was announced in this Abbey on this day
week; which thrilled this congregation with the awful
news—That one of the most gifted men in Europe; the
most eloquent of all our preachers—the most energetic
of all our prelates; the delight of so many of the most
refined and cultivated; the comforter of so many pious
souls, not only by his sermons, not only by his secret
counsels, but by those exquisite Confirmation addresses,
to have lost which is a spiritual loss incalculable—those
Confirmation addresses which touched and ennobled
the hearts alike of children and of parents, and made so
many spirits, young and old, indebted to him from
thenceforth for ever—That this man, with his enormous
capacity and will for doing his duty like a valiant man,
and doing each duty better than any of us his clergy had
ever seen it done before—with his genius too, now so
rare, and yet so needed, for governing his fellow-men—
That he, in the fulness of his power, his health, his
practical example, his practical success, should vanish in
a moment : and that immense natural vitality, that organism of forces so various and so delicate, just as it was
developing to perfection under long and careful self-
education, should be lost for ever to this earth : leaving
England, and her colonies, and indeed all Christendom,
so much the poorer, so much the more weak; and
inflicting—forget not that—a bitter pang on hundreds of

loving hearts : and all by reason of the stumbling of a horse.

And why? Our reason, our conscience, our moral sense ; that, by virtue of which we are not brutes, but men, forces us to ask that question : even if no answer be found to it in earth or heaven. What was the important *why* which lay hid behind that little how ?—The means were so paltry: the effect was so vast—There must have been a final cause, a purpose, for that death : or the fact would be altogether hideous—a scribble without a meaning—a skeleton without a soul. Why did he die ?

"I became dumb and opened not my mouth; for it was Thy doing."

So says the Burial psalm. So let us say likewise.

"I became dumb:" not with rage, not with despair; but because it was Thy doing; and therefore it was done well. It was the deed, not of chance, not of necessity: for had it been, then those who loved him might have been excused had they cursed chance, cursed necessity, cursed the day in which they entered a universe so cruel, so capricious. Not so. For it was the deed of The Father, without whom a sparrow falls not to the ground; of The Son, who died upon the Cross in the utterness of His desire to save; of The Holy Ghost, who is the Lord and Giver of life to all created things.

It was the deed of One who delights in life and not in death; in bliss and not in woe; in light and not in darkness; in order and not in anarchy; in good and not in evil. It had a final cause, a meaning, a purpose: and that purpose is very good.   What it is, we know not: and we need not know.   To guess at it would be indeed to meddle with matters too high for us.   So let us be dumb: but dumb not from despair, but from faith; dumb not like a wretch weary with calling for help which does not come, but dumb like a child sitting at its mother's feet; and looking up into her face, and watching her doings; understanding none of them as yet, but certain that they all are done in Love.

SERMON XXVI.

GOD AND MAMMON.

MATTHEW VI. 24.

Ye cannot serve God and Mammon.

THIS is part of the Gospel for this Sunday; and a specially fit text for this day, which happens to be St Matthew's Day.

On this day we commemorate one who made up his mind, once and for all, that whoever could serve God and money at once, he could not: and who therefore threw up all his prospects in life—which were those of a peculiarly lucrative profession, that of a farmer of Roman taxes—in order to become the wandering disciple of a reputed carpenter's son. He became, it is true, in due time, an Apostle, an Evangelist, and a Martyr; and if posthumous fame be worth the ambition of any man, Matthew the publican—Saint Matthew as we call him—has his share thereof, because he discovered, like a wise man, that he could not serve God and money; and therefore, when Jesus saw him sitting at the receipt of custom, and bade him "Follow Me," he rose up, and left his money-bags, and followed Him, whom he afterwards discovered to be no less than God made man.

"Ye cannot serve God and Mammon."

It is very difficult to make men believe these words. So difficult, that our Lord Himself could not make the Jews believe them, especially the rich and comfortable religious people among them. When He told them that they could not serve two masters; that they could not worship God and money at the same time, the Pharisees, who were covetous. derided Him. They laughed to scorn the notion that they could not be very religious, and respectable, and so forth, and yet set their hearts on making money all the while. They thought that they could have their treasure on earth and in heaven also; and they went their way, in spite of our Lord's warnings; and made money, honestly no doubt, if they could, but if not, why then dishonestly; for money must be made, at all risks.

St Paul warned them, by his disciple Timothy, of their danger. He told them that the love of money is the root of all evil; and that those who will be rich fall into temptation and a snare, and into many foolish and hurtful lusts, which drown men in destruction and perdition.

St James warned them even more sternly; and told the rich men among the Jews of his day to weep and howl for the miseries which were coming on them. They had heaped up treasure for the last days, when it would be of no use to them. They were fattening their hearts —he told them—against a day of slaughter.

But they listened to St Paul and St James no more than they did to our Lord. After the fall of Jerusalem, even more than before, they became the money-makers and the money-lenders of the whole world. And what befel them? Their wealth stirred up the envy and the suspicion of the Gentiles. They were persecuted, robbed, slaughtered, again and again for the sake of their money. And yet they would not give up their ruinous passion. Throughout all the middle ages, here in England, just as much as on the Continent, they lent money at exorbitant interest; and then their debtors, to escape payment, turned on them for not being Christians; accused them of poisoning the wells, and what not; massacred them, burnt them alive, and committed the most horrible atrocities; fulfilling the warnings of our Lord and His Apostles, only too terribly and brutally, again and again.

Do I say this to make any man dislike or despise the Jews? God forbid. The Jews have noble qualities in them, by which they have prospered, and for the sake of which—as I believe—God's blessing rests on them to this day. They have prospered: not by their love of money, not even by their extraordinary courage, persistence, and intellectual power; but by their keeping two at least of the commandments, as no other people on earth has kept them. They have kept the second commandment; and hated idolatry, and any approach to it, with a stern and noble hatred, which would God that all who call themselves Christians would imitate. They have kept, likewise, the fifth commandment; and have honoured their parents, as no other people on earth have done, except it may be the Chinese, who prosper still, in spite of many sins. Their family affections are so intense, their family life is so pure and sound, that they put to shame too many Christians; and where the family life is sound, the heart of a people is sure to be sound likewise; and all will come right with them at last: and meanwhile the days of the Jews will be long in whatsoever land the Lord their God shall give them, till the day of which St Paul prophesied, when the vail shall be taken off their hearts, and they shall acknowledge that Christ, whom their forefathers crucified in their blindness, for their King, and Lord, and God; and so all Israel shall be saved. Amen. Amen.

And meanwhile, who are we that we should complain of the Jews now, or the Jews of our Lord's time, for being too fond of money? Is anything more certain, than that we English are becoming given up, more and more, to the passion for making money at all risks, and by all means fair or foul? Our covetousness is—alas! that it should be so—become a by-word among foreign nations; while our old English commercial honesty— which was once our strength, and protected us from, and all but atoned for, our covetousness—is going fast; and leaving us, feared indeed for our power; but suspected for our chicanery; and odious for our arrogance.

And it is most sad, but most certain, that we are like those Pharisees of old in this also, that we too have made up our mind that we can serve God and Mammon at once; that the very classes among us who are most utterly given up to money-making, are the very classes which, in all denominations, make the loudest religious profession; that our churches and chapels are crowded on Sundays by people whose souls are set, the whole week through, upon gain and nothing but gain; who pretend to reverence Scripture, while they despise the warning of Scripture, that the love of money is the root of all evil.

Have we not seen in our own days persons of the highest religious profession, whose names were the foremost on every charitable subscription list, so devoured by this mad love for money for its own sake, that though they had already more money than they could spend, or enjoy in any way soever, save by saying to themselves— I have got it, I have got it—they must needs, in the mere lust for becoming richer still, ruin themselves and others by frantic speculations? Have we not seen—but why should I defile myself, and you, and this holy place by telling you what I have seen; and what I hope, and hope alas! in vain, that I shall never see again, among those who must needs serve God and Mammon? Has not the love of money become such a chronic disease among us, that we can actually calculate, now, when the disease will come to a head; and relieve itself for a while: though alas! only for a while?

About every eleven years, I am informed, we are to expect a commercial crisis; panics, bankruptcies, and misery and ruin to hundreds; a sort of terrible but beneficent thunderstorm, which clears the foul atmosphere of our commercial system at the expense, alas! not merely of the guilty, but of the innocent; involving

the widow and the orphan, the poor and the simple, in
the same fate as the rich and powerful whom they have
trusted to their own ruin. And yet we boast of our
civilization and of our Christianity; and hardly one, here
and there, lays the lesson to heart, but each man, like a
moth about a candle, unwarned by the fate of his fellows,
fancies that he at least can flutter round the flames and
not be burned; that whoever else cannot serve God and
Mammon, he can do it; and holds, by virtue of his
superior prudence, a special dispensation from the plain
warnings of Holy Scripture.

But every reasonable man knows what advantages
money, and nothing but money, will obtain, not only for
a man himself but for his children; and answers me—If
I wish to rise in life, if I wish my children to rise in
life, how can I do it, without making money?

God forbid that I should check an honourable ambition, and a desire to rise in life. We all ought to rise
in life, and to rise far higher than most of us are likely
to rise. But I ask you to consider very seriously what
you mean by rising in life.

Do you mean by rising in life, merely becoming a
richer man; living in a larger house, eating, drinking,
clothing, better; having more servants, carriages, plate?
Is that to be the highest triumph of all your labours? Is
that your notion of rising in life? If it is, you are not
singular in your notion. There are thousands who call
themselves civilized and Christians, and yet have no
higher notion of what man's highest good may be. But
do you mean by rising in life, simply becoming a nobler,

because a better man?   For if you mean that latter, I seriously advise you to hearken to what the Creator and Governor of all heaven and earth, Jesus Christ our Lord, has told you on that matter, when He said—"Seek ye first the kingdom of God, and His righteousness, and all these things shall be added unto you."

Seek ye first the kingdom of God.   Alas! this money-making generation talks a great deal about religion and saving their souls, being quite indifferent to the serious question—whether their souls are worth saving or not: but as for the kingdom of God, of which our Lord and His Apostles speak so often, they have forgotten altogether what it is.   They talk too, a great deal, about the righteousness of Christ: but they have forgotten also what the righteousness of Christ, which is also the righteousness of God, is like.

The kingdom of God; the government of God; the laws and rules by which Christ, King of kings, and King, too, of every nation and man on earth, whether they know it or not, governs mankind, that is what you have to seek, because it is there already.   You are in Christ's kingdom.   If you wish to prosper in it, find out what its laws are.   That will be true wisdom.   For in keeping the commandments of God, and in obeying His laws; in that alone is life; life for body and soul; life for time and for eternity.

And the righteousness of God, which is the righteousness of Christ;—find out what that is, and pray to Christ to give it to you; for so alone will you be what a man should be, created after God in righteousness and true holiness, and renewed into the image and likeness of God. You will find plenty of persons now, as in all times, who will tell you that you need not do that; that all you need, for this world or the world to come, is some righteousness of the Scribes and Pharisees; calling that—oh shame that such a glorious and eternal truth should be so caricatured and degraded by man—justification by faith: while all they mean is, justification not by faith, but by mere assent; assenting to certain doctrines; keeping certain religious watch-words in your mouth, and, over and above, leading a tolerably respectable life. But what says our Lord? "Except your righteousness exceed the righteousness of the Scribes and Pharisees, ye shall in no wise enter into the kingdom of heaven." Not merely— not dwell in it for ever, but not even enter it, not even get through the very gate, and cross the very threshold, of it. The merely assenting, merely respectable, even the so-called religious and orthodox life will not let you into the kingdom of heaven, either in this life or the life to come. No. That requires the noble life, the pure life, the just life, the gentle life, the generous life, the heroic life, the Godlike life, which is perfect even as our Father in heaven is perfect, because He lets His sun shine on the evil and on the good, and His rain fall on the just and on the unjust. But how will this help you to rise in life? Our Lord Himself answers—and our Lord should surely know—" Seek ye first the kingdom of God and His righteousness, and all these things shall be added to you." Have faith in God, and in His promise; and your faith in God shall be rewarded. You shall find that your heavenly Father knows that you have need of all these things; and has arranged His kingdom, and the whole universe, accordingly. The very good things of this world—wealth, honour, power, and the rest, for the sake of which worldly men quarrel, and envy, and slander, and bully, and cringe, and commit all basenesses and crimes—all these shall come to you of their own accord by the providence of your Father in heaven and by His everlasting Laws, if you will but learn and do God's will, and lead the Christlike and the Godlike life. Honour and power, wealth and prosperity, as much of them as is justly good for you, and as much of them as you deserve—that is, earn and merit by your own ability and self-control—shall come to you by the very laws of the universe and by the very providence of God. You shall find that godliness hath the promise of this life, as well as of the life which is to come. You shall find that God's kingdom is a well-made and well-ordered kingdom; and that His laws are life, and are far more worth trusting in than the maxims of that ill-made and ill-ordered world of man, which you all renounced at your baptism. You shall find that the promises of Scripture are no dreams, but actual practical living truths, which come true, and fulfil themselves, in the lives and histories of men.

Choose, young men; choose now; and make up your minds which way you will rise in life; by merely getting money; or by getting wisdom and honour and virtue. The Psalmists of old, yea our Lord Himself, tell you what will happen in each case. If you want only to be rich, why then be rich; if you are clever enough.   The Lord may give you what you want, in this evil world.   He may give you your portion in this life, and fill you with His hid treasure.   He may let you heap up money which you do not know how to spend, and be a laughing-stock to others while you live; and after you die, your children will probably squander what you have hoarded; while you will carry away nothing when you die, neither will your pomp follow you: and take care lest you wake, after all, like Dives in the torment, to hear the fearful but most reasonable words— "Son, thou in thy lifetime receivedst thy good things, and therefore thou art tormented." Those words too, I fear, will come true, in this very generation, of many a wretched soul who while he lived counted himself a happy man; and had all men speaking well of him, because he did well unto himself.   On whose souls may God have mercy.

Choose, young men: choose; now in the golden days of youth, and strength, and honour, ere you have laid a yoke on your own shoulders—even the yoke of money-worship;—not light and easy, like the yoke of Christ, but heavier and heavier as the years roll on, while you, with fading intellect, fading hopes, and it may be fading credit, and certainly fading power of any rational enjoyment, have still, like the doomed souls in Dante's Inferno, to roll up hill the money-bags which are perpetually slipping back.   I have seen that, and more than once or twice; and it is, I think, the saddest sight on earth—save one.

Choose, I say again, then, young men, before you

have spread a net round your own feet, which, as in disturbed dreams, grows and tangles more and more each time you move—even the net of greed and craft, which men set for their neighbours; and are but too apt, ere all is done, to be taken in themselves; the net of truly bad society, of the society of men who have set their hearts on making money, somehow or other; and with whom, if you cast in your lot, you may descend—O God, I know full well what I am saying—to depths from which your young spirits now would shrink; till your higher nature be subdued to the element in which it works; and the poet's curse on all who bind themselves to natures lower than their own come true of you—

Thou shalt lower to their level, day by day,
All that once was fine within thee growing coarse to sympathize
    with clay.

Or you may choose—God grant that you may choose —the other path; the path of the law of Christ, and of the Spirit of Christ; the kingdom of God and His righteousness. And then shall come true of you, as far as God shall see good for your immortal soul, those other promises—

"Come, ye children, and hearken unto me, and I will teach you the fear of the Lord. What man is he that loves life, and would fain see good days? Let him keep his tongue from evil, and his lips that they speak no deceit. Let him eschew evil and do good; let him seek peace and pursue it. For the eyes of the Lord are over the righteous, and His ears are open to their prayers...

For the Lord ordereth a good man's going, and maketh his way acceptable to Himself. Though he fall he shall not be cast away, for the Lord upholdeth him with His hand...I have been young, and now am old, and yet never saw I the righteous forsaken, nor his seed begging their bread. Flee from evil, and do the thing that is good, and dwell for evermore. For the Lord loveth the thing that is righteous. He forsaketh not His that be godly, but they are preserved for ever."

Choose that; the better part which shall not be taken from you; for it is according to the true laws of political and social economy, which are the laws of the Maker of the Universe, and of the Redeemer of Mankind. And then, whether or not you leave your children wealth, you will, at all events, leave them an example by which they, and their children's children, must prosper to the world's end. And your prayer will be, more and more, as you grow old and weary with the hard work of life—

"I will go forth in the strength of the Lord God, and make mention of His righteousness only. Thou, O God, hast taught me from my youth up until now. Therefore will I tell of Thy wondrous works. Forsake me not, O Lord, in my old age, when I am grey-headed, till I have shewn Thy strength unto this generation ; and Thy power unto those that are yet to come."

To which end may Christ bring us all, of His infinite mercy. Amen.

SERMON XXVII.

THE BEATIFIC VISION.

PSALM LVII.

A Psalm of David when he fled from Saul in the cave.

Be merciful unto me, O God, be merciful unto me, for my soul trusteth in Thee, and under the shadow of Thy wings shall be my refuge, until this tyranny be over-past. I will call unto the most high God, even unto the God that shall perform the cause which I have in hand. He shall send from heaven, and save me from the reproof of him that would eat me up. God shall send forth His mercy and truth: my soul is among lions. And I lie even among the children of men, that are set on fire, whose teeth are spears and arrows, and their tongue a sharp sword. Set up Thyself, O God, above the heavens, and Thy glory above all the earth. They have laid a net for my feet, and pressed down my soul: they have digged a pit before me, and are fallen into the midst of it themselves. My heart is fixed, O God, my heart is fixed: I will sing, and give praise. Awake up, my glory; awake, lute and harp: I myself will awake right early. I will give thanks unto Thee, O Lord, among the people, and I will sing unto Thee among the nations. For the greatness of Thy mercy reacheth unto the heavens, and Thy truth unto the clouds. Set up Thyself, O God, above the heavens, and Thy glory above all the earth.

SOME people now-a-days would call this poetry; and so it is. But what poetry! They would call it a Hebrew song, a Hebrew lyric; and so it is. But what a song!

There is something in us, if we be truly delicate and high-minded people, which will surely make us feel a deep difference between it and common poetry, or common songs; which made our forefathers read or chant it in church, and use it, as many a pious soul has ere now, in private devotion.

David did not compose it in church or in temple. He never meant it, perhaps, to be sung in public worship. He little dreamed that we, and millions more, in lands of which he had never heard, should be repeating his words in a foreign tongue in our most sacred acts of worship. He was thinking, when he composed it, mainly of himself and his own sorrows and dangers. He intends, he says, to awake early, and sing it to lute and harp. Perhaps he had composed it in the night, as he lay either in the cave of Adullam or Engedi, hiding from Saul among the cliffs of the wild goats; and meant to go forth to the cave's mouth, and there, before the sun rose over the downs, he would, to translate his words exactly, "awake the dawning" with his song in the free air and the clear sky, singing to his little band of men.

And to some one more than man, my friends. For his poetry was poetry concerning God. His song was a song to God. He does not sing of his own sorrows to himself, as too many poets have done ere now. He does not sing to his men; though he no doubt wished them to hear him, and learn from him, and gain faith and comfort and courage from his song. He sings of his sorrows to God Himself; to the God who made heaven and earth; the God who is above the heavens, and His glory above all the earth.

This is the secret, the virtue, the charm of the song; that it sings to God. This is why it has passed into many lands, into many languages, through hundreds and hundreds of years, and is as fresh, and mighty, and full of meaning and of power, now, here, to us in England, as it was to David, when he was a poor outlaw, wandering in the hills of the little country of Judæa, more than 2000 years ago.

The poet says,

A thing of beauty is a joy for ever,

and this psalm is most beautiful, and a joy for ever to delicate and noble intellects. But more, a thing of truth is a help for ever. And this psalm is most true, and a help for ever to all sorrowing and weary hearts. For the Spirit of truth it was, who put this psalm into David's heart and brain; and taught him to know and say what was true for him, and true for all men; what was true then, and will be true for ever.

And what in it is true for ever? The very figures, the metaphors of the psalm are true for ever. "Under the shadow of Thy wings shall be my refuge"—that is a noble figure; can we not feel its beauty? And more. Do none of us know that it is true? David did not believe any more than we do, that God had actual wings. But David knew—and it may be some of us know too— that God does at times strangely and lovingly hide us; keep us out of temptation; keep us out of harm's way;

as it is written, "Thou shalt hide them privately in Thy presence from the provoking of all men. Thou shalt keep them in Thy tabernacle from the strife of tongues." Ah, my dear friends, in such a time as this, when the strife of tongues is only too loud, have you never had reason to thank God for being, by some seemingly mere accident, kept out of the strife of tongues and out of your chance of striving too, and of making a fool of yourself like too many others? The image of the mother bird, hiding her brood under her wings, seemed to David just to express that act of God's fatherly love, in words which will be true for ever, as long as a brooding bird is left on the earth, to remind us of David's song; and of One greater than David, too, who said—"O Jerusalem, Jerusalem, how often would I have gathered thy children, as a hen gathereth her chickens under her wings, and thou wouldest not." God grant that we all may do, when our time comes, that which those violent conceited Jews would not do; and therefore paid the awful penalty of their folly.

And the darker and more painful figures of the psalm: are they not true still? Is not a man's soul, even in this just and peaceful land, and far oftener in lands which are still neither just nor peaceful—Is not a man's soul, I say, sometimes among lions?—among greedy, violent, tyrannous persons, who are ready to entangle him in a quarrel, shout him down, ay, or shoot him down; literally ready to eat him up? Are not the children of men still too often set on fire; on fire with wild party cries, with superstitions which they do not half understand, with brute excitements which pander to their basest passions, running like fire from head to head, and heart to heart, till whole classes, whole nations sometimes, are on fire, ready like fire to consume and destroy all they touch; and like fire, to consume and destroy themselves likewise?

Are there none now, too, whose teeth are spears and arrows, and their tongue a sharp sword? Such use the pen now, rather than the tongue: but they know, as well as those whom David met, how to handle the spears and arrows of slander, and the sharp sword of insult. Are there none left, who set nets for their neighbours' feet, by gambling, swindling, puffing, by tricks of trade and tricks of party?—none who, like the Scribes of old, try to entangle men in their talk, and make them offenders for a word; and who, like David's enemies, fall now and then into the very pit which they have digged, and ruin themselves in trying to ruin others?

My friends, such men will be, as long as there is sin upon the earth. Their weapons are very different now from what they were in David's time: but their hearts are the same as they were then. "The works of the flesh they do, which are manifest;" and a very ugly list they make; as all who read St Paul's Epistles know full well.

But such men have their wages. God is merciful in this; that He rewards every man according to his work. And He is merciful to the whole human race, in rewarding such men according to their work. To the flesh they sow, and of the flesh they shall reap corruption. Of old it was written—"The wages of sin are death ;" and that, like all God's words, is a Gospel and good news to poor human beings. For if the wages of sin were not death, what end could there be to sin, and therefore to misery?

But while such men exist, how shall a man escape them? How shall he defend himself from them? Not by craft and falsehood, not by angry replies, not by fighting them with their own weapons. The honest man is no match for them with those. The man who has a conscience is no match for the man who has none. The man who has no conscience does what he wills; everything is fair to him in war; and there—in his unscrupulousness—lies his evil strength. The man who has a conscience dares not do what he likes. His scruples—in plain words, his fear of God—hamper him, and put him at a disadvantage, which will always defeat him, as often as he borrows the devil's tools to do God's work withal.

He must give up those weapons, as David threw off Saul's armour, when he went to fight the giant. It was strong enough, doubt not: but he could not go in it, he said; he was not accustomed to it. He would take simpler weapons, to which he was accustomed ; and fight his battle with them, trusting not in armour, but in the name of the living God.

In the name of the living God. That is the only sure weapon, and the only sure defence. In that David trusted, when he went to fight the giant. In that he trusted, when he was hid in the cave. And because he trusted in God, he prayed to God. He spoke to

God. Remember that, and understand how much it means. David, the simple yeoman's son, the outlaw, the wanderer, despised and rejected by men, one who was no scholar either, who very probably could neither read nor write, and knew neither sciences nor arts, save how to play, in some simple way, upon his harp— this man found out that, however oppressed, miserable, ignorant he was in many respects, he had a right to speak face to face with the Almighty and Infinite God, who had made heaven and earth. He found out that that great God cared for him, protected him, and would be true to him, if only he would be true to God and to himself. What a discovery was that! Worth all the wealth and power, ay, worth all the learning and science in the world.—To have found the pearl of great price, the secret of all secrets; I, David, may speak to God.

Ah, my friends, consider the meaning of that. Consider it, I say. For when that great thought has once flashed across a man's mind, he is a new creature thenceforth. He need speak to no father-confessor or director; to no saints or angels; to no sages or philosophers. For he can speak to God Himself, and he need speak to no one else. Nay, at times he dare speak to no one else. If he can tell his story to God, why tell it to any of God's creatures?

He is in the presence of God Himself, God his Father, God his Saviour, God his Comforter; Father, Son, and Holy Ghost. God is listening to him. To God he can tell all his sorrows, all his wrongs, all his doubts, all his sins, all his weaknesses, as David told his;

and God will hear him; and instead of striking him dead for his presumption or for his sinfulness, will comfort him; comfort him with a feeling of peace, of freedom, of being right, and of being safe, such as he never had before; till all the troubles and dangers of this life shall seem light to him. Let the world rage. Let the foolish people deal foolishly, and the treacherous ones treacherously. For if God be with a man, who can be against him? He has no fears left now. He has nothing to do, save to thank God for his boundless condescension; and to trust on. To trust on. If he has set his heart on the Lord, he need not fear what man will do to him. If his heart is fixed; if he is sure that God cares for him, he will, as it were by instinct, sing and give praise to God, as the bird sings when the rain is past, and the sun shines out once more.

But I think that when a man has reached that state of mind, as David reached it, he will rise, as David rose, to a higher state of mind still. He will rise, as David rises in this psalm, from thoughts about his own soul, to thoughts about God. In one word, he will rise from religion to that which is above even religion, namely theology.

His first cry to God was somewhat selfish. He went to God about himself; about his own sorrows and troubles. That is natural and harmless. The child in pain and terror cries to its mother selfishly to be helped out of its own little woes. But when it is helped, and comforted, and safe in its mother's bosom, and its sobbing is over, then it forgets itself, and looks up into its mother's face, and thinks of her, and her alone.

And so it should be with the man whom God has comforted. When the deliverance has come; when the peace of mind has come; then surely, if he be worthy of the name of man, he will forget himself, and his own petty sorrows; and look up to God, to God Himself, and say within his heart—This great awful Being, eternal, infinite, omnipotent, who yet condescends to take care of a tiny creature like me, who am, in comparison with Him, less than the worm which crawls upon the ground, less than the fly which lives but for an hour—This God, so mighty and yet so merciful: who is He? What is He like? He is good to me. Is He not good to all? He is merciful to me. Is not His mercy over all His works? Nay, is he not good in Himself? The One Good? Must not God be The One Good, who is the cause and the fountain of all other goodness in man, in angels, in all heaven and earth? But if so—what a glorious Being He must be. Not merely a powerful, not merely a wise, but a glorious, because perfect, God. Then will he cry, as David cries in this very psalm—"Oh that men could see that. Oh that men could understand that. Oh that they would do God justice; and confess His glorious Name. Oh that He would teach them His Name, and shew them His glory, that they might be dazzled by the beauty of it, awed by the splendour of it. Oh that He would gladden their souls by the beatific vision of Himself, till they loved Him, worshipped Him, obeyed Him, for His own sake; not for anything which they might obtain from Him, but solely because He is The perfectly Good. Oh that God would set up Himself above the heavens, and His glory above all the earth; and that men would lift up their eyes above the earth, and above the heavens likewise, to God who made heaven and earth; and would cry—Thou art worthy, O Lord, to receive glory and honour and power; for Thou hast made all things, and for Thy pleasure they are and were created; and Thy pleasure is, Peace on Earth, and Goodwill toward men. Thou art the High and Holy One, who inhabitest eternity. Yet Thou dwellest with him that is of a contrite spirit, to revive the heart of the feeble, and to comfort the heart of the contrite. We adore the glory of Thy power; we adore the glory of Thy wisdom: but most of all we adore the glory of Thy justice, the glory of Thy condescension, the glory of Thy love."

And now, friends—almost all friends unknown—and alas! never to be known by me—you who are to me as people floating down a river; while I the preacher stand upon the bank, and call, in hope that some of you may catch some word of mine, ere the great stream shall bear you out of sight—oh catch, at least, catch this one word—the last which I shall speak here for many months, and which sums up all which I have been trying to say to you of late.

Fix in your minds—or rather, ask God to fix in your minds—this one idea of an absolutely good God; good with all forms of goodness which you respect and love in man ; good as you, and I, and every honest man, understand the plain word good. Slowly you will acquire that grand and all-illuminating idea ; slowly, and most imperfectly at best : for who is mortal man that he should conceive and comprehend the goodness of the infinitely good God? But see then whether, in the light of that one idea, all the old-fashioned Christian ideas about the relations of God to man ; whether a Providence, Prayer, Inspiration, Revelation ; the Incarnation, the Passion, and the final triumph, of the Son of God— whether all these, I say, do not begin to seem to you, not merely beautiful, not merely probable ; but rational, and logical, and necessary, moral consequences from the one idea of An Absolute and Eternal Goodness, the Living Parent of the Universe.

And so I leave you to the Grace of God.

CAMBRIDGE: PRINTED BY C. J. CLAY, M.A. AND SONS, AT THE UNIVERSITY PRESS.

THE WORKS OF CHARLES KINGSLEY.

A New and Cheaper Edition.

Crown 8vo. 3s. 6d. each.

Westward Ho!   With Portrait.
Hypatia.
Yeast.
Alton Locke.
Two Years Ago.
Hereward.
Poems.
The Heroes.   With Illustrations.
The Water Babies.   With Illustrations by Linley Sam-
  bourne.
Madam How and Lady Why.   With Illustrations.
At Last.   With Illustrations.
Prose Idylls.
Plays and Puritans : and other Historical Essays.
The Roman and the Teuton.
Sanitary and Social Lectures and Essays.
Historical Lectures and Essays.
Scientific Lectures and Essays.
Literary and General Lectures.
The Hermits.   With Illustrations.
Glaucus ; or, The Wonders of the Sea-shore.   With
  Coloured Illustrations.
Village Sermons and Town and Country Sermons.
The Water of Life : and other Sermons.
The Good News of God.
Sermons for the Times.
Sermons on National Subjects.
The Pentateuch : and David.
Westminster Sermons.
Discipline : and other Sermons.
All Saints' Day : and other Sermons.

MACMILLAN AND CO., LONDON.

CHARLES KINGSLEY'S WORKS.

Poems. Pocket Edition. 18mo. Cloth. 1s. 6d.

The Water Babies: A Fairy Tale for a Land Baby. New Edition. With 100 Pictures by LINLEY SAMBOURNE. Fcap. 4to. 12s. 6d.

Glaucus ; or, The Wonders of the Shore. With coloured Illustrations. Extra cloth, gilt edges. *Presentation Edition.* Crown 8vo. 7s. 6d.

The Heroes ; or, Greek Fairy Tales for my Children. With Illustrations. Extra cloth, gilt edges. *Gift-book Edition.* Crown 8vo. 7s. 6d.

Selections from the Writings. With Portrait. Crown 8vo. 6s.

Health and Education. Crown 8vo. 6s.

Out of the Deep. Words for the Sorrowful. From the Writings of CHARLES KINGSLEY. Extra fcap. 8vo. 3s. 6d.

Daily Thoughts. Selected from the Writings of CHARLES KINGSLEY by his Wife. Crown 8vo. 6s.

From Death to Life. Fragments of Teaching to a Village Congregation. With Letters on the Life after Death. Edited by his Wife. Fcap. 8vo. 2s. 6d.

True Words for Brave Men. 2s. 6d.

"No English author has ever appeared in a more charming form. . . . This is not an *Edition de Luxe*, but it is that much better thing for work-a-day readers, an edition of admirable taste and most pleasant use."—*Pall Mall Gazette*.

Now ready, on fine paper, complete in XIII. Vols. Globe 8vo. 5s. each.

Eversley Edition.

CHARLES KINGSLEY'S NOVELS AND POEMS.

Westward Ho ! Two Vols.	**Yeast.** One Vol.
Two Years Ago. Two Vols.	**Alton Locke.** Two Vols.
Hypatia. Two Vols.	**Hereward.** Two Vols.

Poems. Two Vols.

SIXPENNY EDITION.

CHARLES KINGSLEY'S NOVELS.

Medium 8vo. Sewed. 6d. each.

Westward Ho !	**Alton Locke.**
Hypatia.	**Two Years Ago.**
Yeast.	**Hereward.**

CHARLES KINGSLEY: His Letters and Memoirs. Abridged Edition. 2 Vols. 12s. Popular Edition. Crown 8vo. 6s.

MACMILLAN AND CO., LONDON.

10.1.93.